taste of home Christmas 2009

taste of home BOOKS

taste of home

Editor in Chief: **Catherine Cassidy**

Vice President, Executive Editor/Books:
Heidi Reuter Lloyd

Creative Director: **Ardyth Cope**

Food Director: **Diane Werner RD**

Senior Editor/Books: **Mark Hagen**

Editor: **Janet Briggs**

Project Editor: **Julie Schnittka**

Art Director: **Edwin Robles, Jr.**

Content Production Supervisor: **Julie Wagner**

Design Layout Artists: **Catherine Fletcher, Emma Acevedo**

Proofreaders: **Linne Bruskewitz, Amy Glander**

Recipe Asset System: **Coleen Martin, Sue A. Jurack**

Premedia Supervisor: **Scott Berger**

Food Editors: **Karen Scales, Wendy Stenman**

Recipe Testing & Editing: **Taste of Home Test Kitchen**

Food Photography: **Taste of Home Photo Studio**

Editorial Assistant: **Barb Czysz**

Chief Marketing Officer: **Lisa Karpinski**

Vice President, Book Marketing: **Dan Fink**

Creative Director/Creative Marketing: **Jim Palmen**

The Reader's Digest Association, Inc.

President and Chief Executive Officer: **Mary G. Berner**

President, Food & Entertaining: **Suzanne M. Grimes**

President, Consumer Marketing: **Dawn Zier**

International Standard
Book Number (10): 0-89821-733-4

International Standard
Book Number (13): 978-0-89821-733-9

International Standard Serial Number: 1948-8386

Cover Photography

Photographers: **Dan Roberts, Rob Hagen, Mark Derse**

Food Stylists: **Jim Rude, Julie Herzfeldt**

Set Stylists: **Grace Natoli Sheldon, Sherry Bahr**

Pictured on front cover (clockwise from top left):
Decorated Christmas Cutout Cookies (p. 116), Hint-of-Berry Bonbons (p. 138), Broccoli Saute (p. 34), Painted Santa Star (p. 182) and Turkey with Apple Stuffing (p. 33).

Pictured on back cover (from left to right):
Mint Chocolate Torte (p. 163), Chicken with Mushroom Wine Sauce (p. 52) and Little Soft Snowman (p. 210).

Printed in U.S.A.

Contents

From *Crafts* to *Cooking*, This *Treasury* Has It All!

Baking an assortment of festive cookies...serving a special, sit-down Yuletide dinner...creating heart-felt, homemade gifts. Christmas is more than just a one-day event. The preparations begin months in advance...and the celebrations continue into the New Year!

To help you make moments to remember this spectacular season, we're pleased to introduce Taste of Home Christmas 2009, a photo-filled keepsake offering 215 recipes, 28 decorating ideas and 21 hand-crafted gifts in nine inspiring chapters:

Party Starters & Beverages. Get gatherings off to a delicious beginning with appealing appetizers and drinks, such as Chicken Bacon Bites, Hot Crab Dip, Prosciutto & Pine Nut Bruschetta and White Christmas Sangria.

Christmas Dinners. From Herb-Crusted Prime Rib and Turkey Apple Stuffing to Festive Roast Chicken and Apple Cider-Glazed Ham, Taste of Home Christmas 2009 offers several sensational menu ideas for special sit-down dinners.

Carefree Entertaining. You don't have to fuss in order to serve guests scrumptious, flavorful food! Turn to this chapter's 27 easy—yet impressive—dishes, including Chicken with Mushroom Wine Sauce, Roasted Garlic & Onion Linguine and Mini Orange-Raspberry Trifles.

Seasonal Get-Togethers. There are countless reasons to gather with family and friends over the holidays. Inside this classic book, you'll find merry menus for a Christmas-morning brunch, a casual holiday movie night, a fun-filled open house and an after-caroling party.

Gifts from the Kitchen. Yuletide treats are always welcome gifts! From sweet surprises to savory bites, this chapter has something for everyone...even those hard-to-shop-for folks on your list!

Cookie Tray Delights. Family and friends will be sweet on such treats as Almond Toffee, Wreath Cookies, Coconut Cream Rounds and Marshmallow Pecan Fudge.

Fabulous Desserts. With easy recipes, such as Cranberry Orange Cheesecake, Peppermint Angel Roll and Brandy Snap Cannoli, your holiday parties are guaranteed to have happy endings!

Deck the Halls. It's fun to adorn your humble home with such seasonal decor as Holiday Luminarias, a Dazzling Ornament Wreath and a Mini Gingerbread House.

Gifts to Give. From a Fun Felted Handbag to a Snowflake Afghan, presents made with your own hands are a great way to express your fond feelings in a merry (and economical) way!

With all of the fuss-free recipes, seasonal decor and gift ideas in this treasured edition of Taste of Home Christmas 2009, your holiday planning and preparation is wrapped up in one pretty, practical package!

Party Starters
& BEVERAGES

Brie in Puff Pastry

PREP: 15 MIN. **BAKE:** 20 MIN. + STANDING
YIELD: 10 SERVINGS

My husband was in the Air Force so we've entertained guests in many parts of the world. I acquired this recipe while in California. It's one of my favorite special appetizers.

Sandra Twait ★ Tampa, Florida

- 1 round (13.2 ounces) Brie cheese
- 1/2 cup crumbled blue cheese
- 1 sheet frozen puff pastry, thawed
- 1/4 cup apricot jam
- 1/2 cup slivered almonds, toasted
- 1 egg, lightly beaten

Assorted crackers

Slice Brie horizontally in half. Sprinkle one cut side of Brie with blue cheese; top with remaining Brie. On a lightly floured surface, roll out pastry into a 14-in. square. Cut off corners to make a circle. Spread jam to within 1 in. of pastry edge; sprinkle with nuts. Place Brie on top; fold pastry over the cheese and pinch edges to seal.

Place seam side down on an ungreased baking sheet. Brush the top and sides of pastry with egg. Bake at 400° for 20 minutes or until golden brown. Immediately remove from the baking sheet. Let stand for 1 hour before serving. Serve with crackers.

Pomegranate Ginger Spritzer

PREP: 10 MIN. + CHILLING **YIELD:** 7 CUPS

A pitcher of this nonalcoholic beverage can conveniently be made hours before holiday guests arrive. Add the club soda just before serving. Tart pomegranate juice keeps it from being too sweet. So this fabulous flavor appeals to all!

- 1/2 cup sliced fresh gingerroot
- 1 medium lime, sliced
- 3 cups pomegranate juice
- 3/4 cup orange juice
- 3 cups club soda

Place ginger and lime slices in a pitcher; stir in pomegranate and orange juices. Refrigerate overnight.

Just before serving, strain and discard ginger and lime. Stir club soda into juice mixture.

Mediterranean Layered Dip

PREP/TOTAL TIME: 15 MIN.   **YIELD:** 20 SERVINGS

This quick and easy dip begins with purchased hummus. It's then flavored with the Mediterranean flavors of feta cheese, olives and lemon.

Patterson Watkins ★ Philadelphia, Pennsylvania

2-1/2   cups roasted garlic hummus
  3/4   cup chopped roasted sweet red peppers
  1   cup fresh baby spinach, coarsely chopped
  3   tablespoons lemon juice
  2   tablespoons olive oil
  2   tablespoons coarsely chopped fresh basil
  1   tablespoon coarsely chopped fresh mint
  1/2   cup crumbled feta cheese
  1/2   cup Greek olives, sliced
  1/4   cup chopped red onion
Assorted fresh vegetables *or* baked pita chips

Spread hummus onto a 12-in. round serving platter; top with roasted peppers.

In a small bowl, combine the spinach, lemon juice, oil, basil and mint. Using a slotted spoon, spoon spinach mixture over peppers. Top with cheese, olives and onion. Serve with vegetables or pita chips.

Editor's Note: You can make homemade pita chips by cutting a package of pita bread into wedges. Toss with 2 tablespoons olive oil, 1 teaspoon pepper and 1 teaspoon coarse salt. Place in a single layer on a baking sheet; bake at 350° for 15 to 20 minutes or until golden brown. Cool; store in an airtight container.

Smoky Potato Rounds

PREP: 15 MIN.   **BAKE:** 55 MIN.   **YIELD:** 1-1/2 DOZEN

I love potato skins but decided to top them with barbecue sauce to kick up the flavor a notch. Once the potatoes are baked, these appetizers come together in a hurry.

Rebecca Dozier ★ Kouts, Indiana

- 2 large baking potatoes
- 1/3 cup barbecue sauce
- 1/2 cup shredded cheddar cheese
- 6 bacon strips, cooked and crumbled
- 1/2 cup sour cream
- 3 green onions, thinly sliced

Scrub and pierce potatoes. Bake at 375° for 45 minutes or until almost tender.

When cool enough to handle, cut each potato widthwise into 1/2-in. slices. Place on a greased baking sheet. Brush with barbecue sauce; sprinkle with cheese and bacon.

Bake for 8-10 minutes or until potatoes are tender and cheese is melted. Top with sour cream and onions.

Simple Syrup

PREP: 15 MIN. + COOLING   **YIELD:** 1-2/3 CUPS

Simple syrup is used in a variety of mixed drinks. But it can also be used to sweeten iced tea or coffee.

- 2 cups sugar
- 1 cup water

In a small saucepan, combine sugar and water. Bring to a boil over medium heat. Reduce heat; simmer, uncovered, for 3-5 minutes or until the sugar is dissolved, stirring occasionally. Remove from the heat and cool to room temperature.

Transfer to a container with a tight-fitting lid. Store in the refrigerator for up to 2 weeks.

Champagne Versus Sparkling Wine

Although "champagne" is often used generically to describe any sparkling wine, true Champagne is made in the region of France with the same name.

The flavor of Champagne can range from very sweet (often labeled "doux") to very dry ("brut").

Honey Champagne Fondue

PREP/TOTAL TIME: 30 MIN.   **YIELD:** 3 CUPS

This special Champagne fondue has wonderful flavor from Swiss cheese and honey. It clings well to the dippers.

Scotts Grace ★ Taste of Home Online Community

- 1/4 cup finely chopped shallot
- 1 garlic clove, minced
- 1 tablespoon butter
- 1-1/4 cups Champagne
- 4 teaspoons cornstarch
- 1 teaspoon ground mustard
- 1/4 teaspoon white pepper
- 1/3 cup honey
- 4 cups (16 ounces) shredded Swiss cheese
- 2 tablespoons lemon juice

Pinch ground nutmeg

French bread cubes, tart apple slices *or* pear slices

In a large saucepan, saute shallot and garlic in butter until tender. Combine the Champagne, cornstarch, mustard and pepper until smooth; gradually stir into pan. Bring to a boil; cook and stir for 2 minutes or until thickened.

Stir in honey; heat through. Remove from the heat. Combine cheese and lemon juice; gradually stir into Champagne mixture until melted. Keep warm. Sprinkle with nutmeg. Serve with bread cubes, apple or pear slices.

Pomgaritas

PREP/TOTAL TIME: 5 MIN.   **YIELD:** 4 SERVINGS

Pomegranate juice gives a tart and tasty twist to the traditional margarita. The ruby color is great for Christmas, but we enjoy the refreshing beverage all year long.

Bernice Knutson ★ Danbury, Iowa

- 1/2 cup Triple Sec
- 1/2 cup tequila
- 1/2 cup pomegranate juice
- 1/3 cup lime juice
- 1/4 cup simple syrup

Ice cubes

Orange slices, optional

In a pitcher, combine the first five ingredients; stir well. Serve over ice; garnish with orange slices if desired.

Crab-Stuffed Baby Portobellos

PREP: 45 MIN. **BAKE:** 25 MIN. **YIELD:** 3 DOZEN

Our Christmas is capped off with these savory appetizers.
You can use white mushrooms if portobellos are unavailable.

Debbie Johnston ★ Owatonna, Minnesota

- 1 pound baby portobello mushrooms
- 3/4 cup butter, *divided*
- 2 garlic cloves, minced
- 2 cans (6 ounces *each*) crabmeat, drained, flaked and cartilage removed
- 1/4 cup grated Romano cheese
- 1 tablespoon minced fresh parsley
- 3 teaspoons garlic powder
- 1-1/2 teaspoons onion powder
- 1/4 cup grated Parmesan cheese
- 1 teaspoon garlic salt
- 1/2 cup shredded part-skim mozzarella cheese

Remove the stems from the mushrooms; set the caps aside. Finely chop the stems.

In a large skillet, saute chopped mushrooms in 1/4 cup butter for 5 minutes or just until tender. Add garlic; saute 1-2 minutes longer or until garlic is golden. Remove from the heat; stir in the crab, Romano, parsley, garlic powder and onion powder.

Melt remaining butter; pour into a 13-in. x 9-in. baking dish. Fill mushroom caps with crab mixture; place in baking dish. Sprinkle with Parmesan and garlic salt.

Bake, uncovered, at 350° for 20-25 minutes or until the mushrooms are tender. Sprinkle with the mozzarella. Bake 2-4 minutes longer or until cheese is melted. Serve warm.

About Baby Portobellos

Baby portobellos (also called crimini) have a deeper, earthier flavor than white mushrooms.

Purchase portobellos with light tan to rich brown caps and a very firm texture. If refrigerated in a paper bag, they can stay fresh for about 5 days.

Coffee & Cream Martini

PREP/TOTAL TIME: 10 MIN. **YIELD:** 1 SERVING

Made with Kahlua and Irish cream liqueur, this martini is almost like a dessert. It's an after-dinner drink that's easy to mix.

Clara Coulston Minney ★ Washington Court House, Ohio

- 2 tablespoons coarse sugar
- 1 teaspoon finely ground coffee
- Ice cubes
- 1-1/2 ounces vodka
- 1-1/2 ounces Kahlua
- 1-1/2 ounces Irish cream liqueur
- Chocolate syrup, optional

Sprinkle sugar and coffee on a plate. Moisten the rim of a martini glass with water; hold glass upside down and dip rim into sugar mixture.

Fill a mixing glass or tumbler three-fourths full with ice. Add the vodka, Kahlua and liqueur; stir until condensation forms on outside of glass.

Drizzle chocolate syrup on the inside of the prepared martini glass if desired. Strain vodka mixture into glass; serve immediately.

Shrimp and Pineapple Pinwheels

PREP: 40 MIN. + CHILLING **YIELD:** 3 DOZEN

A girlfriend and I are caters and are always dreaming up new recipes. For a festive look, use spinach or tomato tortillas.

Susanne Steele ★ Phoenix, Arizona

- 2 pounds uncooked medium shrimp, peeled, deveined and finely chopped
- 1 tablespoon butter
- 1 tablespoon honey
- 4 flavored flour tortillas (12 inches), room temperature
- 1 package (8 ounces) cream cheese, softened
- 1 can (20 ounces) crushed pineapple, well drained and patted dry
- 1/2 cup minced fresh cilantro

In a large skillet, saute shrimp in butter until shrimp turn pink; remove from the heat. Drizzle with honey and toss to coat; set aside to cool.

Spread each tortilla with a thin layer of cream cheese; top with pineapple, cilantro and shrimp. Roll up tightly; wrap in plastic wrap. Refrigerate for at least 1 hour.

Just before serving, unwrap the roll-ups and cut into 1-in. slices.

Southwestern Seafood Egg Rolls

PREP: 30 MIN.   **BAKE:** 15 MIN.   **YIELD:** 2 DOZEN

Scallops, shrimp, spicy seasonings and phyllo dough combine to make these unique egg rolls. Assemble them in the morning, refrigerate, then bake as guests arrive.

Lori Coeling ★ Hudsonville, Michigan

1/4	pound uncooked bay scallops
1/4	pound uncooked medium shrimp, peeled and deveined
1	teaspoon minced garlic, *divided*
2	tablespoons olive oil, *divided*
1	large tomato, peeled, seeded and chopped
1/4	cup finely chopped onion
3	tablespoons minced fresh parsley
3	tablespoons minced fresh cilantro *or* additional parsley
3/4	teaspoon ground cumin
1/2	teaspoon paprika
1/4	teaspoon salt
1/8	teaspoon pepper

Dash cayenne pepper

Dash ground turmeric

1/4	cup soft bread crumbs
12	sheets phyllo dough (14 inches x 9 inches)
1/2	cup butter, melted

In a large skillet, saute scallops, shrimp and 1/2 teaspoon garlic in 1 tablespoon oil for 2 minutes or until seafood is opaque. With a slotted spoon, remove from the pan and coarsely chop; set aside.

In the same skillet, combine the tomato, onion and remaining garlic and oil; simmer for 5 minutes. Stir in the parsley, cilantro, cumin, paprika, salt, pepper, cayenne and turmeric. Simmer, uncovered, until liquid is evaporated, about 5 minutes. Stir in seafood mixture and bread crumbs.

Cut phyllo dough into 14-in. x 4-1/2-in. strips. Cover with plastic wrap and with a damp towel until ready to use. Lightly brush one strip with the butter. Top with another strip; brush with the butter. Place a tablespoonful of the seafood mixture near one short side; fold in the long sides and roll up. Brush lightly with the butter.

Place on a greased baking sheet. Repeat with remaining phyllo and filling. Bake at 375° for 12-15 minutes or until golden brown.

Apple & Blue Cheese on Endive

PREP/TOTAL TIME: 30 MIN. **YIELD:** 32 APPETIZERS

This elegant appetizer features a creamy blue cheese and apple spread inside crunchy endive leaves. You can use pears instead of apples or use the spread to top crackers.

Katie Fleming ★ Edmonds, Washington

    1   tablespoon lemon juice
    1   tablespoon water
    1   large red apple, finely chopped
    2   celery ribs, finely chopped
  3/4   cup crumbled blue cheese
    3   tablespoons mayonnaise
    4   heads Belgian endive, separated into leaves
  1/2   cup chopped hazelnuts, toasted

In a small bowl, combine lemon juice and water; add apple and toss to coat. Drain and pat dry.

Combine the apple, celery, blue cheese and mayonnaise; spoon 1 tablespoonful onto each endive leaf. Sprinkle with the hazelnuts.

Pumpkin Spice Latte

PREP/TOTAL TIME: 20 MIN. **YIELD:** 5 SERVINGS

Each sip of this spiced-just-right beverage from our home economists tastes like a piece of pumpkin pie!

  1/2   cup ground coffee
1-1/2   cups water
    3   cups fat-free milk
  3/4   cup canned pumpkin
  1/3   cup packed brown sugar
  1/2   teaspoon ground cinnamon
  1/4   teaspoon ground ginger
  1/8   teaspoon ground nutmeg
Whipped cream and additional ground nutmeg, optional

Place the ground coffee in the filter of a drip coffeemaker. Add water; brew according to manufacturer's instructions.

Meanwhile, in a large saucepan, combine the milk, pumpkin, brown sugar and spices. Cook and stir over medium heat until steaming. Divide coffee among five mugs; add pumpkin mixture. Garnish with whipped cream and additional nutmeg if desired.

Ultimate Cheese Ball

PREP: 20 MIN. + CHILLING **YIELD:** 2 CUPS

This cheese ball has been a requested favorite of family and friends for more than 30 years. If I ever bring a different appetizer to a party, people are disappointed!

Sue Franklin ★ Wentzville, Missouri

- 4 ounces cream cheese, softened
- 1/4 cup sour cream
- 1 cup (4 ounces) shredded Swiss cheese
- 1 cup (4 ounces) sharp shredded cheddar cheese
- 1/4 cup finely chopped onion
- 2 tablespoons real bacon bits
- 2 tablespoons finely chopped pecans
- 1 tablespoon diced pimientos
- 1 tablespoon sweet pickle relish

Dash *each* salt and pepper

TOPPING:

- 3 tablespoons real bacon bits
- 2 tablespoons minced fresh parsley
- 2 tablespoons finely chopped pecans
- 1-1/2 teaspoons poppy seeds

Assorted crackers

In a large bowl, beat cream cheese and sour cream until smooth. Stir in the remaining cheeses, onion, bacon, pecans pimientos, relish, salt and pepper. Cover and refrigerate for at least 1 hour.

In a small shallow bowl, combine the bacon, parsley, pecans and poppy seeds. Shape cheese mixture into a ball; roll in bacon mixture. Wrap in plastic wrap; refrigerate for at least 1 hour. Serve with crackers.

Shaping a Cheese Ball

To keep hands and the countertop clean, spoon the cheese mixture onto a piece of plastic wrap.

Working from the underside of the wrap, pat the mixture into a ball. Place coating on another piece of plastic wrap; carefully roll cheese ball in the coating. Wrap the coated cheese ball in a clean piece of plastic wrap; chill.

Pear Mushroom Strudels

PREP: 45 MIN. **BAKE:** 20 MIN.
YIELD: 2 STRUDELS (12 SLICES EACH)

Guests may raise their eyebrows when you tell them the ingredients in this special appetizer. But after one taste, they're raising their hands for the recipe!

Carole Resnick ★ Cleveland, Ohio

- 1 cup finely chopped mushrooms
- 1 small onion, finely chopped
- 1/2 cup butter, *divided*
- 2 small pears, peeled and thinly sliced
- 3/4 cup shredded Gruyere *or* Swiss cheese
- 1/3 cup sliced almonds
- 1 tablespoon whole grain mustard
- 1/2 teaspoon salt
- 1/4 teaspoon pepper
- 10 sheets phyllo dough (14 inches x 9 inches)
- 1/3 cup grated Parmesan cheese

In a large skillet, cook the mushrooms and onion in 2 tablespoons butter until tender. Stir in the pears; cook 3 minutes longer. Remove from the heat; stir in the Gruyere, almonds, mustard, salt and pepper. Cool to room temperature.

Melt remaining butter. Place one sheet of phyllo dough on a work surface; brush evenly with butter. Sprinkle with 1-1/2 teaspoons Parmesan cheese. Layer with four more sheets of phyllo, brushing each sheet with butter and sprinkling with cheese. (Keep remaining phyllo dough covered with plastic wrap and a damp towel to prevent it from drying out.)

Spread half of the pear mixture in a 2-in.-wide strip along a short side of dough. Roll up jelly-roll style, starting with the pear side; pinch seams to seal. Brush with butter. Transfer to a parchment paper-lined 15-in. x 10-in. x 1-in. baking pan. Repeat with remaining phyllo, butter, Parmesan cheese and pear mixture.

Bake at 375° for 16-20 minutes or until golden brown. Cool for 5 minutes. Cut each strudel into 12 slices.

Hot Crab Dip

PREP: 15 MIN. **BAKE:** 25 MIN. **YIELD:** 2-1/2 CUPS

I lightened up a recipe for traditional crab dip with reduced-fat and fat-free sour cream and cheeses. Feel free to experiment with different cheeses to suit your tastes. This is great for a party because you can make it a day ahead and refrigerate it.

Cammy Brittingham ★ Cambridge, Maryland

1	package (8 ounces) fat-free cream cheese
1/2	cup fat-free sour cream
2	tablespoons fat-free mayonnaise
1	teaspoon Worcestershire sauce
1/2	teaspoon seafood seasoning
1/2	teaspoon spicy brown mustard
1/2	teaspoon reduced-sodium soy sauce
1/8	teaspoon garlic salt
2	cans (6 ounces *each*) crabmeat, drained, flaked and cartilage removed *or* 1/2 pound imitation crabmeat, flaked
1/3	cup plus 2 tablespoons shredded reduced-fat cheddar cheese, *divided*
1/3	cup plus 2 tablespoons shredded part-skim mozzarella cheese, *divided*

Melba rounds *or* crackers

In a large bowl, beat cream cheese until smooth. Add the sour cream, mayonnaise, Worcestershire sauce, seafood seasoning, mustard, soy sauce and garlic salt; mix well. Stir in the crab, 1/3 cup cheddar cheese and 1/3 cup mozzarella.

Transfer to a greased shallow 1-qt. baking dish. Sprinkle with remaining cheeses. Bake at 350° for 25-30 minutes or until bubbly around the edges. Serve warm with melba rounds or crackers.

Sweet-Savory Meatballs

PREP: 25 MIN. **BAKE:** 20 MIN. **YIELD:** 5 DOZEN

When I got married years ago, my mom gave me this recipe. The mouth-watering meatballs are easy to make and always disappear quickly.

Jodi Klassen ★ Coaldale, Alberta

1	egg
1/4	cup finely chopped onion
1	tablespoon ketchup
1-1/2	teaspoons salt
1/2	teaspoon pepper
1/2	teaspoon seasoned salt
1/2	teaspoon Worcestershire sauce
2	pounds ground beef
3/4	cup dry bread crumbs

SAUCE:

2	tablespoons plus 1-1/2 teaspoons cornstarch
1	cup orange marmalade
3	to 4 tablespoons soy sauce
2	tablespoons lemon juice
2	garlic cloves, minced

In a large bowl, combine the first seven ingredients. Crumble beef over mixture. Sprinkle with bread crumbs; mix gently. Shape into 1-in. balls.

Place meatballs on a greased rack in a shallow baking pan. Bake, uncovered, at 350° for 20-25 minutes or until meat is no longer pink; drain.

Meanwhile, in a small saucepan, combine the sauce ingredients. Bring to a boil; cook and stir for 2 minutes or until thickened. Transfer meatballs to a serving dish; serve with sauce.

Hot Bacon Cheese Spread

PREP: 10 MIN. **BAKE:** 1 HOUR **YIELD:** 2 CUPS

Made with Monterey Jack and Parmesan cheeses, this creamy spread is sure to warm up your next holiday party. Guests never wander too far from the table when I put out this fragrant dip.

Bonnie Hawkins ★ Elkhorn, Wisconsin

1	unsliced round loaf (1 pound) Italian bread
2	cups (8 ounces) shredded Monterey Jack cheese
1	cup (4 ounces) shredded Parmesan cheese
1	cup mayonnaise
1/4	cup chopped onion
5	bacon strips, cooked and crumbled
1	garlic clove, minced

Cut the top fourth off loaf of bread; carefully hollow out bottom, leaving a 1-in. shell. Cube the removed bread and set aside. Combine the remaining ingredients; spoon into the bread bowl. Replace the top. Place on an ungreased baking sheet.

Bake at 350° for 1 hour or until heated through. Serve with reserved bread cubes.

Editor's Note: Reduced-fat or fat-free mayonnaise is not recommended for this recipe.

Keep Cooked Bacon On Hand

When time allows, dice and cook a whole package of bacon; drain and let cool. Freeze in a heavy-duty plastic bag. Use the diced cooked bacon to flavor a variety of dishes.

Chicken Bacon Bites

PREP: 15 MIN. + MARINATING **BROIL:** 10 MIN.
YIELD: 2 DOZEN

*Ginger and orange marmalade give these rumaki-style snacks
wonderful flavor. I marinate the wrapped chicken earlier in the
day and broil them when guests arrive.*

Betty Pierson ★ Wellington, Florida

- 12 bacon strips, halved
- 10 ounces boneless skinless chicken breasts, cut into 24 cubes
- 1 can (8 ounces) sliced water chestnuts, drained
- 1/2 cup orange marmalade
- 1/4 cup soy sauce
- 2 garlic cloves, minced
- 1 teaspoon grated fresh gingerroot

Sweet-and-sour sauce, optional

Place bacon on a broiler rack. Broil 4 in. from the heat for
1-2 minutes on each side or until partially cooked; cool.

Wrap a piece of bacon around a chicken cube and water
chestnut slice; secure with a toothpick. In a large resealable
plastic bag, combine the marmalade, soy sauce, garlic and
ginger. Add wrapped chicken; seal and carefully turn to
coat. Refrigerate for 2 hours.

Drain and discard the marinade. Broil the chicken for
3-4 minutes on each side or until the chicken is no longer
pink and the bacon is crisp. Serve warm with the sweet-
and-sour sauce if desired.

White Christmas Sangria

PREP/TOTAL TIME: 10 MIN.
YIELD: 21 SERVINGS (3-3/4 QUARTS)

This punch from our Test Kitchen has a pleasant fruity flavor. It's not too sweet so everyone will enjoy it!

- 3 bottles (750 ml *each*) sparkling white grape juice, chilled
- 6 cups white cranberry juice, chilled
- 3/4 cup thawed lemonade concentrate

Just before serving, combine the juices and lemonade concentrate in a punch bowl.

Making an Ice Ring

This large ice ring is ideal for crowd-pleasing holiday punches. You can use whatever size and shape tube cake pan or gelatin mold you have on hand. (For the ice ring shown here, we used an 8-in. star tube pan.) For this layered look, add water to the pan; arrange fruit in pan and freeze. Repeat until you have as many layers as you want.

For faster preparation, add all the water to pan; arrange fruit on top. Freeze.

Festive Ice Ring

PREP: 10 MIN. + FREEZING   **YIELD:** 1 ICE RING

Our home economists suggest you use this colorful, fruit-filled ice ring to keep your favorite punch cold during a party.

- 5 cups water, *divided*
- Assorted fruit (cranberries, cherries, orange and lemon slices)
- Mint sprigs

Lightly coat a decorative tube cake pan or gelatin mold with cooking spray; add 1/2 cup of water. Arrange fruit and mint in pan as desired. Freeze until solid.

Gently add remaining water; arrange more fruit and mint as desired. Freeze until ready to use.

To unmold, wrap bottom of solidly frozen mold in a warm towel until loosened, or dip mold in a pan of warm water. Float ice ring, fruit side up, in a bowl of cold punch.

Editor's Note: If preparation time for the ice ring is short, just add the water to the pan and arrange the fruit on top. Freeze until solid.

Wonton Wonders

PREP/TOTAL TIME: 30 MIN.   **YIELD:** 4 DOZEN

Two days before your party, bake these wontons; store in an airtight container at room temperature. Prepare the filling; cover and chill. Fill the shells just before serving.

Carol Moth ★ Windsor, Colorado

- 12 wonton wrappers
- 1/3 cup plain yogurt
- 1/4 cup mango chutney
- 3 tablespoons peanut butter
- 1 tablespoon lime juice
- 1-1/2 teaspoons green curry paste
- 1/2 teaspoon salt
- 3 cups finely chopped cooked chicken breast
- 3 green onions, thinly sliced

Cut wonton wrappers into quarters; press into greased miniature muffin cups. Bake at 350° for 5-7 minutes or until lightly browned. Remove to wire racks to cool.

In a large bowl, combine the yogurt, chutney, peanut butter, lime juice, curry paste and salt. Fold in chicken.

Just before serving, place rounded teaspoonfuls of filling onto wontons. Sprinkle with onions.

Editor's Note: This recipe was tested with Thai Kitchen green curry paste. Look for it in the Asian food aisle of your grocery store.

Shrimp Salsa

PREP: 15 MIN. + CHILLING   **YIELD:** ABOUT 1-1/3 CUPS

Every time I take this salsa to a party, it's the first thing to go. I was skeptical when my mother gave me the recipe but one taste won me over.

Monique Jacketta ★ West Bountiful, Utah

- 1/3 pound frozen cooked shrimp, thawed and deveined
- 1/4 cup chopped peeled avocado
- 3 tablespoons chopped onion
- 3 tablespoons chopped tomato
- 3 tablespoons chopped radishes
- 4-1/2 teaspoons lime juice
- 1 tablespoon minced fresh cilantro
- 2 teaspoons chopped jalapeno pepper
- 2 teaspoons olive oil
- 1/4 teaspoon salt

Dash pepper
Tortilla chips

Cut shrimp into small pieces; place in a small serving bowl. Stir in the next 10 ingredients. Cover and refrigerate for at least 1 hour. Serve with tortilla chips.

Editor's Note: When cutting hot peppers, disposable gloves are recommended. Avoid touching your face.

Three-Cheese Dunk

PREP: 10 MIN. + CHILLING   **YIELD:** 3 CUPS

Even folks who don't care for the texture of cottage cheese will gobble up this dip because it's pureed. It can be served with fruit, vegetables and crackers.

Bibs Orr ★ Oceanside, California

- 2 cups (16 ounces) 4% cottage cheese, drained
- 3 tablespoons mayonnaise
- 1 tablespoon prepared horseradish
- 1 tablespoon spicy brown mustard
- 1/4 teaspoon salt
- 1/8 teaspoon pepper
- 1 cup (4 ounces) finely shredded cheddar cheese
- 1/2 cup crumbled blue cheese
- 3 green onions, finely chopped

Sliced fresh pears *or* apples, assorted vegetables *or* crackers

In a food processor, combine cottage cheese, mayonnaise, horseradish, mustard, salt and pepper; cover and process until smooth. Transfer to a small bowl. Fold in the cheddar cheese, blue cheese and onions. Cover and chill for 1 hour. Serve with pears, apples, vegetables or crackers.

Parmesan-Walnut Rounds

PREP: 20 MIN.   **BAKE:** 15 MIN./BATCH   **YIELD:** 3 DOZEN

These cheesy crackers are crisp on the outside and soft on the inside. Enjoy them alone or top the bites with sliced cheese or your favorite spread.

Deirdre Dee Cox ★ Milwaukee, Wisconsin

- 1-1/2 cups grated Parmesan cheese
- 1 cup all-purpose flour
- 1/4 teaspoon cayenne pepper
- 1/2 cup cold butter
- 1/3 cup cold water
- 1/4 cup chopped walnuts
- 2 tablespoons dried parsley flakes

In a large bowl, combine the cheese, flour and cayenne; cut in butter until mixture resembles coarse crumbs. Gradually add water, tossing with a fork just until moistened. Shape into two 6-in. logs. In a shallow bowl, combine walnuts and parsley. Roll each log in walnut mixture to coat edges.

Cut each log into 1/4-in. slices. Place 1 in. apart on ungreased baking sheets. Bake at 375° for 12-15 minutes or until bottoms are lightly browned. Remove to cool wire racks to cool.

Prosciutto & Pine Nut Bruschetta

PREP/TOTAL TIME: 25 MIN.   **YIELD:** 3 DOZEN

Prosciutto, Parmesan and pine nuts tastefully top French bread slices in these handheld appetizers. Make the topping the day before, then the next day, spread on bread and broil.

- 1 cup butter, softened
- 1 cup grated Parmesan cheese
- 1/4 teaspoon garlic powder
- 1 cup chopped pine nuts, toasted
- 6 thin slices prosciutto, chopped
- 1 French bread baguette (10-1/2 ounces), cut into 1/4-inch slices

Minced fresh parsley *or* chives

In a small bowl, combine the butter, cheese and garlic powder. Stir in pine nuts and prosciutto. Spread over one side of each bread slice.

Place on a baking sheet. Broil 3-4 in. from the heat for 3-4 minutes or until golden brown. Sprinkle with parsley. Serve immediately.

Mexican Cheesecake

PREP: 20 MIN. **BAKE:** 30 MIN. + CHILLING
YIELD: 24 SERVINGS

People will rave over this super-easy cheesecake appetizer. I've made this recipe several times at parties, and people were so surprised it was low fat. Make it a day ahead for convenience, adding salsa just before serving.

Sandy Burkett ★ Galena, Ohio

2	packages (8 ounces *each*) reduced-fat cream cheese
1-1/4	cups reduced-fat sour cream, *divided*
1	envelope taco seasoning
3	eggs, lightly beaten
1-1/2	cups (6 ounces) shredded sharp cheddar cheese
1	can (4 ounces) chopped green chilies
1	cup chunky salsa, drained

Tortilla chips *or* fresh vegetables

In a large bowl, beat cream cheese, 1/2 cup sour cream and taco seasoning until smooth. Add eggs; beat on low speed just until combined. Stir in cheddar cheese and chilies.

Transfer to a greased 9-in. springform pan. Place on a baking sheet. Bake at 350° for 25-30 minutes or until center is almost set. Spread remaining sour cream evenly over top. Bake 5-8 minutes longer or until topping is set.

Cool on a wire rack for 10 minutes. Carefully run a knife around the edge of the pan to loosen; cool 1 hour longer. Refrigerate overnight.

Just before serving, spread salsa over cheesecake. Serve with tortilla chips or vegetables.

Christmas
DINNERS

Savory Beef Dinner

Herb-Crusted Prime Rib
pg. 27

Four-Cheese
French Onion Soup
pg. 29

Orange-Shallot Salad
pg. 28

Garlic-Cheddar
Baked Potatoes
pg. 30

Raspberry Lemon Cake
pg. 31

Herb-Crusted Prime Rib

PREP: 20 MIN. **BAKE:** 1-3/4 HOURS + STANDING
YIELD: 8 SERVINGS

Prime rib always makes an impression on a holiday dinner table. But it's actually easy to prepare. This roast is wonderfully flavored with lots of fresh herbs.

Jennifer Dennis ★ Alhambra, California

- 1 large shallot, coarsely chopped
- 6 garlic cloves, quartered
- 3 tablespoons minced fresh rosemary *or* 1 tablespoon dried rosemary
- 2 tablespoons minced fresh oregano *or* 2 teaspoons dried oregano
- 2 tablespoons minced fresh thyme *or* 2 teaspoons dried thyme
- 2 tablespoons minced fresh sage *or* 2 teaspoons rubbed sage
- 2 tablespoons olive oil
- 3 teaspoons pepper
- 1 teaspoon salt
- 1 bone-in beef rib roast (4 pounds), trimmed

AU JUS:
- 1-1/2 cups reduced-sodium beef broth
- 1 cup dry red wine *or* additional reduced-sodium beef broth
- 1 teaspoon butter
- 1/2 teaspoon salt

Place the first six ingredients in a food processor; cover and pulse until finely chopped. Add oil, pepper and salt; cover and process until blended. Rub over roast. Place on a rack in a large roasting pan.

Bake, uncovered, at 350° for 1-3/4 to 2-1/4 hours or until meat reaches desired doneness (for medium-rare, a meat thermometer should read 145°; medium, 160°; well-done, 170°).

Remove roast to a serving platter and keep warm; let stand for 15 minutes. Meanwhile, in a small saucepan, bring broth and wine to a boil; cook until liquid is reduced to 1 cup. Remove from the heat; stir in butter and salt. Slice roast; serve with au jus.

Carving a Standing Rib Roast

1. To carve a standing rib roast, place meat on a cutting board with large side down and rib bones to one side. Make about a 1- to 2-in. cut along the curve of the bone to separate the meat from the bone.

2. Slice the meat horizontally from the top edge of the meat to the bones into 1/4-in. to 1/2-in.-thick slices. Repeat slicing, loosening the meat from the bone as necessary.

Orange-Shallot Salad

PREP/TOTAL TIME: 40 MIN.   **YIELD:** 8 SERVINGS

Creating recipes with my husband and grown daughter is family fun time at our house. Honey-roasted sliced almonds add appealing crunch and sweetness to this pretty salad.

Elaine Hailey ★ Chesterfield, Virginia

2 tablespoons chopped shallots
2 tablespoons plus 1/2 cup olive oil, *divided*
1/2 cup pomegranate juice
1/4 cup orange juice
2 tablespoons red wine vinegar
1 teaspoon sugar
1/4 teaspoon pepper
1/8 teaspoon salt
2 packages (4-1/2 ounces *each*) torn mixed salad greens
1 can (11 ounces) mandarin oranges, drained
1 small onion, halved and thinly sliced
1/3 cup shredded Parmesan cheese
1/3 cup honey-roasted sliced almonds

In a small skillet, cook shallots in 2 tablespoons oil over medium heat for 1-2 minutes or until tender. Stir in the juices and vinegar. Bring to a boil over medium heat. Reduce heat; simmer, uncovered, for 15 minutes or until dressing is reduced to about 1/4 cup.

Stir in the sugar, pepper and salt; cool. Strain and discard shallots. Transfer dressing to a small bowl; whisk in remaining oil.

In a serving bowl, combine the salad greens, oranges and onion. Drizzle with dressing; toss to coat. Sprinkle with cheese and almonds. Serve immediately.

Editor's Note: This recipe was tested with Sunkist Almond Accents.

Four-Cheese French Onion Soup

PREP: 25 MIN. **COOK:** 50 MIN. **YIELD:** 8 SERVINGS

This beef broth is slightly sweet...not too salty like so many other soups. Serve this as a first course on special occasions or as a meal by itself with a green salad.

Gail Van Osdell ★ St. Charles, Illinois

1/3	cup butter, cubed
2	tablespoons olive oil
12	cups thinly sliced onions
2	teaspoons salt
1	teaspoon sugar
1/4	cup all-purpose flour
2	cartons (32 ounces *each*) reduced-sodium beef broth
1-1/2	cups white wine *or* additional reduced-sodium beef broth
8	slices French bread (1/2 inch thick)
1-1/3	cups shredded Swiss cheese
2/3	cup shredded cheddar cheese
1/2	cup shredded part-skim mozzarella cheese
2	tablespoons grated Parmesan cheese

In a Dutch oven, melt butter with oil. Add the onions, salt and sugar; cook over medium heat for 15-20 minutes or until lightly browned, stirring frequently.

Sprinkle flour over onion mixture; stir until blended. Gradually stir in broth and wine. Bring to a boil; cook and stir for 2 minutes. Reduce heat; cover and simmer for 30 minutes, stirring occasionally.

Place bread slices on an ungreased baking sheet. Broil 3-4 in. from the heat for 3-5 minutes on each side or until lightly browned; set aside. Combine the cheeses.

Ladle soup into ovenproof bowls. Top each with a slice of toast; sprinkle with cheese mixture. Place bowls on a baking sheet. Broil for 2-3 minutes or until the cheese is lightly golden.

Make-Ahead Soup Steps

Get a head start on preparing Four-Cheese French Onion Soup for your holiday party. Here are a few things that can be done the day before.

• Measure the salt, sugar and flour; loosely cover and keep on your countertop. • Thinly slice the onions; refrigerate in a tightly covered container. • Slice the French bread and broil as directed. Let cool; store in a resealable plastic bag at room temperature. • Combine the cheeses; cover and refrigerate.

Garlic-Cheddar Baked Potatoes

PREP: 1-1/2 HOURS   **BAKE:** 15 MIN.   **YIELD:** 16 SERVINGS

Having been raised in Italy, I include garlic in a lot of my cooking. The horseradish flavor in these potatoes is mild, making them a great addition to any meal.

Pasqualina Pasko ★ Parrish, Florida

8	large baking potatoes
1	whole garlic bulb
1/2	teaspoon olive oil
1/2	cup butter, softened
3/4	cup milk
2	tablespoons prepared horseradish
1	teaspoon salt
1/4	teaspoon pepper
1-1/2	cups (6 ounces) shredded cheddar cheese, *divided*

Scrub and pierce potatoes. Bake at 400° for 65-75 minutes or until tender. Meanwhile, remove papery outer skin from garlic (do not peel or separate cloves). Cut top off garlic bulb; brush with oil. Wrap in heavy-duty foil. Bake for 40-45 minutes or until softened.

Cool garlic for 10-15 minutes. Squeeze softened garlic into a large bowl. When potatoes are cool enough to handle, cut in half lengthwise. Scoop out the pulp, leaving thin shells.

Add potato pulp and butter to softened garlic; mash. Stir in the milk, horseradish, salt and pepper. Spoon half of the mixture into potato shells. Sprinkle with half of the cheese; top with remaining potato mixture.

Place on a baking sheet. Sprinkle with remaining cheese. Bake for 15-20 minutes or until heated through and cheese is melted.

Raspberry Lemon Cake

PREP: 1-1/4 HOURS + CHILLING   **BAKE:** 20 MIN. + CHILLING
YIELD: 12 SERVINGS

*Want a change from chocolate desserts? Try this elegant
lemon cake...it's packed with refreshing lemon flavor, from
the cake to the homemade lemon curd and creamy frosting.
It won a blue-ribbon at an Alaska State Fair and it's
definitely a winner with me.*

Shirley Warren ★ Thiensville, Wisconsin

LEMON CURD:

3	eggs
3/4	cup sugar
1/2	cup lemon juice
1/4	cup butter, cubed
1	tablespoon grated lemon peel

CAKE:

1	package (3 ounces) lemon gelatin
1/2	cup boiling water
1/2	cup butter, softened
1/2	cup canola oil
1-3/4	cups sugar, *divided*
4	eggs
1/2	cup lemon juice
4	teaspoons grated lemon peel
1	teaspoon lemon extract
1	teaspoon vanilla extract
2-1/2	cups all-purpose flour
2-1/2	teaspoons baking powder
1/2	teaspoon salt
1/2	cup evaporated milk
3/4	cup thawed lemonade concentrate

FROSTING:

2	packages (3 ounces *each*) cream cheese, softened
6	tablespoons butter, softened
3-3/4	to 4 cups confectioners' sugar
4-1/2	teaspoons lemon juice
1-1/2	teaspoons grated lemon peel
3/4	teaspoon vanilla extract
3/4	cup seedless raspberry jam

Fresh raspberries, optional

For lemon curd, in a heavy saucepan, beat eggs and sugar. Stir in the lemon juice, butter and lemon peel. Cook and stir over medium-low heat for 15 minutes or until mixture is thickened and reaches 160°. Cool for 10 minutes. Cover and chill for 1-1/2 hours or until thickened.

For cake, in a small bowl, dissolve gelatin in boiling water until gelatin is dissolved; set aside to cool.

In a large bowl, beat the butter, oil and 1-1/2 cups sugar until combined, about 5 minutes. Add eggs, one at a time, beating well after each addition. Stir in the gelatin mixture, lemon juice, lemon peel and extracts. Combine the flour, baking powder and salt; add to the creamed mixture alternately with milk.

Pour into three greased and floured 9-in. round baking pans. Bake at 350° for 20-25 minutes or until a toothpick inserted near the center comes out clean.

In a microwave-safe bowl, combine the lemonade concentrate and remaining sugar. Microwave, uncovered, on high for 2 minutes or until sugar is dissolved, stirring occasionally. Poke holes in warm cakes with a fork; pour lemonade mixture over cakes. Cool for 10 minutes before removing from pans to wire racks to cool completely.

For frosting, in a large bowl, beat cream cheese and butter until fluffy. Add the confectioners' sugar, lemon juice, lemon peel and vanilla; beat until blended.

To assemble, place one cake layer on a serving plate; spread with 6 tablespoons raspberry jam. Repeat layers. Top with remaining cake layer. Spread 1 cup frosting over sides of cake. Using a shell pastry tip and remaining frosting, pipe a shell border along top and bottom edges. Fill center with 1/2 cup lemon curd (save remaining curd for another use). Garnish with raspberries if desired. Chill for 1 hour.

Turkey with Apple Stuffing

PREP: 20 MIN. **BAKE:** 3-3/4 HOURS + STANDING
YIELD: 10-12 SERVINGS

Complementing your golden bird, the well-seasoned bread stuffing is sparked with a sweetness from apples and raisins.

Nancy Zimmerman ★ Cape May Court House, New Jersey

1-1/2	cups chopped celery
3/4	cup chopped onion
3/4	cup butter, cubed
9	cups day-old cubed whole wheat bread
3	cups finely chopped apples
3/4	cup raisins
1-1/2	teaspoons salt
1-1/2	teaspoons dried thyme
1/2	teaspoon rubbed sage
1/4	teaspoon pepper
1	turkey (14 to 16 pounds)

Additional butter, melted

In a Dutch oven, saute celery and onion in butter. Remove from heat; stir in bread cubes, apples, raisins and seasonings.

Just before baking, loosely stuff turkey with 4 cups stuffing. Place remaining stuffing in a greased 2-qt. baking dish; refrigerate until ready to bake. Skewer turkey openings; tie drumsticks together. Place breast side up on a rack in a roasting pan. Brush with melted butter.

Bake, uncovered, at 325° for 3-3/4 to 4 hours or until a meat thermometer reads 180° for the turkey thigh and 165° for the stuffing, basting occasionally with pan drippings. (Cover loosely with foil if turkey browns too quickly.)

Bake additional stuffing, covered, for 20-30 minutes. Uncover; bake 10 minutes longer or until lightly browned. Cover turkey and let stand for 20 minutes before removing stuffing and carving. If desired, thicken pan drippings for gravy.

Stuffing a Turkey

Combine the stuffing ingredients as recipe directs. Do not stuff the turkey until you're ready to place it in the oven. Spoon the stuffing loosely into neck cavity.

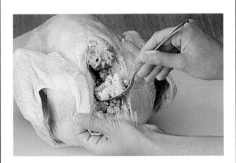

Gorgonzola Pear Salad

PREP: 15 MIN. **BAKE:** 25 MIN. **YIELD:** 12 SERVINGS

Tired of tossed salads? Here's an irresistible variation featuring pears that makes an attractive and tasty first course. The cheese and pecans are nice additions. You'll appreciate how easy it is.

Melinda Singer ★ Tarzana, California

6	medium pears, quartered and cored
1/3	cup olive oil
1	teaspoon salt
12	cups spring mix salad greens
4	plum tomatoes, seeded and chopped
2	cups crumbled Gorgonzola cheese
1	cup pecan halves, toasted
1-1/2	cups balsamic vinaigrette

Place pears in an ungreased 13-in. x 9-in. baking dish. Drizzle with oil and sprinkle with salt. Bake, uncovered, at 400° for 25-30 minutes, basting occasionally with the cooking juices. This step can be done a day ahead. Reheat just before serving.

In a large salad bowl, combine the greens, tomatoes, cheese and pecans. Drizzle with dressing and toss to coat. Divide among 12 serving plates; top each with two pear pieces.

Broccoli Saute

PREP/TOTAL TIME: 15 MIN.   **YIELD:** 10 SERVINGS

I invented this recipe while looking for a different way to cook broccoli that was lower in fat and sodium. Quick, colorful and tasty, it makes an easy accompaniment to a variety of meals.

Jim MacNeal ★ Waterloo, New York

1	cup chopped onion
1	cup julienned sweet red pepper
1/4	cup olive oil
12	cups fresh broccoli florets
1-1/3	cups water
3	teaspoons minced garlic
1/2	teaspoon salt
1/2	teaspoon pepper

In a Dutch oven, saute onion and red pepper in oil for 2-3 minutes or until crisp-tender. Stir in the broccoli, water, garlic, salt and pepper.

Cover and cook over medium heat for 5-6 minutes or until broccoli is crisp-tender.

Broccoli Basics

You'll need about 3-1/2 pounds fresh broccoli to get the 12 cups of florets called for in the Broccoli Saute recipe. Buy firm yet tender stalks of broccoli with compact, dark green or slightly purplish florets. Store unwashed in an open plastic bag in the refrigerator crisper drawer for up to 4 days. Wash before using.

Candied Corn Medley

PREP/TOTAL TIME: 30 MIN. **YIELD:** 8 SERVINGS

This was my kids' favorite holiday dish when they were growing up. They're now adults and still ask me to make it when they visit.

Eleanor Townsend ★ Punta Gorda, Florida

1	medium potato, peeled and diced
4	medium carrots, diced
5	bacon strips, chopped
1	medium onion, chopped
1	tablespoon olive oil
3	cups frozen corn, thawed
2	tablespoons maple syrup
1/2	teaspoon salt
1/8	teaspoon pepper

Place potato in a large saucepan and cover with water. Bring to a boil. Reduce heat; cover and cook for 8-10 minutes or until tender, adding carrots during the last 5 minutes; drain.

Meanwhile, in a large skillet, cook bacon over medium heat until crisp. Using a slotted spoon, remove to paper towels; drain, reserving 1 tablespoon drippings.

In the same pan, saute onion in oil and reserved drippings until tender. Stir in the corn, syrup, salt, pepper and bacon. Drain potato mixture; add to skillet. Heat through.

Roasted Garlic Mashed Potatoes

PREP: 15 MIN. **BAKE:** 30 MIN. + COOLING
YIELD: 8 SERVINGS

For a crowd-pleasing dinner addition that's lighter than you might think, try these tasty mashed potatoes. I use reduced-fat cream cheese and plenty of fresh garlic to flavor the rich side dish.

Nikki Dolan ★ Largo, Florida

1	whole garlic bulb
1	teaspoon canola oil
6	medium red potatoes (about 2-1/4 pounds), cubed
1	package (8 ounces) reduced-fat cream cheese, cubed
1/4	cup milk
1/2	teaspoon salt
1/4	teaspoon pepper

Remove papery outer skin from garlic (do not peel or separate cloves). Cut top off garlic bulb; brush with oil. Wrap in heavy-duty foil. Bake at 425° for 30-35 minutes or until softened. Cool for 10-15 minutes.

Meanwhile, place the potatoes in a large saucepan and cover with water. Bring to a boil. Reduce heat; cover and cook for 15-20 minutes or until tender. Drain. Squeeze softened garlic into a large bowl. Add the potatoes, cream cheese, milk, salt and pepper; beat until blended.

Almond-Cranberry Squash Bake

PREP: 20 MIN.   **BAKE:** 50 MIN.   **YIELD:** 8 SERVINGS

When my husband and I visit family in North Dakota, I bring along the ingredients to make this casserole. It gets rave reviews every time I serve it.

Ronica Skarphol Brownson ★ Madison, Wisconsin

  4   cups mashed cooked butternut squash
  4   tablespoons butter, softened, *divided*
1/2 teaspoon salt
1/2 teaspoon ground cinnamon
1/4 teaspoon ground allspice
1/4 teaspoon ground nutmeg
  1   can (16 ounces) whole-berry cranberry sauce

1/2 cup sliced almonds
1/4 cup packed brown sugar

In a large bowl, combine the squash, 2 tablespoons butter, salt, cinnamon, allspice and nutmeg. Transfer to a greased 2-qt. baking dish. Stir cranberry sauce until softened; spoon over squash.

Combine the almonds, brown sugar and remaining butter; sprinkle over cranberry sauce.

Bake, uncovered, at 350° for 50-60 minutes or until golden brown and bubbly.

Truffle Torte

PREP: 35 MIN.   **BAKE:** 30 MIN. + CHILLING
YIELD: 18 SERVINGS

The biggest sweet tooths are satisfied with just a small slice of this rich, decadent torte. A white-chocolate pattern on top gives it an elegant finish.

Mary Choate ★ Spring Hill, Florida

3/4	cup butter, cubed
8	squares (1 ounce *each*) semisweet chocolate, chopped
6	eggs
3/4	cup sugar
1	teaspoon vanilla extract
3/4	cup ground pecans
1/4	cup all-purpose flour

GANACHE:

4	squares (1 ounce *each*) semisweet chocolate, chopped
1/2	cup heavy whipping cream
2	tablespoons butter

GARNISH:

2	squares (1 ounce *each*) white baking chocolate
3/4	cup finely chopped pecans

Pecan halves, optional

Line the bottom of a greased 9-in. springform pan with waxed paper; grease the paper and set aside.

In a small saucepan, melt butter and chocolate over low heat. Cool. In a large bowl, beat eggs until frothy; gradually add sugar, beating for 4-5 minutes or until mixture triples in volume. Gradually beat in chocolate mixture and vanilla. Combine pecans and flour; fold into batter. Pour into prepared pan.

Bake at 350° for 30-35 minutes or until cake springs back when lightly touched. Cool on a wire rack for 15 minutes. Run a knife around edge of pan; remove sides of pan. Invert cake onto wire rack; carefully remove pan bottom and waxed paper. Cool completely.

In a small saucepan, melt chocolate with cream over low heat; stir until blended. Remove from the heat. Stir in butter until melted.

Transfer to a small bowl; cover and refrigerate until mixture reaches spreading consistency, stirring occasionally. Place cake on a serving plate. Pour ganache over cake and quickly spread to edges.

In a microwave, melt white chocolate; stir until smooth. Transfer to a heavy-duty resealable plastic bag; cut a small hole in a corner of bag. Pipe thin horizontal lines 1 in. apart over ganache. Use a sharp knife to draw right angles across the piped lines. Press pecans onto side of torte. Top with pecan halves if desired. Cover and refrigerate for 30 minutes or until set.

Holiday Ham Menu

Apple Cider-Glazed Ham
pg. 39

Merry Berry Salad
pg. 41

Overnight Honey-Wheat
Rolls
pg. 40

Dijon Green Beans
pg. 41

Gingered Strawberry Tart
pg. 43

Apple Cider-Glazed Ham

PREP: 15 MIN.   **BAKE:** 2-1/2 HOURS
YIELD: 10 SERVINGS (1 CUP SAUCE)

*When I wanted to try something new with our holiday ham,
I created this cider glaze. It's slightly sweet but still has the
spicy flavor my family craves.*

Rebecca LaWare ★ Hilton, New York

1/2 fully cooked bone-in ham (6 to 7 pounds)
2 cups apple cider
1 cup honey
1/2 cup cider vinegar
1/4 cup Dijon mustard
1 tablespoon butter
2 teaspoons chili powder
1/2 teaspoon apple pie spice

Place ham on a rack in a shallow roasting pan. Score the
surface of the ham, making diamond shapes 1/2 in. deep.
Cover and bake at 325° for 2 hours.

Meanwhile, in a saucepan, combine the cider, honey,
vinegar and mustard; bring to a boil. Reduce heat; simmer,
uncovered, for 15 minutes, stirring frequently. Stir in the
butter, chili powder and apple pie spice. Set aside 1 cup
for serving.

Cook the remaining sauce until thickened; spoon over
ham. Bake, uncovered, 30-35 minutes longer or until a meat
thermometer reads 140°. Warm reserved sauce; serve with ham.

Harvest Pumpkin Soup

PREP: 25 MIN.   **COOK:** 45 MIN.
YIELD: 8 SERVINGS (2 QUARTS)

*A drizzle of maple syrup is the crowning touch to this thick
and creamy soup. You can also substitute 4 cups mashed
butternut squash for the fresh pumpkin.*

Lesley Pew ★ Lynn, Massachusetts

1 cup chopped shallots
3/4 cup chopped celery
1 tablespoon butter
1 can (29 ounces) solid-pack pumpkin
2 cups chopped peeled pears
2 cans (14-1/2 ounces *each*) reduced-sodium chicken broth
1 cup white wine *or* additional reduced-sodium chicken broth
1/2 cup water
1 bay leaf
1/2 teaspoon salt
1/8 teaspoon pepper
1/2 cup maple syrup

In a large saucepan, saute shallots and celery in butter until
tender.

Stir in the pumpkin, pears, broth, wine, water, bay leaf,
salt and pepper. Bring to a boil. Reduce heat; cover and
simmer for 30-40 minutes or until pears are tender. Discard
bay leaf. Cool slightly.

In a blender, process soup in batches until smooth.
Return all to the pan. Stir in syrup; heat through.

Holiday Ornament Centerpiece

This centerpiece can be easily assembled
using simple holiday items you may
already have in your home. Start with a
shallow dish with a low lip. Arrange round
ornaments of various sizes in the dish.
Add little wrapped ornaments and a
snowflake or two. For an elegant, mono-
chromatic look, use all one color or add
a pop of color with some small balls (like
the red ones we used).

Overnight Honey-Wheat Rolls

PREP: 30 MIN. + CHILLING **BAKE:** 10 MIN.
YIELD: 1-1/2 DOZEN

These yeast rolls don't require kneading, and the make-ahead dough saves you time on the day of your meal. I love the hint of honey, too.

Lisa Varner ★ Greenville, South Carolina

1	package (1/4 ounce) active dry yeast
1-1/4	cups warm water (110° to 115°), *divided*
2	egg whites
1/3	cup honey
1/4	cup canola oil
1	teaspoon salt
1-1/2	cups whole wheat flour
2-1/2	cups all-purpose flour

Melted butter, optional

In a small bowl, dissolve yeast in 1/4 cup warm water. In a large bowl, beat egg whites until foamy. Add the yeast mixture, honey, oil, salt, whole wheat flour and remaining water. Beat on medium speed for 3 minutes or until smooth. Stir in enough all-purpose flour to form a soft dough (dough will be sticky). Cover and refrigerate overnight.

Punch dough down. Turn onto a well-floured surface; divide in half. Shape each portion into nine balls. To form knots, roll each ball into a 10-in. rope; tie into a knot. Tuck ends under. Place rolls 2 in. apart on greased baking sheets.

Cover and let rise until doubled, about 50 minutes. Bake at 375° for 10-12 minutes or until golden brown. Brush with melted butter if desired.

Dijon Green Beans

PREP/TOTAL TIME: 20 MIN.   **YIELD:** 10 SERVINGS

I love this recipe because it combines the freshness of garden green beans with a warm and tangy mustard dressing. It's a wonderful, quick and easy side dish.

Jannine Fisk ★ Malden, Massachusetts

- 1-1/2 pounds fresh green beans, trimmed
- 2 tablespoons red wine vinegar
- 2 tablespoons olive oil
- 2 teaspoons Dijon mustard
- 1/2 teaspoon salt
- 1/4 teaspoon pepper
- 1 cup grape tomatoes, halved
- 1/2 small red onion, sliced
- 2 tablespoons grated Parmesan cheese

Place beans in a large saucepan and cover with water. Bring to a boil. Cook, uncovered, for 8-10 minutes or until crisp-tender.

Meanwhile, for dressing, whisk the vinegar, oil, mustard, salt and pepper in a small bowl. Drain beans; place in a large bowl. Add tomatoes and onion. Drizzle with dressing and toss to coat. Sprinkle with Parmesan cheese.

Merry Berry Salad

PREP/TOTAL TIME: 20 MIN.   **YIELD:** 10 SERVINGS

Dried cranberries, crunchy apple chunks and toasted almonds dress up this crisp green salad. It's drizzled with a sweet-tart dressing that's a snap to blend.

- 1 package (10 ounces) mixed salad greens
- 1 medium red apple, diced
- 1 medium green apple, diced
- 1 cup (4 ounces) shredded Parmesan cheese
- 1/2 cup dried cranberries
- 1/2 cup slivered almonds, toasted

DRESSING:
- 1 cup fresh cranberries
- 1/2 cup sugar
- 1/2 cup cider vinegar
- 1/4 cup thawed apple juice concentrate
- 1 teaspoon salt
- 1 teaspoon ground mustard
- 1 teaspoon grated onion
- 1 cup canola oil

In a large salad bowl, toss the first six ingredients.

In a blender, combine the cranberries, sugar, vinegar, apple juice concentrate, salt, mustard and onion; cover and process until blended. While processing, gradually add oil in a steady stream.

Drizzle desired amount of dressing over salad and toss to coat. Serve immediately. Refrigerate any leftover dressing.

Gingered Strawberry Tart

PREP: 35 MIN. + CHILLING   **YIELD:** 8 SERVINGS

This strawberry delight is delicious with or without the crystallized ginger. It looks elegant, and tastes great, too.

Marie Rizzio ★ Interlochen, Michigan

- 24   gingersnap cookies (about 1 cup)
- 2   tablespoons plus 1/3 cup sugar, *divided*
- 1/4   cup butter, melted
- 2   tablespoons cornstarch
- 1   teaspoon finely chopped crystallized ginger, optional
- 3   cups chopped fresh strawberries
- 1/4   cup water

TOPPING:
- 2   cups sliced fresh strawberries
- 5   tablespoons seedless strawberry jam

In a food processor, combine the gingersnaps, 2 tablespoons sugar and butter. Cover and process until blended. Press onto the bottom and up the sides of a 9-in. fluted tart pan with a removable bottom; set aside.

In a large saucepan, combine the cornstarch, ginger if desired and remaining sugar. Stir in the chopped strawberries and water. Bring to a boil; cook and stir for 2 minutes. Reduce heat; simmer, uncovered, for 4-6 minutes or until thickened. Cool for 30 minutes. Pour into crust. Cover and refrigerate 2 hours or until set.

Arrange sliced berries over filling. In a small microwave-safe bowl, heat jam on high for 15-20 seconds or until pourable; brush over berries.

Celery-Onion Popovers

PREP: 15 MIN.   **BAKE:** 40 MIN.   **YIELD:** 1 DOZEN

I found this handwritten recipe in a cookbook I received from my mom. With onion and celery, these pleasing popovers taste a little like stuffing.

Barbara Carlucci ★ Orange Park, Florida

- 2   cups all-purpose flour
- 1   teaspoon onion salt
- 1/8   teaspoon celery salt
- 4   eggs
- 1-1/2   cups milk
- 1/4   cup grated onion
- 1/4   cup grated celery
- 2   tablespoons butter, melted

In a large bowl, combine the flour, onion salt and celery salt. Combine the eggs, milk, onion, celery and butter; whisk into the dry ingredients just until blended. Grease and flour the bottom and sides of 12 popover cups; fill two-thirds full with batter.

Bake at 450° for 15 minutes. Reduce heat to 350° (do not open oven door). Bake 25 minutes longer or until deep golden brown (do not underbake). Immediately cut a slit in the top of each popover to allow steam to escape.

Festive Roast Chicken

PREP: 20 MIN.   **BAKE:** 2-1/4 HOURS + STANDING
YIELD: 6 SERVINGS (5 CUPS GRAVY)

With rosemary, apples, cranberries and ginger, this is not your ordinary roasted chicken! It's a great alternative to turkey for a smaller holiday gathering.

Sue Gronholz ★ Beaver Dam, Wisconsin

1/4   cup butter, softened
  5   teaspoons minced fresh rosemary, *divided*
  1   roasting chicken (6 to 7 pounds)
1/2   teaspoon salt
1/4   teaspoon pepper
  4   medium apples, peeled and cubed
  1   large sweet onion, thinly sliced
  1   cup fresh *or* frozen cranberries
  1   can (14-1/2 ounces) reduced-sodium chicken broth, *divided*
  3   tablespoons lemon juice
  4   garlic cloves, minced
  1   tablespoon minced fresh gingerroot
  1   cup unsweetened apple juice
1/4   cup balsamic vinegar
1/4   cup honey

In a small bowl, combine butter and 3 teaspoons rosemary. Place chicken breast side up on a rack in a roasting pan; tie drumsticks together with kitchen string. Rub butter mixture over chicken; sprinkle with salt and pepper. In a large bowl, combine the apples, onion, cranberries, 3/4 cup broth, lemon juice, garlic, ginger and 1 teaspoon rosemary; place around chicken.

Bake, uncovered, at 350° for 1 hour. Pour apple juice over chicken. Bake 1-1/4 to 1-3/4 hours longer or until a meat thermometer reads 180° in the chicken thigh, basting every 30 minutes. Cover loosely with foil if chicken browns too quickly. Cover and let stand for 15 minutes before carving.

Pour drippings and apple mixture into a blender; skim fat. Cover and process until blended. Transfer to a large saucepan. Stir in the vinegar, honey and remaining broth and rosemary; heat through. Serve with chicken.

Elegant Scalloped Potatoes

PREP: 30 MIN.   **BAKE:** 15 MIN.   **YIELD:** 10-12 SERVINGS

I wanted a different side dish one night, so I dressed up my usual scalloped potatoes with bacon, green onions and extra cheddar cheese, which made it even more delicious.

Krista Wilson ★ Edgerton, Kansas

  8 large baking potatoes
  6 tablespoons butter, cubed
  6 tablespoons all-purpose flour
  1 to 2 teaspoons garlic powder
1/2 teaspoon salt
1/2 teaspoon pepper
3-1/2 cups milk
 12 ounces process cheese (Velveeta), cubed
1/3 cup crumbled cooked bacon
  1 cup (4 ounces) shredded cheddar cheese
1/4 cup sliced green onions

Scrub and pierce potatoes; place on a microwave-safe plate. Microwave on high for 15-20 minutes or until potatoes are tender. Cool slightly.

In a saucepan, melt butter. Stir in the flour, garlic powder, salt and pepper until smooth; gradually whisk in milk. Bring to a boil; cook and stir for 2 minutes or until thickened. Add the process cheese and bacon; stir until cheese is melted. Remove from the heat; set aside.

Cut potatoes into 1/4-in. slices. Place a third of the slices in a greased 13-in. x 9-in. baking dish; top with a third of the cheese sauce. Repeat layers twice. Sprinkle with cheddar cheese and onions.

Bake, uncovered, at 350° for 15 minutes or until the cheese is melted.

Editor's Note: This recipe was tested in a 1,100-watt microwave.

Making Soft Bread Crumbs

To make soft bread crumbs, tear several slices of fresh white, French or whole wheat bread into 1-in. pieces. Place in a food processor or blender; cover and push the pulse button several times to make coarse crumbs. One slice of bread yields about 1/2 cup crumbs.

Balsamic-Glazed Brussels Sprouts

PREP/TOTAL TIME: 30 MIN.   **YIELD:** 8 SERVINGS

My relatives claim to hate brussels sprouts, which I took as a challenge to come up with a recipe they'd love. When I served this at my Christmas buffet, there wasn't a sprout left in the bowl!

Carol Bess White ★ Portland, Oregon

  2 pounds fresh brussels sprouts
1/2 pound sliced bacon, cut into 1/2-inch pieces
  1 medium onion, sliced
1/4 cup white balsamic vinegar
  2 tablespoons stone-ground mustard
1/2 teaspoon garlic powder
1/8 teaspoon salt
1/2 cup soft bread crumbs

Cut an "X" in the core of each brussels sprout. Place in a large saucepan; add 1 in. of water. Bring to a boil. Reduce heat; cover and simmer for 8-10 minutes or until vegetables are crisp-tender.

Meanwhile, in a large ovenproof skillet, cook bacon over medium heat until crisp. Using a slotted spoon, remove to paper towels; drain, reserving 2 tablespoons drippings.

Saute onion in drippings until tender. Stir in the vinegar, mustard, garlic powder, salt, brussels sprouts and bacon; cook 2-3 minutes longer.

Sprinkle with bread crumbs; broil 4-6 in. from the heat for 2-3 minutes or until golden brown.

Broccoli-Apple Salad with Bacon

PREP: 30 MIN. + CHILLING   **YIELD:** 10 SERVINGS

Crunchy and colorful, this salad is hard to resist with bacon, apples and cranberries. During the busy holiday season, you'll especially appreciate its make-ahead convenience.

Jennifer Thornley ★ Butler, Pennsylvania

- 2 cups coarsely chopped fresh broccoli florets
- 1 cup coarsely chopped fresh cauliflowerets
- 2 medium carrots, chopped
- 1/2 cup dried cranberries
- 1 medium red apple, chopped
- 1 medium Granny Smith apple, chopped
- 2 tablespoons lemon juice, *divided*
- 1/2 cup mayonnaise
- 2 tablespoons maple syrup
- 1 pound sliced maple-flavored bacon, cooked and crumbled
- 1/2 cup sunflower kernels

In a large bowl, combine the broccoli, cauliflower, carrots and cranberries. Toss apples with 1 tablespoon lemon juice; add to vegetable mixture and toss.

In a small bowl, whisk the mayonnaise, syrup and remaining lemon juice. Stir into broccoli mixture. Cover and refrigerate for at least 1 hour.

Just before serving, stir in bacon and sunflower kernels.

Citrus Fennel Salad

PREP/TOTAL TIME: 20 MIN.   **YIELD:** 8 SERVINGS

I guarantee guests will love the taste of this unique salad. The pleasant orange flavor pairs well with tender pieces of fennel.

Marion Karlin ★ Waterloo, Iowa

2	large fennel bulbs
2	tablespoons olive oil
1	tablespoon butter
6	tablespoons orange juice
3	tablespoons lemon juice
1	teaspoon salt
1/2	teaspoon coarsely ground pepper
2	large navel oranges, peeled and cut into segments

Leaf lettuce

Remove fronds from fennel bulbs; set aside for garnish. Cut bulbs into thin slices. In a large skillet, saute fennel slices in oil and butter until crisp-tender.

Stir in the juices, salt and pepper. Bring to a boil; reduce heat to medium. Cook and stir for 5-6 minutes or until fennel is tender.

Remove from the heat; stir in orange segments. Serve over lettuce leaves; garnish with reserved fennel fronds.

New England Clam Chowder

PREP: 40 MIN.   **COOK:** 15 MIN.   **YIELD:** 1-3/4 QUARTS

I left a cruise ship with a great souvenir...the recipe for this splendid clam chowder! It's a traditional soup that stands the test of time.

Agnes Ward ★ Stratford, Ontario

12	fresh cherrystone clams
3	cups cold water
2	bacon strips, diced
1	small onion, chopped
2	medium potatoes, peeled and finely chopped
1/4	teaspoon salt
1/4	teaspoon pepper
2	tablespoons all-purpose flour
1	cup milk
1/2	cup half-and-half cream

Tap clams; discard any that do not close. Place clams and water in a large saucepan. Bring to a boil. Reduce heat; cover and simmer for 5-6 minutes or until clams open. Discard any clams that do not open.

Remove meat from the clams; chop meat and set aside. Strain the liquid through a cheesecloth-lined colander; set aside.

In a large saucepan, cook bacon over medium heat until crisp. Using a slotted spoon, remove to paper towels. Saute onion in drippings until tender.

Return bacon to the pan; add clam meat and reserved liquid. Stir in the potatoes, salt and pepper. Bring to a boil. Reduce heat; cover and simmer for 10-12 minutes or until potatoes are tender.

Combine the flour and milk until smooth; gradually stir into the soup. Bring to a boil; cook and stir for 2 minutes or until thickened. Reduce heat. Gradually stir in the cream; heat through (do not boil).

Creamed Pearl Onion Casserole

PREP: 30 MIN.   **COOK:** 20 MIN.   **YIELD:** 10 SERVINGS

This rich and creamy onion casserole is great alongside any roasted meat. Feel free to use frozen pearl onions (and skip the first step of the recipe) if you're pressed for time.

Sandra Law ★ Tucson, Arizona

3/4	pound pearl onions
4	celery ribs, chopped
5	green onions, chopped
2	garlic cloves, minced
6	tablespoons butter
1/4	cup all-purpose flour
1/2	teaspoon salt
1/4	teaspoon pepper
3-1/2	cups half-and-half cream
1/4	teaspoon hot pepper sauce
1-1/2	cups shredded Parmesan cheese
1/8	teaspoon paprika

In a Dutch oven, bring 6 cups water to a boil. Add pearl onions; boil for 3 minutes. Drain and rinse in cold water; peel and set aside.

In a large saucepan, saute the celery, green onions and garlic in butter until tender. Stir in the flour, salt and pepper until blended; gradually add the cream and hot pepper sauce. Bring to a boil; cook and stir for 2 minutes or until thickened.

Stir in pearl onions and cheese. Transfer to a greased 8-in. square baking dish; sprinkle with paprika. Bake, uncovered, at 350° for 20-25 minutes or until bubbly.

Cranberry-Swirl Cornmeal Loaves

PREP: 40 MIN. + RISING **BAKE:** 35 MIN. + COOLING
YIELD: 2 LOAVES (16 SLICES EACH)

When my cranberry and cornmeal cookie won a contest at our state fair, I decided to use those ingredients in a yeast bread. My family prefers it to raisin bread.

Mary Volcko ★ Camillus, New York

2	packages (1/4 ounce *each*) active dry yeast
2-1/4	cups warm milk (110° to 115°)
1/3	cup butter-flavored shortening
1/3	cup sugar
2	eggs
2	teaspoons salt
6	to 6-1/2 cups all-purpose flour
1	cup cornmeal

FILLING:

1-1/2	cups dried cranberries
1	tablespoon water
1/4	cup sugar
1/4	cup packed brown sugar
2	teaspoons grated orange peel
1	teaspoon ground cinnamon
1/4	teaspoon ground nutmeg
1	tablespoon milk, optional

In a large bowl, dissolve yeast in warm milk. Add the shortening, sugar, eggs, salt and 3 cups flour; beat until smooth. Stir in cornmeal and enough remaining flour to form a soft dough.

Turn onto a floured surface; knead until smooth and elastic, about 6-8 minutes. Place in a greased bowl, turning once to grease the top. Cover and let rise in a warm place until doubled, about 1 hour.

For filling, place cranberries and water in a small microwave-safe bowl. Cover and microwave on high for 1 minute; set aside. In another bowl, combine the sugars, orange peel, cinnamon and nutmeg.

Punch dough down. Turn onto a lightly floured surface; divide in half. Roll each portion into a 15-in. x 7-in. rectangle. Lightly brush dough with water; sprinkle the sugar mixture to within 1/2 in. of the edges. Sprinkle with the cranberries.

Roll up jelly-roll style, starting with a short side. Pinch seams to seal. Place seam side down in two greased 9-in. x 5-in. loaf pans. Cover and let rise in a warm place until doubled, about 1 hour.

Brush with milk if desired. Bake at 375° for 35-40 minutes or until golden brown. Remove from pans to wire racks to cool.

Broken Glass Gelatin

PREP: 50 MIN. + CHILLING **YIELD:** 10 SERVINGS

Small pieces of gelatin give this old-fashioned salad a mosaic look. I like the fact that I don't need a special mold to make it. Serve this as a salad or dessert.

Suzy Horvath ★ Sheridan, Oregon

1	package (3 ounces) cherry gelatin
3-3/4	cups boiling water, *divided*
1-1/2	cups cold water, *divided*
1	package (3 ounces) lime gelatin
1	package (3 ounces) orange gelatin
1	package (3 ounces) lemon gelatin
1/4	cup sugar
1/2	cup lemonade
1-3/4	cups whipped topping

Additional whipped topping, optional

In a small bowl, dissolve cherry gelatin in 1 cup boiling water; stir in 1/2 cup cold water. Pour into an 8-in. square dish coated with cooking spray. Refrigerate until set.

Repeat with lime and orange gelatin, using separate 8-in. square dishes for each.

In a large bowl, dissolve the lemon gelatin and sugar in remaining boiling water; stir in the lemonade. Cover and refrigerate until slightly thickened. Fold in the whipped topping.

Cut the cherry, lime and orange gelatin into 1/2-in. cubes. Fold into lemon gelatin mixture. Pour into individual serving dishes. Cover and refrigerate for at least 4 hours. Garnish with additional whipped topping if desired.

Party Planner Timeline

The following timeline starts your party-planning process well in advance and ensures you won't overlook any aspect of the upcoming event. Give yourself plenty of time and keep lists of things to do and to buy. As a result, you'll remain stress free and keep last-minute glitches to a minimum.

4 to 6 Weeks Before

Select a date and time for the party...and a date by when guests should reply.

Create the guest list.

Determine your budget—then make sure you stick to it!

Plan your menu and beverages.

Make a list of tasks that can be done in advance and that should be done the day of the party.

2 to 3 Weeks Before

Make party favors, napkin folds and/or nonperishable centerpieces.

Send out invitations or call guests. Make it clear what type of food will be served and what time you plan on serving it.

Take inventory of plates, serving platters, napkins, cutlery, glasses, etc. Shop for any needed items.

Prepare two grocery lists—one for nonperishable items to purchase now and one for perishable items to purchase a few days before the party. Have separate lists for different stores.

Order your fresh meat or fresh turkey.

Make a list of cleaning tasks.

1 Week Before

Call guests who haven't responded.

Buy nonperishable items.

Do preliminary housecleaning.

Check that the table linens are laundered.

Prepare and freeze any recipes you can.

Plan seating, food and drink areas.

Take stock of the bar.

2 to 3 Days Before

Clean out your refrigerator.

Buy remaining grocery items.

Set out decorations and candles.

Thaw any frozen meat.

Bake any desserts or breads that will keep well.

Make ice for drinks.

1 Day Before

Make any dishes that will hold and can be heated the next day.

Precut vegetables for recipes. Measure and place in containers.

Wash and dry greens for salads. Make salad dressing.

Make a list of last-minute tasks for the day of the party.

Have bathrooms well stocked with towels, toilet paper and tissues.

Prepare a cooking timeline for the next day. Decide what time you'd like to serve dinner and work backwards to determine when to begin cooking the foods.

Set the table.

Assemble the floral centerpiece if you're using one.

The Big Day

In the morning, make any appetizers.

Have garnishes ready for desserts or other dishes.

Plan on being ready for guests 1 hour before they're scheduled to arrive. This cushion helps if unforeseen problems arise.

Cook according to your cooking timeline.

Take one more walk around the house and straighten up. If needed, put hard-to-hide clutter in a large laundry basket and stow it away in an unused room.

Start the music and light the candles 30 minutes before your guests arrive.

Carefree
ENTERTAINING

Chicken with Mushroom Wine Sauce

(pictured on page 51)

PREP: 30 MIN.   **COOK:** 20 MIN.   **YIELD:** 6 SERVINGS

A visit to Napa Valley wine country inspired me to experiment with one of my mom's scrumptious chicken dishes. This elegant entree is so easy to prepare.

Jill Bonanno ★ Loma Linda, California

  4 bacon strips, diced
  6 boneless skinless chicken breast halves (5 ounces *each*)
  3 tablespoons butter, *divided*
1/2 pound sliced fresh mushrooms
3/4 cup sliced green onions
  1 large carrot, thinly sliced
  1 garlic clove, minced
  2 tablespoons all-purpose flour
  1 teaspoon salt
1/2 teaspoon dried thyme
1/8 teaspoon pepper
3/4 cup chicken broth
3/4 cup white wine *or* additional chicken broth
  1 bay leaf
  2 tablespoons minced fresh parsley

In a large skillet, cook bacon over medium heat until crisp. Using a slotted spoon, remove to paper towels; drain and discard drippings. In the same skillet, brown chicken on both sides in 2 tablespoons butter. Remove and keep warm.

Saute mushrooms, onions, carrot and garlic in remaining butter until tender. Stir in the flour, salt, thyme and pepper until smooth. Gradually add broth, wine and bay leaf.

Bring to a boil; cook and stir for 2 minutes or until thickened. Return chicken to the pan. Reduce heat; cover and simmer for 10 minutes or until chicken juices run clear. Discard bay leaf. Garnish with parsley and bacon.

Holiday Spinach Salad

(pictured on page 51)

PREP/TOTAL TIME: 25 MIN.   **YIELD:** 8 SERVINGS

We don't care for cooked spinach. But we can't get enough of fresh spinach in salads, especially when paired with strawberries, oranges and peanuts!

Jake Haen ★ Ocala, Florida

  1 package (6 ounces) fresh baby spinach
  4 cups torn red leaf lettuce
  1 cup sliced fresh strawberries
  1 can (11 ounces) mandarin oranges, drained
1/4 cup honey-roasted peanuts
1/4 cup sliced green onions

CITRUS VINAIGRETTE:
1/4 cup canola oil
1/4 cup orange juice
  2 tablespoons sugar
  2 tablespoons white wine vinegar
  1 tablespoon lemon juice
1/2 teaspoon grated orange peel
1/4 teaspoon salt

In a large salad bowl, combine the spinach, lettuce, strawberries, oranges, peanuts and onions.

In a small bowl, whisk the vinaigrette ingredients until blended. Drizzle over the salad and toss to coat. Serve immediately.

Roasted Garlic & Onion Linguine

(pictured on page 51)

PREP: 10 MIN.   **BAKE:** 30 MIN. + COOLING
YIELD: 6 SERVINGS

Instead of offering holiday company ordinary buttered noodles, make this garlic-infused linguine. Pass extra Parmesan around the table for guests who'd like more cheesy flavor.

Mariah Maliska ★ Keene, New Hampshire

  1 whole garlic bulb
  1 teaspoon canola oil
  2 small onions, halved
 12 ounces uncooked linguine
1/4 cup grated Parmesan cheese
1/4 cup reduced-sodium chicken broth
1/4 teaspoon salt
1/4 teaspoon coarsely ground pepper

Remove papery outer skin from the garlic (do not peel or separate cloves). Cut top off garlic bulb; brush with the oil. Wrap bulb and onions in heavy-duty foil.

Bake at 425° for 30-35 minutes or until softened. Cool for 10-15 minutes.

Meanwhile, cook the linguine according to the package directions. Squeeze softened garlic into a food processor. Add the cheese, broth, salt, pepper and onions; cover and process until blended. Drain linguine; toss with garlic mixture.

Parmesan Scones

PREP/TOTAL TIME: 25 MIN. **YIELD:** 1 DOZEN

Unlike most other scones, these are nice and moist...thanks to heavy whipping cream! You can even stir in some basil or oregano if you like.

Jolie Stinson ★ Lebanon, Oregon

2 large onions, chopped
2 tablespoons olive oil
6 garlic cloves, minced
4 cups all-purpose flour
2 cups grated Parmesan cheese
4 teaspoons baking powder
1 teaspoon salt
2 cups heavy whipping cream

In a large skillet, saute onions in oil until tender. Add garlic; saute 1 minute longer.

In a large bowl, combine flour, cheese, baking powder and salt. Stir in the cream just until moistened. Stir in the onion mixture.

Turn onto a floured surface; knead 10 times. Divide the dough in half. Pat each portion into a 6-in. circle. Cut each circle into six wedges. Separate the wedges and place on a greased baking sheet.

Bake at 400° for 10-12 minutes or until light golden brown. Serve warm.

Spinach & Shells Soup

PREP/TOTAL TIME: 25 MIN.   **YIELD:** 4 SERVINGS

I played around with this recipe for 15 years before I got it just right! Served with oven-fresh bread, it makes a wonderful wintertime lunch.

Joyce Toney ★ Peoria, Arizona

- 3 cups reduced-sodium chicken broth
- 1 can (14-1/2 ounces) stewed tomatoes, cut up
- 1 cup uncooked small pasta shells
- 1 teaspoon reduced-sodium chicken bouillon granules
- 1 garlic clove, minced
- 1 can (15 ounces) white kidney or cannellini beans, rinsed and drained
- 1 cup chopped fresh spinach
- 1/2 teaspoon dried basil
- 1/2 teaspoon dried oregano
- 1/4 teaspoon pepper
- 2 tablespoons grated Parmesan cheese

In a large saucepan, combine the broth, tomatoes, pasta, bouillon and garlic. Bring to a boil. Reduce heat; simmer, uncovered, for 5-7 minutes or until pasta is almost tender.

Stir in the beans, spinach, basil, oregano and pepper; cover and simmer for 10 minutes or until heated through and pasta is tender. Sprinkle with Parmesan cheese.

Oat Nut Bread

PREP: 15 MIN.   **BAKE:** 3 HOURS
YIELD: 1 LOAF (1-1/2 POUNDS, 16 SLICES)

A bread machine makes the process of preparing homemade bread so much easier. Toasted nuts enhance the flavor of this lovely loaf.

Diane Morrill ★ Grand Forks, North Dakota

- 1-1/4 cups warm milk (70° to 80°)
- 2 tablespoons plus 1 teaspoon butter, melted, *divided*
- 1/4 teaspoon vanilla extract
- 2 tablespoons brown sugar
- 1 teaspoon salt
- 2-1/2 cups bread flour
- 1/2 cup whole wheat flour
- 1 teaspoon bread machine yeast
- 1/2 cup old-fashioned oats
- 1/4 cup finely chopped walnuts, toasted
- 1/4 cup finely chopped hazelnuts, toasted

In bread machine pan, place all the ingredients in the order suggested by manufacturer. Select basic bread setting. Choose crust color and loaf size if available. Bake according to bread machine directions (check dough after 5 minutes of mixing; add 1 to 2 tablespoons of water or flour if needed).

Just before final kneading (your machine may audibly signal this), add the oats and nuts.

Brush the baked loaf with the remaining butter.

Dressed-Up Candle

Add a little flair to a plain pillar candle by embellishing it with costume jewelry.

Raid your jewelry box for long chain or beaded necklaces. Using T-pins or U-pins to hold them in place, wrap several necklaces around a large pillar candle. (The pins are available at craft stores.) Mix and match colors and textures as desired to create a unique focal point.

Orange Honey Carrots

PREP/TOTAL TIME: 25 MIN. **YIELD:** 6 SERVINGS

With a subtle honey flavor, these colorful carrots would pair well with any entree. Family and friends find them on many of my menus.

Judy Parker ★ Albuquerque, New Mexico

- 3 tablespoons honey
- 2 tablespoons butter
- 2 to 3 teaspoons poppy seeds, optional
- 1/2 teaspoon grated orange peel
- 1/4 teaspoon salt
- 1 pound carrots, julienned

In a large saucepan, combine the honey, butter, poppy seeds if desired, orange peel and salt. Bring to a boil. Stir in the carrots. Cook and stir until carrots are crisp-tender, about 10 minutes.

Pomegranate Fluff Salad

PREP: 40 MIN. **YIELD:** 26 SERVINGS (3/4 CUP EACH)

My sister-in-law brought this salad to Thanksgiving one year and we all loved it. It's a fun way to introduce folks to pomegranates.

Jennie Richards ★ Riverton, Utah

- 5 cups pomegranate seeds (about 3 large pomegranates)
- 3 cans (11 ounces *each*) mandarin oranges, drained
- 1 package (10-1/2 ounces) pastel miniature marshmallows
- 3 medium apples, chopped
- 2 medium bananas, sliced
- 1/2 cup flaked coconut
- 1/2 cup chopped walnuts
- 2 cups heavy whipping cream
- 1/3 cup confectioners' sugar
- 1 teaspoon vanilla extract

In a large bowl, combine the first seven ingredients. In another bowl, beat cream until it begins to thicken. Add confectioners' sugar and vanilla; beat until stiff peaks form. Gently fold into the fruit mixture. Serve immediately.

Sweet Citrus Punch

PREP/TOTAL TIME: 5 MIN.
YIELD: 12 SERVINGS (ABOUT 3 QUARTS)

The wonderful rosy color of this beverage makes it a natural choice to serve at Christmas. I keep the ingredients on hand to prepare at a moment's notice.

Mary Ann Kosmas ★ Minneapolis, Minnesota

- 1 can (12 ounces) frozen orange juice concentrate, thawed
- 1 can (12 ounces) frozen lemonade concentrate, thawed
- 1 cup grenadine syrup
- 2 quarts ginger ale, chilled

Ice ring *or* shaved ice, optional

Just before serving, combine the concentrates, grenadine and ginger ale in a punch bowl. Add an ice ring or shaved ice if desired.

Opening a Pomegranate

1. Cut off the crown of the fruit and discard. Score the fruit into quarters, taking care not to cut into the red juice sacs or arils (also referred to in recipes as the seeds.)

2. Place the sections in a bowl of water and soak for 5 minutes. Break sections open with your fingers and gently push out the seed clusters. Discard skin and white membrane. Drain water, reserving arils. Dry on paper towels. The arils may be eaten whole, seeds and all.

Peanut Butter Pie

PREP: 10 MIN. + CHILLING **YIELD:** 8 SERVINGS

You don't have to be a kid—only a kid at heart!—to relish this mile-high pie packed with peanut butter. The chocolate crust is a nice complement.

Peter Mitchell ★ Watertown, Wisconsin

12	ounces cream cheese, softened
1	cup creamy peanut butter
3-3/4	cups confectioners' sugar
1	carton (16 ounces) frozen whipped topping, thawed
1	chocolate crumb crust (9 inches)
1/3	cup miniature semisweet chocolate chips

In a large bowl, beat the cream cheese, peanut butter and confectioners' sugar until smooth. Fold in whipped topping.

Spread into crust. Sprinkle with chocolate chips. Refrigerate for at least 2 hours before serving.

Editor's Note: You can make a homemade chocolate crumb crust. Combine 1-1/4 cups crumbs (about 20 chocolate wafers), 1/4 cup sugar and 1/4 cup melted butter; blend well. Press onto the bottom and up the sides of an ungreased 9-in. pie plate. Chill 30 minutes before filling.

Warm Pork and Pear Salad

PREP: 35 MIN. **COOK:** 20 MIN. **YIELD:** 4 SERVINGS

Convenient items—like a salad mix and marinated pork loin—are the secret to this speedy salad that's tossed with a special sweet-and-sour dressing.

Patricia Harmon ★ Baden, Pennsylvania

- 1 cup sliced sweet onion
- 1 tablespoon plus 1/3 cup canola oil, *divided*
- 1/4 cup cider vinegar
- 1 teaspoon molasses
- 1 teaspoon sugar
- 1/2 teaspoon salt
- 1/8 teaspoon pepper

SALAD:

- 1 package (1.7 pounds) lemon-garlic center cut pork loin fillet
- 2 tablespoons canola oil
- 1 package (10 ounces) Italian romaine and radicchio salad mix
- 2 medium pears, sliced
- 1/2 cup seedless red grapes
- 1/2 cup coarsely chopped walnuts, toasted
- 1/2 cup crumbled Gorgonzola cheese

In a large skillet, cook the onion in 1 tablespoon oil over medium heat for 10-15 minutes or until golden brown. Cool to room temperature.

Place onion and vinegar in a blender; cover and process until onion is chopped. Add the molasses, sugar, salt and pepper; cover and process until blended. While processing, gradually add the remaining oil in a steady stream. Pour the dressing into a microwave-safe bowl; set aside.

Cut the pork into 1/4-in. slices. In a large skillet, cook the pork in oil until no longer pink. Remove and cut into strips; keep warm.

Microwave dressing on high for 30-60 seconds or until warmed; whisk until blended. Toss salad mix with 1/2 cup dressing; place on a serving platter. Top with pears, grapes and pork. Drizzle with remaining dressing; sprinkle with walnuts and cheese. Serve immediately.

Chicken Fajita Pasta

PREP: 20 MIN. **COOK:** 15 MIN. **YIELD:** 8 SERVINGS

The flavor of fajitas shines through in this quick and easy pasta dish. A simple green salad completes the meal.

Stacy Myers ★ Wapakoneta, Ohio

- 1 pound boneless skinless chicken breasts, cut into thin strips
- 2 tablespoons fajita seasoning mix, *divided*
- 2 tablespoons canola oil, *divided*
- 8 ounces uncooked penne pasta
- 1 *each* medium green, sweet red and yellow pepper, sliced
- 1 medium onion, sliced
- 1 jar (16 ounces) salsa
- 1/2 cup water
- 1/4 cup shredded cheddar cheese
- 1 tablespoon minced fresh cilantro

Sour cream, optional

Sprinkle the chicken with 1 tablespoon fajita seasoning. In a large skillet over medium heat, cook the chicken in 1 tablespoon oil for 6-8 minutes or until juices run clear. Meanwhile, cook pasta according to package directions.

Remove chicken and keep warm. In the same skillet, saute peppers and onion in remaining oil. Sprinkle with remaining fajita seasoning; stir until blended. Add the salsa, water and chicken; heat through.

Drain pasta; toss with chicken mixture. Sprinkle with cheese and cilantro. Serve with sour cream if desired.

Lake Charles Dip

PREP: 15 MIN. + CHILLING **YIELD:** 1-1/2 CUPS

Italian salad dressing mix gives this simply delicious dip its wonderful taste. Serve it with fresh veggies or crackers for an easy appetizer.

ScottsGrace ★ Taste of Home Online Community

- 1 cup (8 ounces) sour cream
- 2 tablespoons reduced-fat mayonnaise
- 1 tablespoon Italian salad dressing mix
- 1/3 cup finely chopped avocado
- 1 teaspoon lemon juice
- 1/2 cup finely chopped seeded tomato

In a small bowl, combine the sour cream, mayonnaise and dressing mix. Toss avocado with lemon juice; stir into sour cream mixture. Stir in tomato. Cover and refrigerate for at least 1 hour.

Brisket with Cranberry-Horseradish Gravy

PREP: 15 MIN.   **COOK:** 6 HOURS   **YIELD:** 10 SERVINGS

Need a fix-it-and-forget-it entree for Christmas? Give this slow cooker specialty a try. I like to round out this dinner with boiled red potatoes.

Jeannie Mangan ★ Spokane, Washington

- 1 teaspoon onion powder
- 1 teaspoon salt
- 1 teaspoon coarsely ground pepper
- 1/2 teaspoon ground allspice
- 1 fresh beef brisket (5 pounds)
- 1 can (16 ounces) whole-berry cranberry sauce
- 3/4 cup horseradish sauce
- 2 teaspoons lemon juice
- 1 bay leaf
- 3 tablespoons cornstarch
- 1/4 cup cold water

Combine the onion powder, salt, pepper and allspice; rub over brisket. Cut brisket in half; place in a 5-qt. slow cooker.

Combine the cranberry sauce, horseradish, lemon juice and bay leaf; pour over beef. Cover and cook on low for 6-7 hours or until tender.

Remove brisket and keep warm. Strain cooking juices; discard bay leaf. Transfer 3 cups cooking juices to a small saucepan.

Combine cornstarch and cold water until smooth; stir into juices. Bring to a boil; cook and stir for 2 minutes or until thickened. Thinly slice beef across the grain; serve with gravy.

Editor's Note: This is a fresh beef brisket, not corned beef.

Trim Beans in No Time

There's a faster way to trim the ends of fresh beans instead of snapping off the ends one by one.

Simply line up the ends of several beans on a cutting board. Using a chef's knife, slice off the ends. Repeat on the other side.

Stir-Fried Beans with Pecans

PREP/TOTAL TIME: 20 MIN.   **YIELD:** 5 SERVINGS

Made with fresh-from-the-garden green beans and onions, this side dish gets gobbled up by our six kids. Pecans add a bit of crunch.

Kathy Klingensmith ★ Riesel, Texas

- 1/2 pound fresh green beans, trimmed
- 1/2 pound fresh wax beans, trimmed
- 2 tablespoons canola oil
- 1 large onion, sliced
- 1/2 cup pecan halves
- 3/4 teaspoon salt

In a large skillet or wok, stir-fry the beans in oil for 4-5 minutes. Add the remaining ingredients; stir-fry for 2-3 minutes longer or until the vegetables are crisp-tender.

Eggplant Muffuletta

PREP: 35 MIN. **BROIL:** 5 MIN. **YIELD:** 18 SERVINGS

I often rely on this recipe when hosting a casual holiday party. It's a marvelous meatless sandwich that is sure to make each gathering special.

Elizabeth Dumont ★ Boulder, Colorado

1	jar (8 ounces) roasted sweet red peppers, drained
1	cup pimiento-stuffed olives
1	cup pitted ripe olives
1	cup giardiniera
3/4	cup olive oil, *divided*
1/4	cup packed fresh parsley sprigs
3	tablespoons white wine vinegar
4	garlic cloves, halved
1-1/2	teaspoons salt, *divided*
1/2	teaspoon pepper, *divided*
1	pound sliced fresh mushrooms
1	large onion, thinly sliced
2	tablespoons butter
1	cup all-purpose flour
1	medium eggplant, cut into nine slices
3	loaves (10 ounces *each*) focaccia bread
2	large tomatoes, sliced
9	slices provolone cheese
9	slices part-skim mozzarella cheese

In a food processor, combine the red peppers, olives, giardiniera, 1/4 cup oil, parsley, vinegar, garlic, 1 teaspoon salt and 1/4 teaspoon pepper. Cover and process until blended; set aside.

In a large skillet, saute mushrooms and onion in butter and 1/4 cup oil. Remove and keep warm.

In a large resealable plastic bag, combine the flour and remaining salt and pepper. Add the eggplant, a few slices at a time, and shake to coat. In the same skillet, cook eggplant in remaining oil for 2-3 minutes on each side or until golden brown.

Split each loaf of focaccia in half lengthwise. Spread the reserved olive mixture over each focaccia bottom; top with eggplant, mushroom mixture, tomatoes and cheeses.

Place on a baking sheet. Broil 2-3 in. from the heat for 2-4 minutes or until the cheese is melted. Replace focaccia tops. Cut each loaf into six wedges.

About the Muffuletta

The muffuletta sandwich was created in 1906 at Central Grocery in New Orleans. Made on a large loaf of bread, this sandwich is typically layered with meats and cheeses and topped with a marinated olive salad.

Save time when making meatless Eggplant Muffuletta by preparing the pepper-olive mixture in advance and refrigerating it.

Mediterranean Mahi Mahi

PREP: 30 MIN.   **BAKE:** 10 MIN.   **YIELD:** 4 SERVINGS

I created this entree years ago when a friend gave me some fresh-caught mahi mahi. Shortly after, I entered the recipe in a contest and won! I think you'll agree it's a keeper.

Virginia Anthony ★ Jacksonville, Florida

1	medium onion, chopped
1	medium green pepper, chopped
4-1/2	teaspoons olive oil, *divided*
1	garlic clove, minced
3/4	cup salsa
1/2	cup white wine *or* chicken broth
1/4	cup halved Greek olives
1/2	teaspoon Greek seasoning
4	mahi mahi fillets (6 ounces *each*)
1/4	teaspoon salt
1/4	teaspoon pepper
1/4	cup crumbled tomato and basil feta cheese

In a large ovenproof skillet, saute onion and green pepper in 1-1/2 teaspoons oil until tender. Add the garlic; saute 1 minute longer.

Stir in the salsa, wine, olives and Greek seasoning. Bring to a boil. Reduce heat; simmer, uncovered, for 5 minutes or until slightly thickened. Transfer to a bowl; set aside.

Sprinkle mahi mahi with salt and pepper. In the same skillet, lightly brown fillets in remaining oil for 2 minutes on each side. Spoon salsa mixture over fillets.

Bake, uncovered, at 425° for 6 minutes. Sprinkle with the cheese; bake 2-3 minutes longer or until the fish just turns opaque.

Pina Colada Fruit Dip

PREP/TOTAL TIME: 15 MIN. **YIELD:** 2-1/2 CUPS

A taste of the tropics will be welcomed by your holiday guests. The cool and creamy dip can be served as either an appetizer or a dessert.

Shelly Fisher ★ Hermiston, Oregon

- 1 package (8 ounces) cream cheese, softened
- 1 jar (7 ounces) marshmallow creme
- 1 can (8 ounces) crushed pineapple, drained
- 1/2 cup flaked coconut

Assorted fresh fruit *or* cubed pound cake

In a small bowl, beat cream cheese and marshmallow creme until fluffy. Fold in pineapple and coconut. Cover and chill until serving. Serve with fruit or pound cake.

Lemon-Oat Cheesecake Bars

PREP: 20 MIN. **BAKE:** 25 MIN. + COOLING **YIELD:** 32 BARS

Because it's prepared in a jelly-roll pan, this dessert is easier than a traditional cheesecake. But it still has the same great flavor.

Sarah Miller ★ Wauconda, Washington

- 2 cups all-purpose flour
- 1-1/2 cups packed brown sugar
- 1/2 teaspoon salt
- 1 cup cold butter
- 1-1/2 cups quick-cooking oats
- 2 packages (8 ounces *each*) cream cheese, softened
- 1/2 cup sugar
- 3 eggs, lightly beaten
- 1/4 cup lemon juice
- 1/4 cup milk
- 1 teaspoon vanilla extract

In a large bowl, combine the flour, brown sugar and salt; cut in butter until crumbly. Stir in the oats. Set aside 1-1/2 cups for topping.

Press the remaining oat mixture into a greased 15-in. x 10-in. x 1-in. baking pan. Bake at 350° for 10-12 minutes or until golden brown.

Meanwhile, in a large bowl, beat cream cheese and sugar until smooth. Add the eggs; beat on low speed just until combined. Stir in the lemon juice, milk and vanilla. Pour over crust. Sprinkle with reserved oat mixture.

Bake for 24-26 minutes or until the edges are lightly browned and filling is set. Cool on a wire rack. Cut into bars. Store in the refrigerator.

Italian Appetizer Meatballs

PREP: 40 MIN. **COOK:** 2 HOURS **YIELD:** 4 DOZEN

Store-bought spaghetti sauce speeds up the preparation of these homemade meatball appetizers. Leftovers make terrific sub sandwiches.

Rene McCrory ★ Indianapolis, Indiana

- 2 eggs, beaten
- 1/2 cup dry bread crumbs
- 1/4 cup milk
- 2 teaspoons grated Parmesan cheese
- 1 teaspoon salt
- 1/4 teaspoon pepper
- 1/8 teaspoon garlic powder
- 1 pound ground beef
- 1 pound bulk Italian sausage
- 2 jars (26 ounces *each*) spaghetti sauce

In a large bowl, combine first seven ingredients. Crumble the beef and sausage over the mixture and mix well. Shape into 1-in. balls.

Place meatballs on a greased rack in a shallow baking pan. Bake, uncovered, at 400° for 15-20 minutes or until no longer pink.

Transfer the meatballs to a 4-qt. slow cooker; add the spaghetti sauce. Cover and cook on high for 2-3 hours or until heated through.

Winter Delight Stew

PREP: 20 MIN. **BAKE:** 1-1/2 HOURS
YIELD: 16 SERVINGS (4 QUARTS)

This home-style stew is loaded with sausage, beans and vegetables. It wins rave reviews from everyone who tries it.

Lee Sauers ★ Mifflinburg, Pennsylvania

- 1 pound bulk Italian sausage
- 4 cups chopped cabbage
- 2 cups sliced fresh carrots
- 2 medium potatoes, chopped
- 1 cup chopped onion
- 2 cups beef *or* chicken broth
- 1 can (16 ounces) kidney beans, rinsed and drained
- 1 can (14-1/2 ounces) diced tomatoes, undrained
- 1/2 cup tomato juice
- 1/8 teaspoon salt

In a Dutch oven, cook the sausage over medium heat until no longer pink; drain.

Stir in the remaining ingredients. Cover and bake at 350° for 1-1/2 to 2 hours or until vegetables are tender.

Olive & Cheese Appetizers

PREP: 10 MIN. + CHILLING   **BAKE:** 10 MIN.   **YIELD:** 3 DOZEN

These pizza-like appetizers are sure to appeal to all people at your party. Prepare the olive mixture in advance. When ready to serve, spread on bread slices and bake.

Germaine Stank ★ Pound, Wisconsin

- 1 jar (5 ounces) pimiento-stuffed olives, drained and chopped
- 3/4 cup shredded Monterey Jack cheese
- 3/4 cup shredded cheddar cheese
- 3 green onions, chopped
- 1/2 cup mayonnaise
- 3/4 teaspoon chili powder
- 1 French bread baguette (10-1/2 ounces), cut into 1/4-inch slices

In a small bowl, combine the olives, cheeses, green onions, mayonnaise and chili powder. Cover; chill for 2-3 hours.

Spread over bread slices. Place on an ungreased baking sheet. Bake at 400° for 8-10 minutes until cheese is melted and bubbly. Serve immediately.

Honey Sweet Potato Biscuits

PREP: 20 MIN.   **BAKE:** 15 MIN.   **YIELD:** 10 BISCUITS

I make at least one batch of these hearty biscuits each week. They pair well with soups, stews and even breakfast entrees!

Mary Ellen Swanson ★ Rainsville, Alabama

- 1 cup plus 3 tablespoons all-purpose flour
- 3/4 cup whole wheat flour
- 1/2 cup toasted wheat germ
- 2 teaspoons baking powder
- 1/2 teaspoon baking soda
- 1/2 teaspoon salt
- 1-1/4 cups buttermilk
- 2/3 cup mashed sweet potato
- 1/4 cup butter, melted
- 2 tablespoons honey

In a large bowl, combine first six ingredients. In another bowl, whisk the buttermilk, sweet potato, butter and honey; stir into dry ingredients just until moistened.

Turn onto a lightly floured surface; knead 8-10 times. Pat or roll dough out to 3/4-in. thickness; cut with a floured 2-1/2-in. biscuit cutter.

Place 2 in. apart on a greased baking sheet. Bake at 400° for 15-20 minutes or until golden brown. Serve warm.

Bacon-Cheese Biscuit Bites

PREP: 20 MIN.   **BAKE:** 15 MIN.   **YIELD:** 20 APPETIZERS

As a busy stay-at-home mom, I like great-tasting recipes that are easy and that the kids can help prepare. These savory snacks meet both of those requirements.

Margo Lewis ★ Lake City, Michigan

- 4 ounces cream cheese, softened
- 1 egg
- 1 tablespoon milk
- 1/3 cup real bacon bits
- 1/4 cup shredded Swiss cheese
- 1 tablespoon dried minced onion
- 1 large plum tomato, seeded and finely chopped, *divided*
- 1 tube (10.2 ounces) large refrigerated flaky biscuits

In a small bowl, beat the cream cheese, egg and milk until blended. Stir in the bacon, cheese, onion and half of the tomato; set aside.

Cut each biscuit into four pieces; press each piece into a greased miniature muffin cup. Fill with the cream cheese mixture; top with remaining tomato.

Bake at 375° for 14-16 minutes or until golden brown.

Tips for Making Biscuits

For biscuits that are tender and moist instead of tough and dry, be careful not to overmix or overknead the dough.

When reworking the trimmings, handle the dough as little as possible and use as little flour as needed on the working surface.

Biscuits are best served warm but can be frozen for up to 3 months. To reheat defrosted biscuits, wrap in foil and bake at 300° for 10-12 minutes.

Mini Orange-Raspberry Trifles

PREP/TOTAL TIME: 20 MIN.   **YIELD:** 6 SERVINGS

Pound cake, raspberry pie filling and hot fudge topping make trifles hard to resist! For a fun party idea, have each guest assemble their own.

- 1 loaf (10-3/4 ounces) frozen pound cake, thawed and cut into 1/2-inch cubes
- 1/4 cup Triple Sec *or* orange juice
- 1 can (21 ounces) raspberry pie filling
- 3/4 cup hot fudge ice cream topping, warmed
- Additional hot fudge ice cream topping, warmed
- 3/4 cup whipped topping

Place cake cubes in a large bowl. Drizzle with Triple Sec; toss to coat. Spoon 3 tablespoons of the pie filling into each of six parfait glasses or dessert dishes. Top with 1/3 cup cake cubes, 2 tablespoons hot fudge, 1/3 cup cake cubes and 3 tablespoons pie filling. Drizzle with additional fudge topping; dollop with 2 tablespoons whipped topping.

Creamy Vegetable Casserole

PREP: 25 MIN.   **BAKE:** 20 MIN.   **YIELD:** 8 SERVINGS

With four different vegetables, this creamy and comforting casserole has something for everyone.

Christie Nelson ★ Taylorville, Illinois

- 2 cups fresh baby carrots
- 2 cups fresh broccoli florets
- 2 cups fresh cauliflowerets
- 1-3/4 cups sliced fresh mushrooms
- 2 tablespoons butter
- 2 tablespoons all-purpose flour
- 2 cups half-and-half cream
- 1 teaspoon chicken bouillon granules
- 1/2 teaspoon onion powder
- 1/4 teaspoon white pepper
- 1 cup (4 ounces) shredded Swiss cheese
- 1/2 cup crushed butter-flavored crackers (about 15 crackers)

Place the carrots in a steamer basket; place in a large saucepan over 1 in. of water. Bring to a boil; cover and steam for 3 minutes.

Add broccoli and cauliflower; steam 5 minutes longer or until tender. Transfer the vegetables to a greased 2-1/2-qt. baking dish.

In a large skillet, saute mushrooms in butter until tender. Stir in flour until blended. Gradually stir in cream, bouillon, onion powder and pepper. Bring to a boil; cook and stir for 2 minutes or until thickened. Stir in cheese.

Pour over vegetables and stir to coat. Sprinkle with cracker crumbs. Bake, uncovered, at 350° for 20-25 minutes or until bubbly.

Seasoning Steamed Veggies

If serving simple steamed vegetables as a side, consider adding ingredients to steamer basket for more great taste.

For subtle flavor, use fresh herbs (such as basil, thyme, rosemary and garlic cloves) or lemon and lime slices.

Fragrant oils (like hot chili oil) and spices (seasoned salts and curry, for example) pack a robust punch.

You can even add beef, chicken or vegetable granules to the water in the pan.

Carrot Raisin Couscous

PREP: 15 MIN.   **COOK:** 20 MIN.   **YIELD:** 10 SERVINGS

The addition of golden raisins adds a slightly sweet flavor to this unique side dish featuring both couscous and carrots.

Jordan Sucher ★ Brooklyn, New York

1/3	cup port wine *or* chicken broth
1/3	cup golden raisins
1	medium onion, chopped
3	tablespoons olive oil, *divided*
1	package (10 ounces) couscous
2	cups chicken broth
1/4	teaspoon salt, *divided*
1/4	teaspoon pepper, *divided*
4	medium carrots, julienned
1	tablespoon sugar
1	teaspoon molasses

In a small saucepan, heat wine until hot. In a small bowl, soak the raisins in wine for 5 minutes. Drain the raisins, reserving wine.

In a large saucepan, saute onion in 1 tablespoon oil until tender. Stir in the couscous. Cook and stir until lightly browned. Stir in the broth, raisins and half of the salt and pepper. Bring to a boil. Cover and remove from the heat. Let stand for 5 minutes; fluff with a fork.

In a small skillet, saute carrots in remaining oil until crisp-tender. Combine the sugar, molasses, reserved wine and the remaining salt and pepper. Stir into the carrots; heat through.

In a large bowl, combine couscous mixture and carrots; toss to combine.

Seasonal
GET-TOGETHERS

Seasonal Get-Togethers

Christmas morning brunch...holiday movie night...festive open house...after-caroling party. You have countless reasons to gather with family and friends during the Christmas season. Make those moments even more memorable with this chapter's merry array of mouth-watering appetizers, beverages, entrees, side dishes and sinfully, rich desserts!

Santa is done stuffing the stockings. Midnight services have been attended. The excitement of gift-opening is over. But you can extend the celebration on Christmas Day with these eye-opening brunch dishes!

As Ham & Spinach Crepes bake, offer your family glasses of gorgeous Mango Orange Quencher. Vanilla Fruit Salad is dressed with peach pie filling for a sweet side that pairs well with the savory crepes. Oven-fresh Merry Christmas Scones are dotted with colorful red and green candied cherries for a sweet surprise.

Ham & Spinach Crepes

PREP: 40 MIN. + CHILLING   **BAKE:** 25 MIN.
YIELD: 11 SERVINGS

Corn bread crepes hold a creamy, ham-and-cheese filling in this special brunch item. I appreciate that they're made the night before. In the morning, I just pop them in the oven and start brewing the coffee!

Diane Nemitz ★ Ludington, Michigan

1-1/2	cups milk
1	cup water
5	eggs
1/4	cup canola oil
2	cups all-purpose flour
1	package (8-1/2 ounces) corn bread/muffin mix

FILLING:

4	green onions, chopped
2	tablespoons butter
1	pound finely chopped fully cooked ham
2	packages (10 ounces *each*) frozen chopped spinach, thawed and squeezed dry
2	packages (8 ounces *each*) reduced-fat cream cheese, cubed
2	tablespoons Dijon mustard
1/2	teaspoon ground nutmeg
1/8	teaspoon pepper

TOPPING:

3/4	cup dry bread crumbs
2	tablespoons butter, melted
2	tablespoons grated Parmesan cheese

In a large bowl, whisk milk, water, eggs and oil. Combine the flour and corn bread mix; add to the egg mixture and mix well. Cover and refrigerate for 1 hour.

For filling, in a large skillet, saute onions in butter until tender. Add ham, spinach, cream cheese, mustard, nutmeg and pepper. Cook and stir until cheese is melted. Remove from the heat; keep warm.

Heat a lightly greased 8-in. nonstick skillet over medium heat; pour 3 tablespoons of the batter into center of skillet. Lift and tilt pan to evenly coat bottom. Cook until the top appears dry; turn and cook 15-20 seconds longer. Remove to a wire rack. Repeat with the remaining batter, greasing skillet as needed.

Spoon about 3 tablespoons of filling down the center of 22 crepes (save remaining crepes for another use). Roll up and place seam side down in two 13-in. x 9-in. baking dishes. Cover and refrigerate overnight.

Remove from the refrigerator 30 minutes before baking. Cover and bake at 350° for 20 minutes.

Combine the topping ingredients. Remove the foil; sprinkle topping over crepes. Bake 5 minutes longer or until heated through.

Sparkling Candles

This fun table accent takes just a few minutes to assemble. Place glass pebbles in small- to medium-sized clear vases. Arrange slender tapers, also called celebration candles, in the pebbles. Coordinate the color of the glass pebbles and candles to complement your table.

Make-Ahead Fruit Salad

Christmas morning can be hectic as eager kids scramble to the presents under the tree!

So the night before, assemble the ingredients for Vanilla Fruit Salad—but don't add the bananas. Cover and refrigerate. Just before serving, slice the bananas and stir into the mixture.

Vanilla Fruit Salad

PREP/TOTAL TIME: 20 MIN.   **YIELD:** 10 SERVINGS

Peach pie filling is the secret ingredient in this crowd-pleasing salad. Make it throughout the year using whatever fruits are in season.

Nancy Dodson ★ Springfield, Illinois

- 1 pound fresh strawberries, quartered
- 1-1/2 cups seedless red *and/or* green grapes, halved
- 2 medium bananas, sliced
- 2 kiwifruit, peeled, sliced and quartered
- 1 cup cubed fresh pineapple
- 1 can (21 ounces) peach pie filling
- 3 teaspoons vanilla extract

In a large bowl, combine the strawberries, grapes, bananas, kiwi and pineapple. Fold in pie filling and vanilla. Chill until serving.

Mango Orange Quencher

PREP: 10 MIN. + CHILLING   **YIELD:** 13 SERVINGS (2-1/2 QUARTS)

Our home economists suggest you serve this beautiful beverage at your next brunch in place of mimosas. Just chill the base one hour before adding the club soda.

- 4 cups mango nectar
- 2 cups orange juice
- 2 tablespoons lime juice
- 1 bottle (1 liter) club soda, chilled

Lime slices, optional

In a large pitcher, combine nectar and juices. Refrigerate for at least 1 hour.

Just before serving, stir in club soda. Serve in champagne flutes or wine glasses. Garnish with lime slices if desired.

Merry Christmas Scones

PREP: 25 MIN. **BAKE:** 15 MIN. **YIELD:** 1 DOZEN

*I keep a supply of scones in my freezer to pull out and glaze
for drop-in holiday guests. They taste great alongside coffee or
hot chocolate.*

Joan Pecsek ★ Chesapeake, Virginia

- 2 cups all-purpose flour
- 3 teaspoons baking powder
- 1/2 teaspoon salt
- 2 tablespoons cold butter
- 1 cup eggnog
- 1 cup chopped pecans
- 1/2 cup red candied cherries, quartered
- 1/2 cup green candied cherries, quartered

GLAZE:
- 1/2 cup confectioners' sugar
- 1 teaspoon rum extract
- 4 to 5 teaspoons heavy whipping cream

In a large bowl, combine the flour, baking powder and salt;
cut in butter until mixture resembles coarse crumbs. Stir
in the eggnog just until moistened. Stir in the pecans and
candied cherries.

Turn onto a floured surface; knead 10 times. Transfer
dough to a greased baking sheet. Pat into a 9-in. circle.
Cut into 12 wedges, but do not separate.

Bake at 425° for 12-14 minutes or until golden brown.
Combine the glaze ingredients; drizzle over the scones.
Serve warm.

Editor's Note: This recipe was tested with commercially prepared eggnog.

Holiday Movie Night

Have you been dreaming of a White Christmas? Do you agree It's a Wonderful Life? Hoping for a Miracle on 34th Street? If a host of holiday movies inspires you, get together with friends to watch those festive flicks!

The only thing that can make the night better is fabulous food! Stromboli Ring, Pizza Rusticana and Greek Pasta have mouth-watering Mediterranean flavor, while Tijuana Tidbits pack spicy Southwestern flair. Satisfy a sweet tooth with Coconut-Almond Fudge Cups and the evening is complete.

Stromboli Ring

PREP: 20 MIN. + RISING   **BAKE:** 30 MIN.   **YIELD:** 12 SERVINGS

A friend shared this recipe with me many years ago. It's incredibly good. I guarantee it will disappear at your next party!

Barrie Peagler ★ Scottsdale, Arizona

- 1   pound bulk Italian sausage
- 1-1/2   cups (6 ounces) shredded Monterey Jack *or* part-skim mozzarella cheese
- 2   eggs
- 1/2   teaspoon Italian seasoning
- 1   loaf (1 pound) frozen bread dough, thawed
- 1   tablespoon grated Parmesan cheese

Marinara sauce, warmed, optional

In a large skillet, cook sausage over medium heat until no longer pink; drain. Stir in the Monterey Jack cheese, one egg and Italian seasoning.

On a lightly floured surface, roll dough into an 18-in. x 6-in. rectangle. Spoon the sausage mixture over dough to within 1/2 in. of edges. Roll up jelly-roll style, starting with a long side; pinch seam to seal.

Place seam side down on a greased baking sheet; pinch ends together to form a ring. With a scissors, cut from the outside edge to two-thirds of the way toward the center of ring at 1-in. intervals.

Beat remaining egg; brush over dough. Sprinkle with Parmesan cheese. Cover and let rise in a warm place until doubled, about 30 minutes.

Bake at 350° for 28-32 minutes or until golden brown. Serve with marinara sauce if desired.

Pizza Rusticana

PREP: 30 MIN.   **BAKE:** 15 MIN.   **YIELD:** 35 SERVINGS

Refrigerated pizza crust gives this recipe a head start, but feel free to substitute your own homemade crust. The veggies are so tasty you won't miss the sauce or the meat.

Sally Sierak ★ Shoreline, Washington

- 1   tube (13.8 ounces) refrigerated pizza crust
- 4   tablespoons olive oil, *divided*
- 2   large tomatoes, thinly sliced
- 1   tablespoon Italian seasoning
- 2   medium red onions, cut into thin wedges
- 2   medium sweet red peppers, cut into 1/4-inch strips
- 1   large portobello mushroom, cut into 1/8-inch strips
- 2   cups (8 ounces) shredded Parmesan cheese

Unroll crust into a lightly greased 15-in. x 10-in. x 1-in. baking pan; flatten dough and build up edges slightly. Brush crust with 1 tablespoon oil. Bake at 425° for 7 minutes.

Meanwhile, in a small bowl, combine the tomatoes, 1 tablespoon oil and Italian seasoning; set aside.

In a large resealable plastic bag, combine the onion, red peppers, mushroom and remaining oil; seal bag and toss to coat. Place vegetables in a single layer on a greased broiler pan. Broil 4 in. from the heat until skins blister, about 15 minutes.

Arrange the tomatoes over the crust; top with roasted vegetables. Sprinkle with cheese.

Bake at 425° for 12-15 minutes or until golden brown.

Tijuana Tidbits

(pictured on page 76)

PREP: 20 MIN.   **BAKE:** 1 HOUR + COOLING
YIELD: 4-3/4 QUARTS

Tortilla chips, chili powder and cayenne pepper lend to the Mexican flair of this snack mix, while corn syrup and brown sugar add a bit of sweetness. I like to package it in holiday tins to give as gifts.

Beverly Phillips ★ Duncanville, Texas

12	cups popped popcorn
4	cups bite-size tortilla chips
3	cups Crispix
1	can (11-1/2 ounces) mixed nuts
1/2	cup butter, cubed
1/2	cup light corn syrup
1/2	cup packed brown sugar
3	teaspoons chili powder
1/4	teaspoon salt
1/8	to 1/4 teaspoon cayenne pepper
1/8	teaspoon ground cinnamon

In a large greased roasting pan, combine the popcorn, tortilla chips, cereal and nuts. In a small saucepan, combine remaining ingredients. Bring to a boil, stirring constantly. Pour over popcorn mixture and toss to coat.

Bake, uncovered, at 250° for 1 hour, stirring every 20 minutes. Cool on waxed paper. Store in an airtight container.

Greek Pasta

PREP/TOTAL TIME: 25 MIN.   **YIELD:** 15 SERVINGS

Sun-dried tomatoes, black olives and fresh basil are tossed with olive oil and pasta in this easy vegetarian dish. I like to make it in advance so the flavors have a chance to blend.

Jennifer Mento ★ Boston, Massachusetts

1	jar (6 ounces) pitted Greek olives, drained
3/4	cup oil-packed sun-dried tomatoes
1/2	cup grated Romano cheese
1/4	cup olive oil
1	tablespoon capers, drained
1	teaspoon lime juice
1/4	teaspoon pepper
1/4	teaspoon crushed red pepper flakes
3	to 4 drops hot pepper sauce, optional
1	package (16 ounces) spiral pasta
3/4	cup minced fresh basil

Additional grated Romano cheese, optional

In a small bowl, combine the olives, tomatoes, cheese, oil, capers, lime juice, pepper, pepper flakes and pepper sauce if desired; let stand for 10-15 minutes. Meanwhile, cook pasta according to package directions.

Drain pasta; place in a large bowl. Add olive mixture and basil; toss to coat. Serve with additional cheese if desired.

Coconut-Almond Fudge Cups

PREP: 30 MIN.   **BAKE:** 10 MIN./BATCH + COOLING
YIELD: 4 DOZEN

With a coconut filling, the taste of these fudgy bites is reminiscent of a favorite candy bar. The recipe makes a big batch so you'll have plenty to share with others.

Maybrie ★ Taste of Home Online Community

1	package (18-1/4 ounces) chocolate fudge cake mix
1/2	cup butter, melted
1	egg

FILLING:

1/4	cup sugar
1/4	cup evaporated milk
7	large marshmallows
1	cup flaked coconut

TOPPING:

3/4	cup semisweet chocolate chips
1/4	cup evaporated milk
2	tablespoons butter
1/2	cup sliced almonds

In a large bowl, beat the cake mix, butter and egg until well blended. Shape into 1-in. balls; place in foil-lined miniature muffin cups. Bake at 350° for 8 minutes.

Using the end of a wooden spoon handle, make a 1/2-in.-deep indentation in the center of each cup. Bake 2-3 minutes longer or until cake springs back when lightly touched. Remove from pans to wire racks to cool.

For filling, in a microwave-safe bowl, heat sugar and milk on high for 2 minutes, stirring frequently. Add the marshmallows; stir until melted. Stir in coconut. Spoon into cooled cups.

For topping, in another microwave-safe bowl, combine the chocolate chips, milk and butter. Microwave in 10- to 20-second intervals until melted; stir until smooth. Stir in almonds. Spread over filling. Store in the refrigerator.

Editor's Note: This recipe was tested in a 1,100-watt microwave.

Festive Open House

Christmas Eve and Christmas Day often involve the challenge of traveling from house to house. This year, open your home and have everyone come to you! All you need are some hearty appetizers (like Roast Beef and Pear Crostini, Baked Crab Rangoons and Apricot Chicken Wings), a selection of snacks (such as Layered Blue Cheese Spread and Warm Spiced Nuts) and a festive beverage (like Grape Juice Sparkler).

Roast Beef and Pear Crostini

PREP/TOTAL TIME: 30 MIN.   **YIELD:** 40 APPETIZERS

My friends request these each time we get together. They have a tasty combination that everyone falls in love with.

Marie Rizzio ★ Traverse City, Michigan

- 1 French bread baguette (1 pound)
- 3 tablespoons olive oil
- 1 garlic clove, minced
- 1 cup blue cheese salad dressing
- 1 medium pear, diced
- 1/4 cup thinly sliced green onions
- 2 cups diced cooked roast beef
- 1 cup diced seeded tomatoes
- 1/2 teaspoon salt
- 1/4 teaspoon pepper
- 1/2 cup fresh basil leaves, thinly sliced

Cut the baguette into 40 slices. Combine the oil and garlic; brush over one side of each slice of bread. Place on an ungreased baking sheet. Bake at 350° for 6-9 minutes or until lightly toasted.

Combine the salad dressing, pear and onions. Combine the roast beef, tomatoes, salt and pepper. Spread dressing mixture over toasted bread; top with beef mixture and basil.

Apricot Chicken Wings

PREP: 15 MIN. + MARINATING   **BAKE:** 30 MIN.
YIELD: 2 DOZEN

Simple-to-make appetizers are the key to easy entertaining. A five-ingredient marinade flavors these juicy and tender chicken wings.

Robin Spires ★ Tampa, Florida

- 2 pounds chicken wings
- 1 cup apricot preserves
- 2 tablespoons cider vinegar
- 2 teaspoons hot pepper sauce
- 1 teaspoon chili powder
- 1 garlic clove, minced

Cut chicken wings into three sections; discard wing tips. Combine the remaining ingredients; pour 1/2 cup into a large resealable plastic bag. Add chicken; seal bag and turn to coat. Refrigerate for 4 hours or overnight. Cover and refrigerate remaining marinade.

Drain and discard marinade from chicken. Place wings in a greased foil-lined 15-in. x 10-in. x 1-in. baking pan. Bake at 400° for 30-35 minutes or until juices run clear, turning and basting occasionally with remaining marinade.

Editor's Note: Uncooked chicken wing sections (wingettes) may be substituted for whole chicken wings.

Baked Crab Rangoons

PREP/TOTAL TIME: 30 MIN.   **YIELD:** 1 DOZEN

Although these Asian-inspired appetizers feel fancy, they're actually easy to prepare. Baking instead of deep frying not only saves time but reduces the mess.

Sue Bennett ★ Shelburn, Indiana

- 12   wonton wrappers
- 4   ounces cream cheese, softened
- 1/4   cup mayonnaise
- 1   can (6 ounces) crabmeat, drained, flaked and cartilage removed
- 1/4   cup thinly sliced green onions

Press wonton wrappers into greased miniature muffin cups. Bake at 350° for 6-7 minutes or until lightly browned.

Meanwhile, in a small bowl, beat the cream cheese and mayonnaise until smooth. Stir in crab and onions; spoon into wonton cups. Bake for 10-12 minutes or until heated through. Serve warm.

Grape Juice Sparkler

PREP/TOTAL TIME: 15 MIN.   **YIELD:** 10 SERVINGS (2 QUARTS)

For a nice alternative to wine, give this fruity beverage from our home economists a try. The kid-friendly drink will appeal to people of all ages.

- 1   can (11-1/2 ounces) frozen cranberry-raspberry juice concentrate, thawed
- 1   bottle (1 liter) club soda, chilled
- 1   bottle (750 ml) sparkling white grape juice, chilled
- 20   to 30 fresh raspberries

Just before serving, combine juice concentrate with club soda in a large pitcher. Stir in sparkling grape juice. Place two to three raspberries in the bottom of each glass; add the juice.

Editor's Note: Use 2 cans of cranberry-raspberry juice concentrate and 2 teaspoons lemon juice for a sweeter, fruitier beverage.

Layered Blue Cheese Spread

PREP/TOTAL TIME: 25 MIN.   **YIELD:** 4 CUPS

This is an attractive and delicious spread to present guests at holiday parties. Serve it with crackers or even vegetable dippers.

Lillian Julow ★ Gainesville, Florida

> 3 packages (8 ounces *each*) cream cheese, softened, *divided*
> 1 cup (4 ounces) crumbled blue cheese
> 1/4 cup plus 1 tablespoon sour cream, *divided*
> 2 tablespoons minced fresh parsley
> 1 tablespoon minced fresh cilantro
> 1 tablespoon minced chives
> 1/2 teaspoon coarsely ground pepper
> 1/2 cup chopped walnuts
> Assorted breads *or* crackers

On a serving plate, spread the two packages of cream cheese into an 8-in. circle. In a bowl, combine blue cheese, 1/4 cup sour cream, parsley, cilantro, chives and pepper until well blended. Spread over cream cheese layer to within 1/2 in. of the edges.

In a small bowl, beat remaining cream cheese and sour cream until smooth. Spread over blue cheese layer to within 1 in. of the edges. Sprinkle with walnuts just before serving. Serve with breads or crackers.

Warm Spiced Nuts

PREP: 5 MIN.   **BAKE:** 30 MIN.   **YIELD:** 3 CUPS

I like to set out bowls of spiced nuts when hosting holiday parties. Sometimes I stir in M&M's for a sweet and salty snack.

Jill Matson ★ Zimmerman, Minnesota

> 1 cup pecan halves
> 1 cup unblanched almonds
> 1 cup unsalted dry roasted peanuts
> 3 tablespoons butter, melted
> 4-1/2 teaspoons Worcestershire sauce
> 1 teaspoon chili powder
> 1/2 teaspoon garlic salt
> 1/4 teaspoon cayenne pepper

In a large bowl, combine the pecans, almonds and peanuts. Combine butter and Worcestershire sauce; pour over nuts and toss to coat.

Spread in a single layer in an ungreased 15-in. x 10-in. x 1-in. baking pan. Bake at 300° for 30 minutes or until browned, stirring every 10 minutes.

Transfer warm nuts to a bowl. Combine chili powder, garlic salt and cayenne; sprinkle over nuts and stir to coat. Serve warm or cooled. Store in an airtight container.

After-Caroling Warm-Up

After spreading seasonal cheer to neighbors through Christmas carols, welcome friends and family to your home for a cozy meal!

Hot and hearty Round-Up Chili and Tuscan Stew conveniently simmer in slow cookers while you're spreading holiday spirit. So supper is served in a jiffy when guests come in from the cold. Complete the merry meal with Rosemary Garlic Focaccia, California Tossed Salad and Truffle Hot Chocolate with flavored whipped creams.

Round-Up Chili

PREP: 35 MIN. **COOK:** 6 HOURS
YIELD: 12 SERVINGS (3 QUARTS)

Two types of meat make this not-too-spicy chili a hearty meal. Because it's made in the slow cooker, it's a great choice for casual Christmas gatherings.

Linda Stemen ★ Monroeville, Indiana

- 2 pounds lean ground beef
- 1 beef flank steak (1-1/2 pounds), cubed
- 1 medium onion, chopped
- 1 celery rib, chopped
- 1 can (29 ounces) tomato sauce
- 2 cans (14-1/2 ounces *each*) diced tomatoes, undrained
- 1 can (16 ounces) kidney beans, rinsed and drained
- 1 can (15 ounces) pinto beans, rinsed and drained
- 1 can (4 ounces) chopped green chilies
- 2 to 3 tablespoons chili powder
- 3 teaspoons ground cumin
- 2 teaspoons salt
- 2 teaspoons pepper
- 1/2 teaspoon ground mustard
- 1/2 teaspoon paprika
- 1/2 teaspoon cayenne pepper
- 1/4 teaspoon garlic powder

Hot pepper sauce, shredded cheddar cheese and additional chopped onion, optional

In a large skillet, cook the ground beef, flank steak, onion and celery over medium heat until meat is no longer pink; drain.

Transfer to a 6-qt. slow cooker. Stir in the tomato sauce, tomatoes, beans, chilies and seasonings. Cover and cook on low for 6-8 hours.

Serve with hot pepper sauce, cheese and onion if desired.

Rosemary Garlic Focaccia

PREP: 45 MIN. + RISING **BAKE:** 15 MIN.
YIELD: 2 LOAVES (10 WEDGES EACH)

Garlic and fresh rosemary tastefully top a light and airy focaccia. Serve it alone with flavored olive oil for dipping or alongside a chili or spaghetti dinner.

Tammy Bollman ★ Minatare, Nebraska

- 1 cup warm milk (70° to 80°)
- 1 egg
- 1/4 cup water (70° to 80°)
- 1/4 cup butter, softened
- 2-3/4 cups bread flour
- 2 tablespoons sugar
- 1 teaspoon salt
- 2 teaspoons active dry yeast
- 4 teaspoons olive oil
- 4 teaspoons minced fresh rosemary
- 3 garlic cloves, minced
- 1 teaspoon kosher salt

In bread machine pan, place the first eight ingredients in order suggested by the manufacturer. Select dough setting (check the dough after 5 minutes of mixing; add 1 to 2 tablespoons of water or flour if needed).

When cycle is completed, turn dough onto a lightly floured surface (dough will be sticky). Divide into two portions; place on greased baking sheets. Cover and let rest for 10 minutes. Shape each portion into an 8-in. circle. Cover and let rise until doubled, about 30 minutes.

Using the end of a wooden spoon handle, make 1/4-in. indentations in dough. Brush with oil; sprinkle with rosemary, garlic and salt. Bake at 400° for 12-15 minutes or until golden brown. Remove to wire racks.

Truffle Hot Chocolate

PREP/TOTAL TIME: 25 MIN. **YIELD:** 6 SERVINGS

Your company will be delighted with this rich and creamy warm-up. Double the recipe for the group and make several of the flavored whipped creams that follow. Let your guests top off their own hot chocolate.

- 4 cups milk
- 6 ounces 70% cacao dark baking chocolate, chopped
- 3 tablespoons brown sugar
- 1 teaspoon instant espresso powder
- 1 teaspoon vanilla extract

Dash salt

Flavored whipped cream (recipes at right)

Chocolate-Covered Coffee Beans, optional (recipe below)

In a large saucepan, heat the milk over medium heat until bubbles form around sides of pan (do not boil). Remove from the heat; whisk in the chocolate, brown sugar, espresso powder, vanilla and salt until smooth. Return to the heat; cook and stir until heated through. Pour into mugs; top with desired flavor of whipped cream and Chocolate-Covered Coffee Beans if desired.

Chocolate-Covered Coffee Beans

PREP/TOTAL TIME: 30 min. **YIELD:** 1 CUP

Two terrific flavors—coffee and chocolate—come together in this mouth-watering recipe from our Test Kitchen. Enjoy them as a snack or use them to top your favorite mocha desserts.

- 2/3 cup semisweet chocolate chips
- 1-1/2 teaspoons shortening
- 1/2 cup coffee beans

Baking cocoa, optional

In a microwave, melt chocolate chips and shortening; stir until smooth. Dip coffee beans in chocolate; allow excess to drip off. Place on waxed paper; let stand for 10-15 minutes.

Roll in cocoa if desired; let stand until set. Store in an airtight container.

Dulce de Leche Whipped Cream

YIELD: 1 CUP

In a heavy skillet, melt 3 tablespoons sugar until golden. Gradually stir in 1/2 cup heavy whipping cream; cook and stir until sugar is dissolved. Transfer to a small bowl; cover and refrigerate for 4 hours. Beat until stiff peaks form.

Chocolate Whipped Cream

YIELD: 1 CUP

In a small bowl, beat 1/2 cup heavy whipping cream until it begins to thicken. Add 2 tablespoons chocolate syrup; beat until stiff peaks form.

Peppermint Whipped Cream

YIELD: 1 CUP

In a small bowl, beat 1/2 cup heavy whipping cream until it begins to thicken. Add 1 tablespoon sugar and 1/8 teaspoon peppermint extract; beat until stiff peaks form. Garnish with 1 tablespoon crushed peppermint candies.

Coffee Whipped Cream

YIELD: 1 CUP

In a small bowl, beat 1/2 cup heavy whipping cream and 1 teaspoon instant espresso powder until it begins to thicken. Add 1 tablespoon sugar; beat until stiff peaks form.

Irish Whipped Cream

YIELD: 1 CUP

In a small bowl, beat 1/2 cup heavy whipping cream and 1 tablespoon Irish cream liqueur until stiff peaks form.

For garnish, if desired, pipe swirls of melted candy coating on waxed paper. Let stand until set.

Tuscan Pork Stew

PREP: 15 MIN.   **COOK:** 8-1/2 HOURS   **YIELD:** 8 SERVINGS

Tender chunks of pork are slowly cooked in a nicely seasoned, wine-infused sauce...and the results are fantastic!

Penny Hawkins ★ Mebane, North Carolina

- 1   boneless whole pork loin roast (1-1/2 pounds), cut into 1-inch cubes
- 2   tablespoons olive oil
- 2   cans (14-1/2 ounces *each*) Italian diced tomatoes, undrained
- 2   cups reduced-sodium chicken broth
- 2   cups frozen pepper stir-fry vegetable blend, thawed
- 1/2   cup dry red wine *or* additional reduced-sodium chicken broth
- 1/4   cup orange marmalade
- 2   garlic cloves, minced
- 1   teaspoon dried oregano
- 1/2   teaspoon fennel seed
- 1/2   teaspoon pepper
- 1/8   teaspoon crushed red pepper flakes, optional
- 2   tablespoons cornstarch
- 2   tablespoons cold water
- Hot cooked fettuccine, optional

In a large skillet, brown pork in oil until no longer pink; drain. Place pork in a 5-qt. slow cooker.

In a large bowl, combine the tomatoes, broth, vegetable blend, wine, marmalade, garlic, oregano, fennel seed, pepper and pepper flakes if desired; pour over pork. Cover and cook on low for 8 hours or until meat is tender.

Mix cornstarch and water until smooth; stir into stew. Cover and cook on high for 30 minutes or until gravy is thickened. Serve with fettuccine if desired.

California Tossed Salad

PREP: 15 MIN. + CHILLING   **YIELD:** 12 SERVINGS

Even though I'm retired, I'm busier than ever! Served with crusty French bread, this speedy salad is a meal in itself.

Patricia Nieh ★ Portola Valley, California

- 2   jars (7-1/2 ounces *each*) marinated quartered artichoke hearts, undrained
- 2   jars (4-1/2 ounces *each*) whole mushrooms, drained
- 1-1/2   cups cherry tomatoes
- 1-1/2   cups cubed Monterey Jack cheese
- 2   large ripe avocados, peeled and cubed
- 1   can (6 ounces) pitted ripe olives, drained
- 2   tablespoons lemon juice
- 4   cups torn romaine

In a large bowl, combine the first seven ingredients. Cover and refrigerate for at least 1 hour. Just before serving, add the romaine and toss to coat.

Gifts
FROM THE KITCHEN

Cranberry-Pecan Quick Bread

(pictured on page 89)

PREP: 20 MIN. **BAKE:** 35 MIN. + COOLING
YIELD: 2 LOAVES (12 SLICES EACH)

With whole wheat flour, flaxseed, oats, cranberries and pecans, a slice of this quick bread is a very satisfying start to your day.

Wendy Marotta ★ Wilson, New York

1-3/4	cups all-purpose flour
3/4	cup whole wheat flour
3/4	cup sugar
1/4	cup quick-cooking oats
1/4	cup ground almonds
2	tablespoons ground flaxseed
1	teaspoon baking powder
3/4	teaspoon salt
1/2	teaspoon baking soda
2	eggs
1-1/4	cups orange juice
1/4	cup butter, melted
1/4	cup unsweetened applesauce
1	cup dried cranberries
1/4	cup chopped pecans

In a large bowl, combine the first nine ingredients. In a small bowl, whisk the eggs, orange juice, butter and applesauce. Stir into dry ingredients just until moistened. Fold in cranberries and pecans.

Transfer to two greased 8-in. x 4-in. loaf pans. Bake at 350° for 35-40 minutes or until a toothpick inserted near the center comes out clean. Cool for 10 minutes before removing from pans to wire racks.

Rosemary-Parmesan Snack Mix

PREP: 10 MIN. **BAKE:** 30 MIN. + COOLING
YIELD: 2-1/2 QUARTS

Balsamic vinegar, rosemary, basil and Parmesan cheese lend an Italian taste to this easy-to-make snack mix. Folks won't be able to stop eating it!

Carolyn Schmeling ★ Brookfield, Wisconsin

4	cups pretzel snaps *or* miniature pretzels
4	cups Rice Chex
2	cups unblanched almonds
1/4	cup olive oil
2	tablespoons balsamic vinegar
3	teaspoons dried rosemary, crushed
2	teaspoons garlic powder
2	teaspoons dried basil
4	to 5 drops hot pepper sauce
2	teaspoons salt
1/4	cup grated Parmesan cheese

In a large bowl, combine the pretzels, cereal and almonds. Combine the oil, vinegar, rosemary, garlic powder, basil and pepper sauce; pour over cereal mixture and stir to coat.

Spread into two ungreased 15-in. x 10-in. x 1-in. baking pans. Sprinkle with salt. Bake at 300° for 15 minutes.

Sprinkle with cheese and stir. Bake 15 minutes longer. Spread on paper towels to cool. Store in airtight containers.

Parmesan Peppercorn Breadsticks

(pictured at right)

PREP: 35 MIN. + RISING **BAKE:** 20 MIN. + COOLING
YIELD: 2 DOZEN

These crisp breadsticks are just like the ones served in restaurants. When entertaining, use them as a garnish on plate chargers. When guests sit down to dinner, they have an immediate treat!

Mary Beth Jung ★ Hendersonville, North Carolina

2	tablespoons grated Parmesan cheese
1	package (1/4 ounce) quick-rise yeast
2	teaspoons salt
1	teaspoon sugar
1	teaspoon dried rosemary *or* thyme, crushed
1/2	teaspoon coarsely ground pepper
3-1/2	to 4 cups all-purpose flour
1-1/4	cups water
3	tablespoons olive oil
1	egg white
1	tablespoon cold water
2	tablespoons sesame seeds

In a large bowl, combine cheese, yeast, salt, sugar, rosemary, pepper and 2 cups flour. In a small saucepan, heat water and oil to 120°-130°. Add to dry ingredients; beat just until smooth. Stir in enough remaining flour to form a soft dough (dough will be sticky).

Turn onto a floured surface; knead until smooth and elastic, about 6-8 minutes. Place in a greased bowl, turning once to grease top. Cover and let rise in a warm place until doubled, about 30 minutes.

Punch dough down. Turn onto a lightly floured surface. Divide dough in half. Divide each half into 12 pieces. Roll into 12-in. x 1/2-in. strips; place on greased baking sheets.

Beat egg white and cold water until foamy; brush over strips. Sprinkle with sesame seeds.

Bake at 400° for 18-22 minutes or until lightly browned. Cool on wire racks.

For tender breadsticks, serve the same day. Or let stand, uncovered, at room temperature for 1-2 days to dry breadsticks to a cracker-like consistency before packaging.

Warm Pesto Dip

PREP/TOTAL TIME: 20 MIN.　**YIELD:** 2-1/2 CUPS

This pretty green dip is perfect for Christmas, especially when served with red bell pepper strips. You can make it ahead and reheat when ready to serve.

Megan Taylor ★ Washougal, Washington

1/3　cup finely chopped onion
　1　teaspoon olive oil
　1　cup prepared pesto
　1　package (8 ounces) cream cheese, cubed
1/2　cup heavy whipping cream
1/4　cup grated Parmesan cheese
Breadsticks, bread cubes *or* assorted fresh vegetables

In a small saucepan, saute the onion in oil until tender. Stir in the pesto and cream cheese; cook and stir over low heat until smooth.

Stir in cream and Parmesan cheese. Cover and cook over low heat for 10 minutes, stirring occasionally. Serve with breadsticks, bread cubes or vegetables.

Chocolate Chip Biscotti

PREP: 30 MIN. **BAKE:** 40 MIN. + COOLING
YIELD: 3 DOZEN

With a hint of apricots, these chocolate chip biscotti taste great alongside a cup of coffee or tea. Friends and family are always happy to receive a batch for Christmas.

Theresa Smith ★ Lee, New Hampshire

3/4	cup butter, softened
1-1/2	cups plus 1-1/2 teaspoons sugar, *divided*
4	eggs
3	teaspoons vanilla extract
4	cups all-purpose flour
3	teaspoons baking powder
1/2	teaspoon salt
1	cup finely chopped dried apricots
1	cup swirled semisweet and white chocolate chips

In a large bowl, cream the butter and 1-1/2 cups sugar. Add eggs, one at a time, beating well after each addition. Beat in the vanilla. Combine the flour, baking powder and salt; gradually add to creamed mixture. Stir in the apricots and chocolate chips.

Divide dough in half. On ungreased baking sheets, shape each portion into a 12-in. x 2-1/2-in. rectangle. Sprinkle with remaining sugar. Bake at 325° for 30 minutes or until firm. Cool for 5 minutes.

Transfer to a cutting board; cut diagonally with a serrated knife into 1/2-in. slices. Place cut side down on ungreased baking sheets. Bake for 6-8 minutes or until golden brown. Remove to wire racks to cool. Store in an airtight container.

Butterscotch Maple Topping

PREP/TOTAL TIME: 20 MIN. **YIELD:** 2-1/2 CUPS

I came across this recipe when I was given a half-gallon of fresh maple syrup. The sweet topping pairs well with vanilla ice cream.

Janis Kelly ★ Columbia City, Indiana

1	cup packed brown sugar
1	cup maple syrup
1/4	cup butter, cubed
2	teaspoons vanilla extract
1	teaspoon salt
3/4	cup half-and-half cream

Vanilla ice cream

In a small saucepan, combine brown sugar and syrup. Bring to a boil over medium heat, stirring constantly. Cook and stir for 5 minutes.

Remove from the heat; stir in the butter, vanilla and salt. Let stand for 5 minutes.

Add cream; whisk for 1 minute or until well blended. Serve over ice cream. Refrigerate leftovers.

Cranberry Buttermilk Pancake Mix

PREP/TOTAL TIME: 30 MIN.
YIELD: 16 PANCAKES (1-1/2 CUPS SYRUP)

This fruity mix is handy to have in the pantry for fast yet filling breakfasts. Everyone loves the light, fluffy flapjacks.

Helen Schaefer ★ Appleton, Wisconsin

1-1/4	cups all-purpose flour
3/4	cup whole wheat flour
1/2	cup dried cranberries, chopped
1/2	cup buttermilk blend powder
3	tablespoons sugar
1	teaspoon baking soda
3/4	teaspoon ground cinnamon
1/4	teaspoon salt

CINNAMON CRANBERRY SYRUP:

1/4	cup sugar
4	teaspoons cornstarch
2	cups cranberry juice
1	cinnamon stick (3 inches)

ADDITIONAL INGREDIENTS:

2	eggs
1-3/4	cups water

For mix, combine the first eight ingredients. Store in an airtight container in a cool dry place for up to 6 months. **YIELD:** 1 batch.

For the syrup, in a small saucepan, combine the sugar, cornstarch and cranberry juice until smooth; add cinnamon stick. Bring to a boil; cook and stir for 1-2 minutes or until thickened. Remove from the heat. Discard cinnamon stick. Transfer syrup to a storage container; cover and refrigerate for up to 3 weeks.

TO PREPARE PANCAKES: Pour the mix into a large bowl. Whisk the eggs and water; stir into the dry ingredients just until moistened.

Pour batter by 1/4 cupfuls onto a greased hot griddle. Turn when bubbles form on top; cook until second side is golden brown. Reheat syrup if desired; serve with pancakes.

In a large bowl, cream butter and sugars until light and fluffy. Beat in egg and corn syrup. Combine the flour, baking soda, ginger, orange peel, allspice, cloves and nutmeg; gradually add to creamed mixture and mix well.

Shape into four 6-in. rolls; wrap in plastic wrap. Refrigerate overnight.

Unwrap and cut into 1/8-in. slices. Place 2 in. apart on ungreased baking sheets. Sprinkle with additional sugar if desired.

Bake at 400° for 5-6 minutes or until lightly browned. Remove to wire racks to cool.

Making a Special Presentation

Slice & Bake Orange Spice Wafers go great with a cup of tea. To give them as an inexpensive gift, place the wafers in a cellophane bag and tie with a bow. Set inside a tea cup. (Look for unique cups and saucers at garage sales, flea markets and discount stores.) If desired, arrange a tea bag or two on the saucer. Place the cup and saucer on a piece of cellophane. Bring up the ends and secure with a small strand of berry garland or a ribbon.

Slice & Bake Orange Spice Wafers

PREP: 45 MIN. + CHILLING **BAKE:** 5 MIN./BATCH
YIELD: 16 DOZEN

These thin and crispy cookies from our Test Kitchen stack well, making them a great gift to give. Ginger and orange lend to their sweet and spicy flavor.

- 1 cup butter, softened
- 3/4 cup sugar
- 3/4 cup packed brown sugar
- 1 egg
- 2 tablespoons light corn syrup
- 3 cups all-purpose flour
- 2 teaspoons baking soda
- 2 teaspoons ground ginger
- 2 teaspoons grated orange peel
- 1/4 teaspoon *each* ground allspice, cloves and nutmeg

Additional sugar, optional

Raspberry Chocolate Rugalach

PREP: 40 MIN. + CHILLING
BAKE: 20 MIN./BATCH + COOLING
YIELD: 32 COOKIES

Since we celebrate both Hanukkah and Christmas, these cookies are always on the menu. The cookies can be covered and refrigerated overnight or frozen for up to two months.

G.P. Busarow ★ Whitehall, Montana

- 1/2 cup butter, softened
- 4 ounces cream cheese, softened
- 1 cup all-purpose flour
- 1/4 teaspoon salt

FILLING:
- 1/4 cup dried currants
- 2 tablespoons sugar
- 1/2 teaspoon ground cinnamon
- 1/4 cup seedless raspberry jam
- 2/3 cup finely chopped pecans
- 1/4 cup miniature semisweet chocolate chips

In a large bowl, beat butter and cream cheese until smooth. Combine flour and salt; gradually add to creamed mixture and mix well.

Divide dough in half; form into two balls. Flatten to 5-in. circles; wrap in plastic wrap. Refrigerate for 8 hours or overnight.

Place currants in a small bowl. Cover with boiling water; let stand for 5 minutes. Drain well and set aside. Combine sugar and cinnamon; set aside.

On a lightly floured surface or pastry mat, roll one portion of dough into an 11-in. circle. Brush with half of the jam. Sprinkle with half of the cinnamon-sugar, pecans, chocolate chips and currants; press down gently.

Cut into 16 wedges. Roll up wedges from the wide end and place point side down 2 in. apart on a parchment paper-lined baking sheet. Curve ends to form a crescent. Cover and refrigerate for 30 minutes before baking. Repeat with remaining dough and filling.

Bake at 350° for 18-22 minutes or until golden brown. Remove to wire racks to cool.

Java-Spice Rub for Pork

PREP/TOTAL TIME: 10 MIN.   **YIELD:** 4 SERVINGS PER BATCH

Ground coffee is the secret ingredient in this special rub, which could also be used on beef steaks.

Mark Morgan ★ Waterford, Wisconsin

- 1 tablespoon finely ground coffee
- 1 teaspoon kosher salt
- 1 teaspoon brown sugar
- 1 teaspoon chili powder
- 1/2 teaspoon ground cumin
- 1/2 teaspoon ground cinnamon
- 1/2 teaspoon pepper
- 1/4 teaspoon garlic powder

ADDITIONAL INGREDIENTS (FOR EACH BATCH):
- 1 pork tenderloin (1 pound)
- 1 tablespoon canola oil

In a small bowl, combine first eight ingredients. Transfer to a small spice jar. Store in a cool dry place for up to 2 months. **YIELD:** 3 batches (3 tablespoons total).

TO PREPARE PORK TENDERLOIN: Brush pork with oil; rub with 1 tablespoon seasoning mix. Cover and refrigerate at least 2 hours or overnight.

Prepare grill for indirect heat. Grill the pork, covered, over indirect medium-hot heat for 25-30 minutes or until a meat thermometer reads 160°. Let stand for 5 minutes before slicing.

Editor's Note: Pineapple Pepper Salsa (page 103) makes a fabulous accompaniment for this spicy roast.

Ginger Pear Muffins

PREP: 25 MIN.   **BAKE:** 20 MIN.   **YIELD:** 1-1/2 DOZEN

This wonderful recipe has been in my files for years. The chunks of fresh pear make each bite moist and delicious.

Lorraine Caland ★ Thunder Bay, Ontario

- 3/4 cup packed brown sugar
- 1/3 cup canola oil
- 1 egg
- 1 cup buttermilk
- 2-1/2 cups all-purpose flour
- 1 teaspoon baking soda
- 1 teaspoon ground ginger
- 1/2 teaspoon salt
- 1/2 teaspoon ground cinnamon
- 2 cups chopped peeled fresh pears

TOPPING:
- 1/3 cup packed brown sugar
- 1/4 teaspoon ground ginger
- 2 teaspoons butter, melted

In a small bowl, beat the brown sugar, oil and egg until well blended. Beat in buttermilk. In a small bowl, combine the flour, baking soda, ginger, salt and cinnamon; gradually beat into buttermilk mixture until blended. Stir in the pears. Fill paper-lined muffin cups two-thirds full.

For topping, combine brown sugar and ginger. Stir in butter until crumbly. Sprinkle over batter.

Bake at 350° for 18-22 minutes or until a pick inserted near center comes out clean. Cool for 5 minutes before removing from pans to wire racks. Serve warm.

Chewy Soft Pretzels

PREP: 1 HOUR + RISING   **BAKE:** 15 MIN.   **YIELD:** 1 DOZEN

These homemade pretzels never last long around our house. My kids love to make them...and eat them! I serve the pretzels to company with a variety of dips, such as pizza sauce, ranch dressing, spinach dip or hot mustard.

Elvira Martens ★ Aldergrove, British Columbia

- 1 package (1/4 ounce) active dry yeast
- 1-1/2 cups warm water (110° to 115°)
- 1 tablespoon sugar
- 2 teaspoons salt
- 4 to 4-1/4 cups all-purpose flour
- 8 cups water
- 1/2 cup baking soda
- 1 egg, beaten

Kosher salt, sesame seeds, poppy seeds *or* grated Parmesan cheese

In a large bowl, dissolve yeast in warm water. Add the sugar, salt and 2 cups flour; beat until smooth. Stir in enough of the remaining flour to form a stiff dough.

Turn onto a floured surface; knead until smooth and elastic, about 5 minutes. Place in a greased bowl, turning once to grease top. Cover and let rise in a warm place until doubled, about 1 hour.

Punch dough down; divide into 12 portions. Roll each into an 18-in. rope; twist into a pretzel shape.

In a large saucepan, bring the water and baking soda to a boil. Place the pretzels into boiling water, one at a time, for 30 seconds. Remove with a slotted spoon; drain on paper towels.

Place pretzels on greased baking sheets. Brush with egg; sprinkle with desired topping. Bake at 425° for 12-14 minutes or until golden brown. Remove from pans to wire racks. Serve warm.

Orange-Cranberry Coffee Cakes

PREP: 40 MIN. + RISING **BAKE:** 20 MIN. + COOLING
YIELD: 2 COFFEE CAKES (12 SERVINGS EACH)

Baking is my favorite thing to do. So during the holiday season, I can often be found in my kitchen preparing festive baked goods, such as these coffee cakes.

Loraine Meyer ★ Bend, Oregon

1/2	cup sugar
1	package (1/4 ounce) active dry yeast
1-1/4	teaspoons salt
4	to 4-1/2 cups all-purpose flour
1	cup milk
1/2	cup butter, cubed
1/4	cup water
1	egg

FILLING:

1	cup fresh *or* frozen cranberries, thawed
1/4	cup sugar
1/4	cup chopped walnuts
1/4	cup dark corn syrup
1	tablespoon grated orange peel
1/4	teaspoon ground ginger

ICING:

2-1/2	cups confectioners' sugar
3	tablespoons plus 1 teaspoon orange juice
1/4	cup toasted chopped walnuts

In a large bowl, combine the sugar, yeast, salt and 2-1/2 cups flour. In a small saucepan, heat the milk, butter and water to 120°-130°. Add to dry ingredients; beat just until moistened. Add the egg; beat until smooth. Stir in enough remaining flour to form a stiff dough.

Turn onto a floured surface; knead until smooth and elastic, about 6-8 minutes. Place in a greased bowl, turning once to grease the top. Cover and let rise in a warm place until doubled, about 1 hour.

Place cranberries in a blender; cover and process until chopped. Drain well; discard liquid from cranberries. In a small bowl, combine the cranberries with remaining filling ingredients. Set aside.

Punch down dough; turn onto a lightly floured surface. Divide the dough in half. Roll each half into a 16-in. x 10-in. rectangle; spread with filling to within 1 in. of edges. Roll up each jelly-roll style, starting with a long side; seal seams. Place in greased 15-in. x 10-in. x 1-in. baking pans; shape the ends to form crescent shapes.

With kitchen scissors or a small sharp knife, cut a lengthwise slit down the center of each loaf, 1/2 in. deep and stopping 2 in. from the ends. Cover loaves and let rise in a warm place until doubled, about 30 minutes. Bake at 350° for 20-25 minutes or until golden brown. Remove from pans to wire racks to cool.

Combine the confectioners' sugar and orange juice; drizzle over coffee cakes. Top with the walnuts; press onto icing to secure.

Secret Kiss Cookies

PREP: 25 MIN. **BAKE:** 15 MIN./BATCH **YIELD:** 2-1/2 DOZEN

Here's a recipe that's literally sealed with a kiss. This cookie's bound to tickle any sweet tooth.

Karen Owen ★ Rising Sun, Indiana

- 1 cup butter, softened
- 1/2 cup sugar
- 1 teaspoon vanilla extract
- 2 cups all-purpose flour
- 1 cup finely chopped walnuts
- 30 milk chocolate kisses
- 1-1/3 cups confectioners' sugar, *divided*
- 2 tablespoons baking cocoa

In a large bowl, cream the butter, sugar and vanilla until light and fluffy. Gradually add flour and mix well. Fold in walnuts. Refrigerate dough for 2-3 hours or until firm.

Shape into 1-in. balls. Flatten balls and place a chocolate kiss in the center of each; pinch dough together around kiss. Place 2 in. apart on ungreased baking sheets.

Bake at 375° for 12 minutes or until set but not browned. Cool for 1 minute; remove from pans to wire racks.

Sift together 2/3 cup confectioners' sugar and cocoa. While cookies are still warm, roll half in cocoa mixture and half in remaining confectioners' sugar. Cool completely. Store in an airtight container.

Hot Buttered Cider Mix

PREP/TOTAL TIME: 15 MIN. **YIELD:** 64 SERVINGS

Put the butter base for this beverage in a decorative jar and attach a copy of the recipe for a great gift from your kitchen. You can omit the brandy for a kid-friendly version.

- 1 cup butter, softened
- 1 cup packed brown sugar
- 1/2 cup honey
- 1 teaspoon ground cinnamon
- 1/2 teaspoon ground cardamom
- 1/4 teaspoon ground cloves

ADDITIONAL INGREDIENTS (FOR EACH SERVING):

- 3/4 cup apple cider *or* juice
- 1 ounce apple brandy, optional

In a small bowl, cream butter and brown sugar until light and fluffy. Beat in honey and spices. Transfer to an airtight container. Store in the refrigerator for up to 2 weeks. **YIELD:** 2 cups.

TO PREPARE CIDER: In a small saucepan or microwave, heat the apple cider until warm; stir in 1-1/2 teaspoons butter mixture. Pour into a mug. Add brandy if desired.

Olive-Herb Cheese Spread Mix

PREP: 10 MIN. + CHILLING **YIELD:** 1-1/4 CUPS PER BATCH

I combined a blend of dried herbs to create a delicious mix that wonderfully flavors cream cheese. You can even use the spread on sandwiches.

Genise Krause ★ Sturgeon Bay, Wisconsin

- 1 tablespoon dried basil
- 1 tablespoon dried parsley flakes
- 1 tablespoon dried minced chives
- 1 tablespoon dill weed
- 1 tablespoon dried minced onion
- 1/2 teaspoon garlic salt
- 1/4 teaspoon pepper
- 1/8 teaspoon cayenne pepper
- ADDITIONAL INGREDIENTS (FOR EACH BATCH):
- 1 package (8 ounces) cream cheese, softened
- 1 to 2 tablespoons milk
- 1 can (2-1/4 ounces) sliced ripe olives, drained
- Pita chips *or* crackers

In a small bowl, combine first eight ingredients. Transfer to a small spice jar. Store in a cool dry place for up to 6 months. **YIELD:** 5 batches (5 tablespoons total).

   TO PREPARE SPREAD: In a small bowl, beat cream cheese and 1 tablespoon seasoning mix until blended. Beat in enough milk until spread reaches desired consistency. Stir in olives. Cover and refrigerate for 1 hour. Serve with pita chips or crackers.

Salt & Garlic Pita Chips

(pictured at left)

PREP/TOTAL TIME: 25 MIN.   **YIELD:** 6 DOZEN

With just four ingredients, our Test Kitchen staff baked up this easy treat. The sturdy chips hold up well to any dip or spread.

- 1/4 cup olive oil
- 2 garlic cloves, minced
- 6 pita breads (6 inches), split in half
- 3/4 teaspoon kosher salt

In a small bowl, whisk oil and garlic. Brush over rough side of pita halves; sprinkle with salt. Cut each pita half into six wedges. Place rough side up on ungreased baking sheets.

   Bake at 350° for 12-15 minutes or until crisp and golden brown. Cool on wire racks. Store in an airtight container.

Caramel-Cashew Pretzel Rods

PREP: 45 MIN. + CHILLING   **YIELD:** 4 DOZEN

To give these pretzel rods the fun flavor of s'mores, I sometimes use mini marshmallows and coarsely crushed graham crackers in place of the cashews.

Joanne Wright ★ Niles, Michigan

- 1 package (14 ounces) caramels
- 1 tablespoon heavy whipping cream
- 24 pretzel rods
- 3 cups chopped salted cashews *or* chopped pecans, toasted
- 4 ounces dark chocolate candy coating, melted
- 4 ounces white candy coating, melted

In a microwave, heat caramels and cream on high for 2-3 minutes or until caramels are melted, stirring after each minute. Stir until smooth.

   Break the pretzel rods in half. Dip the broken end two-thirds of the way into caramel mixture; allow excess to drip off. Roll in cashews. Place on a waxed paper-lined baking sheet. Chill until set.

   Drizzle dark chocolate over dipped portion of pretzels; chill until set. Drizzle with white coating; chill until set. Store in airtight containers.

Editor's Note: This recipe was tested in a 1,100-watt microwave.

Pretzel Presents

Caramel-Cashew Pretzel Rods make tasty gifts for relatives, neighbors and teachers!

   Simply bundle some pretzels in a festive cellophane bag and tie with a pretty ribbon.

   The pretzels could also be placed in a holiday tin lined with tissue paper.

Candied Pecans

PREP: 20 MIN.   **BAKE:** 40 MIN.   **YIELD:** ABOUT 1 POUND

I packed these crispy pecans in jars, tied with pretty ribbon, for family and friends. My granddaughter gave some to a doctor at the hospital where she works, and he said they were too good to be true!

Opal Turner ★ Hughes Springs, Texas

2-3/4	cups pecan halves
2	tablespoons butter, softened, *divided*
1	cup sugar
1/2	cup water
1/2	teaspoon salt
1/2	teaspoon ground cinnamon
1	teaspoon vanilla extract

Place pecans in a shallow baking pan in a 250° oven for 10 minutes or until warmed. Grease a 15-in. x 10-in. x 1-in. baking pan with 1 tablespoon butter; set aside.

Grease the sides of a large heavy saucepan with the remaining butter; add sugar, water, salt and cinnamon. Cook and stir over low heat until sugar is dissolved. Cook and stir over medium heat until mixture comes to a boil. Cover and cook for 2 minutes to dissolve sugar crystals.

Cook, without stirring, until a candy thermometer reads 236° (soft-ball stage). Remove from the heat; add vanilla. Stir in the warm pecans until evenly coated. Spread onto prepared baking pan. Bake at 250° for 30 minutes, stirring every 10 minutes. Spread on a waxed paper-lined baking sheet to cool.

Editor's Note: We recommend that you test your candy thermometer before each use by bringing water to a boil; the thermometer should read 212°. Adjust your recipe temperature up or down based on your test.

Easy Mint Chocolate Truffles

PREP: 20 MIN.   **COOK:** 10 MIN. + CHILLING
YIELD: 70 TRUFFLES

I make a lot of candy around the holidays. This is one of my favorites because the mixture isn't sticky or messy to work with, and the results are just delicious.

Jean Olson ★ Wallingford, Iowa

   1   tablespoon plus 3/4 cup butter, *divided*
   3   cups sugar
   1   can (5 ounces) evaporated milk
   2   cups (12 ounces) semisweet chocolate chips
   1/2 teaspoon peppermint extract
   1   jar (7 ounces) marshmallow creme
   1   teaspoon vanilla extract
   Baking cocoa, finely chopped nuts *or* chocolate sprinkles

Line a 15-in. x 10-in. x 1-in. pan with foil. Grease the foil with 1 tablespoon butter; set aside.

In a heavy saucepan, combine the sugar, milk and remaining butter. Bring to a boil over medium heat. Cook, stirring constantly, until a candy thermometer reads 234° (soft-ball stage). Remove from the heat; stir in chips and peppermint extract until chocolate is melted. Stir in the marshmallow creme and vanilla until smooth. Spread into prepared pan.

Refrigerate, uncovered, for 3 hours or until firm. Lift out of the pan; cut into 1-1/2-in. squares. Roll into 1-in. balls. Roll the balls in cocoa, nuts or sprinkles. Refrigerate in an airtight container.

Editor's Note: We recommend that you test your candy thermometer before each use by bringing water to a boil; the thermometer should read 212°. Adjust your recipe temperature up or down based on your test.

Pineapple Pepper Salsa

PREP/TOTAL TIME: 10 MIN.   **YIELD:** 2 CUPS

The contrast of sweet and heat makes for a flavorful salsa that both friends and family enjoy. For a spicy variety, use jalapeno jelly instead of sweet red pepper jelly.

Sandy Starks ★ Amherst, New York

   1   can (8 ounces) crushed pineapple, drained
   1/3 cup sweet red pepper jelly
   1/2 cup chopped red onion
   1/2 cup chopped sweet red pepper
   1   teaspoon minced fresh cilantro
   1/8 teaspoon coarsely ground pepper

In a small bowl, combine all ingredients. Serve immediately or refrigerate until serving. Use as a condiment with grilled meats or as a dip with tortilla chips.

Southwestern Dip Mix

PREP/TOTAL TIME: 15 MIN. **YIELD:** 2 CUPS (1-1/2 CUPS TOTAL)

Keep a container of this mix on hand to make dip at a moment's notice. The dip is spiced just right so it will appeal to all palates at potlucks and holiday gatherings.

Tonia Egan ★ Burlington, Massachusetts

- 1/2 cup dried parsley flakes
- 1/3 cup dried minced onion
- 1/3 cup chili powder
- 1/4 cup ground cumin
- 2 tablespoons dried minced chives
- 1 tablespoon salt
- 2 teaspoons paprika
- 1/2 teaspoon crushed red pepper flakes, optional

ADDITIONAL INGREDIENTS (FOR EACH BATCH):
- 1 cup mayonnaise
- 1 cup sour cream

Tortilla chips *or* fresh vegetables

Combine the first eight ingredients. Store in an airtight container in a cool dry place for up to 6 months. **YIELD:** 12 batches (1-1/2 cups total).

   TO PREPARE ONE BATCH OF DIP: Add 2 tablespoons of mix to mayonnaise and sour cream; stir until blended. Serve with chips or vegetables.

Pasta Fagioli Soup Mix

PREP: 20 MIN. + SOAKING   **COOK:** 1-3/4 HOURS
YIELD: 14 SERVINGS (3-1/2 QUARTS)

This meatless soup is both economical and flavorful. Church groups could buy the ingredients in bulk and assemble mixes to give to shut-ins.

Tamera Duncan ★ Castle, Oklahoma

- 1 cup small pasta shells
- 3/4 cup dried great northern beans
- 3/4 cup dried pinto beans
- 3/4 cup dried kidney beans
- 1/4 cup dried minced onion
- 3 tablespoons dried parsley flakes
- 1 teaspoon dried basil
- 1 teaspoon dried oregano
- 1/2 teaspoon dried rosemary, crushed
- 1/4 teaspoon dried minced garlic
- 1 bay leaf

Dash crushed red pepper flakes

ADDITIONAL INGREDIENTS:

- 14 cups water, *divided*
- 1 can (28 ounces) diced tomatoes, undrained
- 3 medium carrots, chopped
- 1 celery rib, chopped
- 1 teaspoon salt

Grated Parmesan cheese, optional

Place pasta in a small resealable plastic bag; place in a 1-qt. glass jar. Layer with beans. Place seasonings in another plastic bag; place in jar. Cover and store in a cool dry place for up to 3 months. **YIELD:** 1 batch.

TO PREPARE SOUP: Remove seasoning packet from jar. Remove beans; sort and rinse. Set pasta aside.

Place beans in a Dutch oven; add 6 cups water. Bring to a boil; boil for 2 minutes. Remove from the heat; cover and let stand for 1 to 4 hours or until beans are softened. Drain and discard liquid.

Return beans to the pan. Add contents of seasoning packet and remaining water. Bring to a boil. Reduce heat; cover and simmer for 1 hour or until beans are tender. Add the tomatoes, carrots, celery and salt; cover and simmer 30 minutes longer, stirring occasionally.

Stir in the pasta. Cover and simmer for 5-10 minutes or until pasta and carrots are tender, stirring occasionally. Remove the bay leaf before serving. Garnish with the cheese if desired.

Use Canning Jars for Mixes

Leftover canning jars are great for giving mixes at Christmastime.

After filling the jar, tie a 5-in. square of fabric onto the top with ribbon or wire garland.

Print or write out a label to stick on the jar with recipe instructions.

Kickin' Red Pepper Jelly

PREP: 30 MIN. + STANDING   **PROCESS:** 10 MIN.
YIELD: 4 HALF-PINTS

Peppers grow like wild fire in our hot Missouri summers. That's when I make spicy jelly to give as gifts at Christmas. The leftover pulp can be frozen in small batches and stirred into chili, pasta sauce, salad dressing and salsa.

Lee Bremson ★ Kansas City, Missouri

- 5   medium sweet red peppers, coarsely chopped
- 3   jalapeno peppers, stemmed and seeded
- 2   garlic cloves, peeled
- 1/2 cup red wine vinegar
- 3   tablespoons balsamic vinegar
- 2   tablespoons bottled lemon juice
- 1   package (1-3/4 ounces) powdered fruit pectin
- 3-1/4 cups sugar

Place the red peppers, jalapenos and garlic in a blender; cover and process until finely chopped. Set aside 1/2 cup; puree remaining pepper mixture.

Line a strainer with four layers of cheesecloth and place over a bowl. Place pureed pepper mixture in strainer; cover with edges of cheesecloth. Let stand for 30 minutes or until liquid measures 1-1/2 cups.

Discard pepper mixture from cheesecloth or save for another use; place liquid in a large saucepan. Stir in the vinegars, lemon juice, pectin and reserved pepper mixture. Bring to a full rolling boil over high heat, stirring constantly. Stir in the sugar; return to a full rolling boil. Boil for 1 minute, stirring constantly.

Remove from the heat; skim off the foam. Ladle the hot liquid into hot half-pint jars, leaving 1/4-in. headspace. Wipe rims and adjust lids. Process for 10 minutes in a boiling-water canner.

Editor's Note: When cutting hot peppers, disposable gloves are recommended. Avoid touching your face. The processing time listed is for altitudes of 1,000 feet or less. Add 1 minute to the processing time for each 1,000 feet of additional altitude.

Instant Latte Mix

PREP/TOTAL TIME: 15 MIN.   **YIELD:** 7 SERVINGS

Do you have to buy a gift for a coffee drinker? This mix is a fantastic, frugal substitution to coffeehouse beverages. Feel free to use chocolate or pumpkin spice pudding in place of the vanilla.

Melody Sroufe ★ Garden Plain, Kansas

- 1   cup nonfat dry milk powder
- 1/2 cup powdered nondairy creamer
- 1/3 cup instant coffee granules
- 1/3 cup sugar
- 1/4 cup instant vanilla pudding mix

ADDITIONAL INGREDIENT FOR HOT LATTE:

- 3/4 cup hot water

ADDITIONAL INGREDIENTS FOR ICED LATTE:

- 1/4 cup hot water
- 1/4 cup cold water
- 1/2 cup ice cubes

In a blender, combine the milk powder, creamer, coffee granules, sugar and pudding mix; cover and process until mixture is a fine powder. Store in an airtight container for up to 6 months. **YIELD:** 1-3/4 cups.

TO PREPARE HOT LATTE: Dissolve 1/4 cup mix in hot water; stir well.

TO PREPARE ICED LATTE: Dissolve 1/4 cup mix in hot water; stir in cold water. Transfer to a blender; add ice. Cover and process until blended.

Toffee Crunch Pretzels

PREP: 20 MIN.   **BAKE:** 1 HOUR + COOLING
YIELD: 3-1/2 QUARTS

The sweet and salty combination of flavors in these lightly coated pretzels makes them hard to resist. Get ready to double the recipe!

Bethany ★ Taste of Home Online Community

- 12 cups miniature pretzels
- 1   cup packed brown sugar
- 1/2 cup butter, cubed
- 1/4 cup light corn syrup
- 1   teaspoon vanilla extract
- 1/2 teaspoon baking soda

Place the pretzels in a greased roasting pan. In a small saucepan, combine the brown sugar, butter and corn syrup. Bring to a boil over medium heat. Boil for 5 minutes, stirring occasionally.

Remove from the heat; stir in vanilla and baking soda (mixture will foam). Pour over pretzels and mix well.

Bake, uncovered, at 200° for 1 hour, stirring every 15 minutes. Spread on waxed paper to cool. Store in an airtight container.

Peppermint Candy

PREP: 25 MIN. + CHILLING   **YIELD:** 5 DOZEN

Pairing peppermint and chocolate is a natural. Family and friends gobble up these sweet confections.

Kandy Clarke ★ Columbia Falls, Montana

1 cup semisweet chocolate chips
1 can (14 ounces) sweetened condensed milk, *divided*
1 cup vanilla *or* white chips
3 teaspoons peppermint extract
2 to 3 drops green food coloring

In a small saucepan, melt the chocolate chips with 3/4 cup condensed milk over low heat, stirring occasionally. Line an 8-in. square dish with waxed paper; butter the paper.

Spread half of melted chocolate mixture into pan; chill for 5-10 minutes (let remaining melted chocolate mixture stand at room temperature).

In another saucepan, melt the vanilla chips. Stir in the remaining condensed milk until smooth. Remove from the heat; add extract and food coloring. Refrigerate until set. Spread over chocolate layer; spread with reserved chocolate mixture. Refrigerate until set. Cut into 1-in. pieces.

Mushroom Barley Soup Mix

PREP: 15 MIN. **COOK:** 45 MIN.
YIELD: 6-1/2 CUPS PER BATCH

Steaming bowls of homemade soup are less than an hour away when you have this lovely layered soup mix on hand. You won't miss the meat in this hearty soup featuring lentils and barley.

- 1-1/2 cups dried lentils
- 3 cups medium pearl barley
- 1 package (1 ounce) dried shiitake *or* porcini mushrooms (about 2 cups)
- 6 bay leaves
- 18 beef bouillon cubes
- 6 tablespoons dried celery flakes
- 6 tablespoons dried parsley flakes
- 6 tablespoons dried minced onion
- 3 teaspoons coarsely ground pepper
- 3 teaspoons garlic salt
- 3 teaspoons dried thyme

ADDITIONAL INGREDIENTS (FOR EACH BATCH):
- 2 quarts water
- 2 medium carrots, chopped

In six pint-size jars or cellophane gift bags, layer 1/4 cup lentils, 1/2 cup barley and 1/3 cup mushrooms. Top with a bay leaf.

In six snack-size resealable plastic bags, place three bouillon cubes, 1 tablespoon celery flakes, 1 tablespoon parsley, 1 tablespoon onion, 1/2 teaspoon pepper, 1/2 teaspoon garlic salt and 1/2 teaspoon thyme; seal bags. Place one in each jar or bag and seal. **YIELD:** 6 batches.

TO PREPARE ONE BATCH OF SOUP: Place mix and seasonings in a large saucepan; add water and carrots. Bring to a boil; stir well. Reduce heat; cover and simmer for 45-60 minutes or until barley and lentils are tender. Remove bay leaf before serving.

Glazed Pfeffernuesse

PREP: 1-1/4 HOURS + CHILLING   **BAKE:** 10 MIN./BATCH
YIELD: ABOUT 10 DOZEN

Our home economists' version of the classic German cookie is nice to serve throughout the holiday season. They stay fresh— and become more intense in flavor—when stored in an airtight container for weeks.

- 1-1/4 cups butter, softened
- 1-1/4 cups packed brown sugar
- 3/4 cup molasses
- 1/2 cup water
- 1 teaspoon anise extract
- 6 cups cake flour
- 1/2 teaspoon baking soda
- 1/2 teaspoon salt
- 1-1/2 teaspoons ground cinnamon
- 1/2 teaspoon ground allspice
- 1/2 teaspoon ground cloves
- 1/4 teaspoon ground nutmeg
- 1/4 teaspoon ground mace
- 1/8 teaspoon pepper
- 1/8 teaspoon ground cardamom
- 2 cups finely chopped nuts

GLAZE:
- 1 cup confectioners' sugar
- 3 tablespoons milk
- 1/4 teaspoon vanilla extract

Additional confectioners' sugar

In a large bowl, cream butter and brown sugar until light and fluffy. Beat in the molasses, water and extract. Combine the flour, baking soda, salt and spices; gradually add to the creamed mixture and mix well. Stir in the nuts. Cover and refrigerate for 1 hour.

Roll dough into 1-in. balls. Place 2 in. apart on greased baking sheets. Bake at 375° for 10-12 minutes or until golden brown.

Meanwhile, in a shallow bowl, combine confectioners' sugar, milk and vanilla. Place additional confectioners' sugar in another shallow bowl. Remove cookies to wire racks; cool 5 minutes. Dip tops of warm cookies in glaze, then dip in confectioners' sugar. Cool completely on wire racks. Store in an airtight container.

Editor's Note: This recipe does not use eggs.

Chardonnay Crackers

PREP: 10 MIN. **BAKE:** 45 MIN. + COOLING **YIELD:** 9 CUPS

Special occasions call for extraordinary snacks. I use white wine and ranch dip mix to dress up plain wheat crackers. They're great to munch on anytime!

Sandra Cole ★ Danville, Pennsylvania

- 2 packages (10 ounces *each*) wheat crackers
- 1/2 cup canola oil
- 1 envelope ranch dip mix
- 1 tablespoon chardonnay *or* other dry white wine
- 1 teaspoon garlic powder
- 1 teaspoon dill weed

Place the crackers in a large bowl. Combine the remaining ingredients; pour over crackers and toss to coat. Transfer to two ungreased 15-in. x 10-in. x 1-in. baking pans.

Bake at 250° for 45 minutes or until crisp, stirring every 15 minutes. Cool on a wire rack. Store the crackers in an airtight container.

Sunflower Oatmeal Loaves

PREP: 45 MIN. + RISING **BAKE:** 20 MIN. + COOLING
YIELD: 4 LOAVES (8 SLICES EACH)

With oats, wheat germ and sunflower kernels, a small slice of this dense bread goes a long way. The glossy top of this lovely loaf is sprinkled with sesame seeds.

Courtney Taglauer ★ Fairfield, Iowa

- 1 cup old-fashioned oats
- 1-1/4 cups boiling water
- 1/2 cup honey
- 2 tablespoons butter
- 3 to 4 cups all-purpose flour
- 1 cup whole wheat flour
- 1/2 cup toasted wheat germ
- 2 packages (1/4 ounce *each*) active dry yeast
- 2 teaspoons salt
- 1/2 cup sunflower kernels
- 1 egg yolk
- 1/4 teaspoon cold water
- 4 teaspoons sesame seeds

Place the oats in a small bowl; add boiling water, honey and butter. Let stand until mixture cools to 120°-130°, stirring occasionally.

In a large bowl, combine 2 cups all-purpose flour, whole wheat flour, wheat germ, yeast and salt. Beat in oat mixture until blended. Stir in sunflower kernels and enough of the remaining flour to form a stiff dough (dough will be sticky).

Turn onto a lightly floured surface; knead until smooth and elastic, about 6-8 minutes. Place in a greased bowl, turning once to grease the top. Cover and let rise in a warm place until doubled, about 1 hour.

Punch dough down; turn onto a lightly floured surface. Divide into four portions; shape into 8-in. x 2-in. loaves. Place on greased baking sheets. Cover and let rise until doubled, about 30 minutes.

Beat the egg yolk and cold water; brush over the loaves. Sprinkle with sesame seeds. With a sharp knife, cut slits in tops of loaves.

Bake at 350° for 20-25 minutes or until golden brown. Remove from pans to wire racks to cool.

Toffee Chip Fudge

PREP: 15 MIN. + CHILLING **COOK:** 10 MIN.
YIELD: 2 POUNDS

My grandchildren savor the job of taste-testing my baking experiments. I combined two recipes to come up with this yummy fudge dotted with crisp toffee bits. The kids gave it a "thumbs-up" before requesting a batch to take home.

Maxine Smith ★ Owanka, South Dakota

1-1/2	teaspoons plus 1/4 cup butter, *divided*
1-1/2	cups sugar
1	can (5 ounces) evaporated milk
1/4	teaspoon salt
1-1/2	cups semisweet chocolate chips
2	cups miniature marshmallows
1/2	cup plus 2 tablespoons English toffee bits *or* almond brickle chips, *divided*
1	teaspoon vanilla extract

Line a 9-in. square pan with foil. Grease the foil with 1-1/2 teaspoons butter; set aside.

In a large heavy saucepan, combine the sugar, milk, salt and remaining butter. Cook and stir over medium heat until the sugar is dissolved. Bring to a rapid boil; boil for 5 minutes, stirring constantly.

Remove from the heat; stir in the chocolate chips and marshmallows until melted. Fold in 1/2 cup toffee bits and vanilla. Pour into a prepared pan. Sprinkle with remaining toffee bits. Chill until firm. Remove from pan and cut into 1-in. squares. Store in the refrigerator.

Pickled Peppers

PREP: 30 MIN. **PROCESS:** 15 MIN. + STANDING
YIELD: 4 PINTS

I'm nearing the age of 80 and still love to can my homegrown produce. I call this recipe "Summer in a Jar." The peppers have a nice combination of tart and spicy flavors.

Edna Clemens ★ West Branch, Michigan

4	to 6 large sweet red peppers, cut into strips
12	banana peppers, halved and seeded
1	medium onion, thinly sliced
8	garlic cloves, peeled
4	teaspoons canola oil
2-1/2	cups water
2-1/2	cups white vinegar
1-1/4	cups sugar
2	teaspoons canning salt

Pack red and banana peppers into four hot 1-pint jars to within 1/2 in. of the top. Divide the onion, garlic and oil among jars.

In a large saucepan, bring the water, vinegar, sugar and salt to a boil. Ladle hot liquid over pepper mixture, leaving 1/2-in. headspace. Remove air bubbles; wipe the rims and adjust lids. Process for 15 minutes in a boiling-water canner.

Editor's Note: The processing time listed is for altitudes of 1,000 feet or less. For altitudes up to 3,000 feet, add 5 minutes; 6,000 feet, add 10 minutes; 8,000 feet, add 15 minutes; 10,000 feet, add 20 minutes.

Packing Cookies for Shipping

When sending home-baked cookies to out-of-town family and friends, ensure the mouth-watering morsels are at their best upon arrival by reviewing these packing pointers.

Many drop, refrigerator and sandwich cookies are fairly sturdy and travel well. Some cutouts and shaped varieties are a little more delicate and more likely to break. Cookies requiring refrigeration are poor choices to ship because they'll spoil. If you are shipping to a warm climate, frostings or chocolate chips might melt.

Pack and ship cookies soon after baking so they're as fresh as possible.

Put crisp and soft cookies and strong-flavored and mild-flavored cookies in separate tins. Consider shipping soft cookies by express mail so they'll be moist upon arrival.

1. Wrap the cookies in bundles of two (for drop cookies, place their bottoms together) with plastic wrap.

2. Line a festive tin or box with crumpled waxed paper to help cushion the cookies. Snugly pack cookies to within 1 inch of the top.

3. Use crumpled waxed paper or bubble wrap to fill gaps between cookies. Add more paper or bubble wrap over the cookies to cushion and prevent shifting.

Snickerdoodles

PREP/TOTAL TIME: 25 MIN.   **YIELD:** 2-1/2 DOZEN

The history of this whimsically named treat is widely disputed, but the popularity of this classic cinnamon-sugar-coated cookie is undeniable!

- 1/2 cup butter, softened
- 1 cup plus 2 tablespoons sugar, *divided*
- 1 egg
- 1/2 teaspoon vanilla extract
- 1-1/2 cups all-purpose flour
- 1/4 teaspoon baking soda
- 1/4 teaspoon cream of tartar
- 1 teaspoon ground cinnamon

In a large bowl, cream butter and 1 cup sugar until light and fluffy. Beat in egg and vanilla. Combine the flour, baking soda and cream of tartar; gradually add to the creamed mixture and mix well. In a small bowl, combine the cinnamon and sugar.

Shape dough into 1-in. balls; roll in cinnamon-sugar. Place 2 in. apart on ungreased baking sheets. Bake at 375° for 10-12 minutes or until lightly browned. Remove to wire racks to cool.

Cookie Tray
DELIGHTS

Almond Toffee

(pictured on page 113)

PREP: 50 MIN. + STANDING   **YIELD:** ABOUT 1-1/2 POUNDS

After trying a co-worker's fabulous toffee, I had to have the recipe! It's now a regular on my Christmas cookie tray. I also entered it at our country fair and received "Best in Show."

Sue Gronholz ★ Beaver Dam, Wisconsin

- 1   tablespoon plus 2 cups butter, *divided*
- 2   cups sugar
- 1   cup slivered almonds
- 1/4 cup water
- 1   teaspoon salt
- 1   teaspoon vanilla extract
- 1   package (11-1/2 ounces) milk chocolate chips, *divided*
- 1/2 cup finely chopped almonds

Grease a 15-in. x 10-in. x 1-in. pan with 1 tablespoon butter; set aside. In a large heavy saucepan, melt the remaining butter. Add the sugar, slivered almonds, water and salt; cook and stir over medium heat until a candy thermometer reads 295° (approaching hard-crack stage). Remove from the heat; stir in vanilla.

Quickly pour into prepared pan. Let stand at room temperature until cool, about 1 hour.

In a microwave, melt 1 cup chocolate chips; spread over toffee. Refrigerate for 45 minutes or until set. Invert onto an ungreased large baking sheet. Melt remaining chips; spread over toffee. Sprinkle with chopped almonds. Let stand for 1 hour. Break into bite-size pieces. Store in an airtight container.

Editor's Note: We recommend that you test your candy thermometer before each use by bringing water to a boil; the thermometer should read 212°. Adjust your recipe temperature up or down based on your test.

Brandied Cherry Balls

PREP: 45 MIN. + CHILLING   **YIELD:** ABOUT 3-1/2 DOZEN

These special candies look impressive but are actually quite easy to prepare. The brandy really complements the cherries and chocolate.

homebody2 ★ Taste of Home Online Community

- 1/2   cup dried cherries, finely chopped
- 1/2   cup cherry brandy
- 1   package (3 ounces) cream cheese, softened
- 1   tablespoon butter, softened
- 3-3/4 cups confectioners' sugar
- 6   ounces dark chocolate candy coating, chopped
- 1   tablespoon shortening

DRIZZLE:
White candy coating, chopped
Pink paste food coloring

Place the cherries in a small bowl. Cover with the brandy; refrigerate overnight.

In a large bowl, beat cream cheese and butter until smooth. Add confectioners' sugar; beat until crumbly. Drain cherries, reserving 2 teaspoons brandy. Add cherries and reserved brandy to cream cheese mixture.

Roll into 1-1/2-in. balls. Place balls on a waxed paper-lined baking sheet. Cover loosely and refrigerate for 1 hour.

In a microwave, melt dark chocolate candy coating and shortening; stir until smooth. Dip balls in chocolate; allow excess to drip off. Return to the baking sheet.

For drizzle, melt a small amount of white candy coating in a microwave; stir in food coloring until smooth. Drizzle over candies. Chill until set.

Coconut Cream Rounds

PREP: 45 MIN. **BAKE:** 10 MIN./BATCH + COOLING
YIELD: 3 DOZEN

With a yummy coconut topping, these cookies are a holiday hit, tea party favorite and potluck dinner "must." I've been using the recipe for more than 50 years.

Sylvia Thurston Davis ★ Auburn, New York

- 1 cup butter, softened
- 1 cup confectioners' sugar
- 2 teaspoons vanilla extract
- 2 cups all-purpose flour
- 1 teaspoon salt

TOPPING:
- 1 package (3 ounces) cream cheese, softened
- 1 cup confectioners' sugar
- 2 tablespoons all-purpose flour
- 1 teaspoon vanilla extract
- 1/2 cup flaked coconut
- 1/2 cup finely chopped walnuts
- 3/4 cup semisweet chocolate chips, melted

In a large bowl, cream butter and confectioners' sugar until light and fluffy. Beat in vanilla. Combine flour and salt; gradually add to creamed mixture and mix well.

Shape into 1-in. balls. Place 2 in. apart on ungreased baking sheets. Using the end of a wooden spoon handle, make a 1/2-in.-deep indentation in the center of each ball.

Bake at 350° for 10-12 minutes or until lightly browned. Remove to wire racks to cool.

For filling, in a small bowl, beat cream cheese and confectioners' sugar until light and fluffy. Beat in flour and vanilla; stir in coconut and walnuts. Mound 1 teaspoonful onto each cookie. Drizzle with chocolate; let stand until set.

Decorated Christmas Cutout Cookies

PREP: 15 MIN. + CHILLING **BAKE:** 10 MIN./BATCH + COOLING
YIELD: 6-7 DOZEN (2-1/2-INCH COOKIES)

Rich, buttery cookies like these never last long at a party. I use seasonal cutters to celebrate the holidays tastefully.

Lynn Burgess ★ Rolla, Missouri

3/4   cup butter, softened
1   cup sugar
2   eggs
1   teaspoon vanilla extract
2-3/4   cups all-purpose flour
1   teaspoon baking powder
1/2   teaspoon salt
Tinted frostings, colored sugars, edible glitter and nonpareils

In a large bowl, cream butter and sugar until light and fluffy. Beat in eggs and vanilla. Combine the flour, baking powder and salt; gradually add to creamed mixture and mix well. Refrigerate for 1 hour or until firm.

On a lightly floured surface, roll out dough to 1/4-in. thickness. Cut out with Christmas cookie cutters of your choice. Using a floured spatula, transfer cookies to greased baking sheets.

Bake at 375° for 8-10 minutes or until lightly browned. Cool completely on wire racks.

Decorate cookies with frosting, sugars and candies.

Millionaire Clusters

PREP: 30 MIN.   **COOK:** 30 MIN. + CHILLING
YIELD: 7 DOZEN

Of the 35 kinds of candy I make each Christmas, this is by far the favorite of family and friends. These treats taste like a million bucks!

Theda Andres ★ Appleton, Wisconsin

    2   tablespoons plus 1 cup butter, *divided*
    2   cups evaporated milk
    1   cup sugar
    1   cup packed brown sugar
    1   cup light corn syrup
  1/8   teaspoon salt
    4   cups chopped pecans
    1   teaspoon vanilla extract
    1   pound milk chocolate candy coating, melted

Grease four baking sheets with 2 tablespoons of butter; set aside.

In a large heavy saucepan, combine the milk, sugars, corn syrup, salt and remaining butter. Bring to a boil, stirring frequently. Cook over medium heat until a candy thermometer reads 238° (soft-ball stage), stirring occasionally.

Remove from the heat. Stir in pecans and vanilla. Drop by tablespoonfuls onto prepared baking sheets. Let stand until set.

Drizzle melted candy coating over clusters; chill for 10 minutes or until set. Store in airtight containers.

Editor's Note: We recommend that you test your candy thermometer before each use by bringing water to a boil; the thermometer should read 212°. Adjust your recipe temperature up or down based on your test.

Chrusciki Bow Tie Cookies

PREP: 1 HOUR   **COOK:** 5 MIN./BATCH   **YIELD:** 4 DOZEN

My mother-in-law gave me the recipe for these traditional Polish "angel wings." She's been gone for years now, but I still make them in memory of her.

Linda Svercauski ★ San Diego, California

    3   egg yolks
    1   egg
  1/4   cup spiced rum
    2   tablespoons vanilla extract
  1/2   teaspoon salt
  1/4   cup confectioners' sugar
    2   cups all-purpose flour
Oil for deep-fat frying
Additional confectioners' sugar

In a large bowl, beat the egg yolks, egg, rum, vanilla and salt until blended. Gradually add confectioners' sugar; beat until smooth. Stir in flour until a stiff dough forms. Turn onto a lightly floured surface; knead seven times.

Divide dough into three portions. Roll one portion into a 1/4-in.-thick rectangle, about 12 in. x 5-1/2 in. Cut in half lengthwise, then cut dough widthwise into 1-1/2-in.-wide strips. Cut a 3/4-in. lengthwise slit down the center of each strip; pull one of the ends through the slit, forming a bow. Repeat with remaining strips.

In an electric skillet or deep-fat fryer, heat oil to 375°. Fry cookies, a few at a time, for 1-2 minutes on each side or until golden brown. Drain on paper towels. Dust with confectioners' sugar.

Chocolate & Vanilla Spritz

PREP: 40 MIN. **BAKE:** 10 MIN./BATCH + COOLING
YIELD: 9 DOZEN

These tender treats are so cute and have a great buttery flavor. The dough is easy to work with and the cookies bake up beautifully every time.

Mary Beth Jung ★ Hendersonville, North Carolina

1-1/2	cups butter, softened
1	cup sugar
1	egg
2	tablespoons milk
1	teaspoon vanilla extract
1/2	teaspoon almond extract
3-1/2	cups all-purpose flour
1	teaspoon baking powder
3	tablespoons baking cocoa

Melted chocolate and chocolate jimmies, optional

In a large bowl, cream the butter and sugar until light and fluffy. Beat in the egg, milk and extracts. Combine the flour and baking powder; gradually add to the creamed mixture and mix well.

Divide dough in half; add cocoa to one portion and mix well. Divide each portion into six pieces; shape each into a 5-in. log. Place a chocolate log and vanilla log together, pressing to form another log.

Using a cookie press fitted with the disk of your choice, press dough 2 in. apart onto ungreased baking sheets. Bake at 375° for 9-11 minutes or until edges are lightly browned. Remove to wire racks to cool.

If desired, dip each cookie halfway into the melted chocolate, allowing excess to drip off. Place on waxed paper; sprinkle with jimmies. Let stand until set.

Creamy Soft Caramels

PREP: 20 MIN. **COOK:** 25 MIN. + COOLING
YIELD: 2-1/2 POUNDS

Rich, creamy, smooth, soft...those are just a few reasons to love these old-fashioned caramels. Store-bought varieties just can't compare.

Sharon Struthers ★ Belgrade, Minnesota

1	teaspoon plus 1 cup butter, *divided*
1-1/4	cups packed brown sugar
1	cup sugar

Dash salt

1	cup light corn syrup
1	can (14 ounces) sweetened condensed milk
1	teaspoon vanilla extract

Making Two-Tone Spritz Cookies

These pretty, bicolored spritz add a touch of sophistication to any dessert tray...and they're easy to make! Make six logs from the chocolate dough and six logs from the vanilla dough. (Each log should be 5 inches long.) Take one chocolate log and one vanilla log; press together to form one large log. Make sure that the new log is not wider than the diameter of your cookie press. If it is, just roll it on the counter to make it a little thinner.

Line a 9-in. square pan with foil. Grease the foil with 1 teaspoon butter; set aside. In a large saucepan, combine the sugars, salt and remaining butter. Bring to a boil over medium heat, stirring constantly. Stir in corn syrup; return to a boil. Remove from the heat; slowly stir in milk.

Cook and stir over medium-low heat until a candy thermometer reads 238° (soft-ball stage). Remove from the heat; stir in vanilla. Pour into prepared pan. Cool. Using foil, lift candy out of pan; cut into 1-in. squares. Wrap individually in waxed paper.

Editor's Note: We recommend that you test your candy thermometer before each use by bringing water to a boil; the thermometer should read 212°. Adjust your recipe temperature up or down based on your test.

Microwave Divinity

PREP: 40 MIN.   **COOK:** 10 MIN. + STANDING
YIELD: ABOUT 2-1/2 DOZEN

Not only is this the best-tasting divinity I've ever made, it's the easiest! Try it with and without the pecans.

LaDonna Reed ★ Ponca City, Oklahoma

2	egg whites
2-1/4	cups sugar
1/2	cup water
1/2	cup light corn syrup
1/8	teaspoon salt
1/2	cup chopped pecans
1-1/2	teaspoons vanilla extract

Place egg whites in the bowl of a heavy-duty stand mixer; let stand at room temperature for 30 minutes.

In a microwave-safe 2-qt. bowl, combine the sugar, water, corn syrup and salt. Microwave, uncovered, on high for 4 minutes; stir until sugar is dissolved. Cook 6-8 minutes longer or until a candy thermometer reads 260° (hard-ball stage), stirring every 2 minutes. Just before the temperature is reached, beat egg whites on medium speed until stiff peaks form.

With mixer running on high speed, carefully pour hot syrup in a slow, steady stream into the bowl. Beat just until candy loses its gloss and holds its shape, about 15-20 minutes. Immediately stir in pecans and vanilla. (Do not overmix, or candy will get stiff and crumbly.)

Working quickly, drop the mixture by tablespoonfuls onto waxed paper. Let stand at room temperature overnight or until dry to the touch. Store in an airtight container at room temperature.

Editor's Note: This recipe was tested in a 1,100-watt microwave. We recommend that you test your candy thermometer before each use by bringing water to a boil; the thermometer should read 212°. Adjust your recipe temperature up or down based on your test.

Crisp Lemon Cookies

PREP: 30 MIN. **BAKE:** 15 MIN./BATCH + COOLING
YIELD: ABOUT 4-1/2 DOZEN

These light, citrus cookies are a nice change of pace from typical Christmas cookies. Melted vanilla chips drizzled over the top is the fantastic finishing touch.

Darlene Dixon ★ Hanover, Minnesota

- 1-1/3 cups butter, softened
- 2 cups confectioners' sugar
- 2 tablespoons lemon juice
- 2 teaspoons grated lemon peel
- 1/2 teaspoon vanilla extract
- 3 cups all-purpose flour
- 1/4 cup sugar
- 3/4 cup vanilla *or* white chips, melted

In a large bowl, cream butter and confectioners' sugar until light and fluffy. Beat in the lemon juice, peel and vanilla. Gradually add flour and mix well.

Shape dough into 1-in. balls. Place 2 in. apart on ungreased baking sheets. Coat the bottom of a glass with cooking spray; dip in sugar. Flatten cookies with glass, redipping in sugar as needed.

Bake at 325° for 11-13 minutes or until edges are lightly browned. Remove to wire racks to cool. Drizzle with melted vanilla chips.

Line an 8-in. square pan with foil and grease the foil with 1 teaspoon butter; set aside.

In a large metal bowl, sprinkle gelatin over 1/2 cup water; set aside. In a large heavy saucepan, combine the sugar, corn syrup, coffee granules and remaining water. Bring to a boil, stirring occasionally. Cook, without stirring, until a candy thermometer reads 250° (hard-ball stage).

Remove from the heat and gradually add to gelatin. Beat on high speed until mixture is thick and the volume doubles, about 10 minutes. Spread into prepared pan. Cover and cool at room temperature for 6 hours or overnight.

Sprinkle cutting board lightly with pecans. Using the foil, lift candy out of pan; invert onto the cutting board. Cut into 1-in. squares; roll in pecans. Store in an airtight container in a cool dry place.

Editor's Note: We recommend that you test your candy thermometer before each use by bringing water to a boil; the thermometer should read 212°. Adjust your recipe temperature up or down based on your test.

Microwave Pralines

PREP: 25 MIN. + STANDING **YIELD:** 2 DOZEN

These are definitely a big hit with the people we give them to at Christmas. Making candy has never been so simple!

Linda Starlin ★ St. Johns, Michigan

1	cup sugar
1	cup packed brown sugar
1/4	cup water
1/4	cup light corn syrup
1	tablespoon butter
1-1/2	cups pecan halves
1	teaspoon vanilla extract

Line two baking sheets with waxed paper; set aside. In a microwave-safe 2-qt. bowl, combine the sugars, water, corn syrup and butter. Microwave, uncovered, on high for 4 minutes; stir until sugar is dissolved. Cook 1-2 minutes longer or until a candy thermometer reads 234° (soft-ball stage), stirring after each minute.

Add pecans and vanilla; stir just until mixture starts to thicken, about 1 minute. Working quickly, drop by rounded tablespoonfuls onto prepared pans. Flatten slightly. Let stand until set. Store in an airtight container.

Editor's Note: This recipe was tested in a 1,100-watt microwave. We recommend that you test your candy thermometer before each use by bringing water to a boil; the thermometer should read 212°. Adjust your recipe temperature up or down based on your test.

Coffee-Pecan Marshmallows

PREP: 35 MIN. **COOK:** 30 MIN. + COOLING
YIELD: 1-1/2 POUNDS

Homemade marshmallows are extraordinary and bear no resemblance to the store-bought variety. These will soon become your signature Christmas candy!

Deirdre Dee Zosha ★ Milwaukee, Wisconsin

1	teaspoon butter
2	envelopes unflavored gelatin
1/2	cup plus 3/4 cup cold water, *divided*
2	cups sugar
3/4	cup light corn syrup
2	tablespoons instant coffee granules
1	cup ground pecans

Caramel Pecan Shortbread

PREP: 30 MIN. + CHILLING
BAKE: 15 MIN./BATCH + COOLING
YIELD: ABOUT 4 DOZEN

My grandchildren look for "Grandma's candy bar cookies" every Christmas. I recommend doubling the recipe for these sweet treats because they go so fast.

Dorothy Buiter ★ Worth, Illinois

- 3/4 cup butter, softened
- 3/4 cup confectioners' sugar
- 2 tablespoons evaporated milk
- 1 teaspoon vanilla extract
- 2 cups all-purpose flour
- 1/4 teaspoon salt

FILLING:
- 28 caramels
- 6 tablespoons evaporated milk
- 2 tablespoons butter
- 1/2 cup confectioners' sugar
- 3/4 cup finely chopped pecans

ICING:
- 1 cup (6 ounces) semisweet chocolate chips
- 3 tablespoons evaporated milk
- 2 tablespoons butter
- 1/2 cup confectioners' sugar
- 1/2 teaspoon vanilla extract

Pecan halves

In a large bowl, cream butter and confectioners' sugar until light and fluffy. Beat in milk and vanilla. Combine flour and salt; gradually add to creamed mixture. Cover and refrigerate for 1 hour or until easy to handle.

On a lightly floured surface, roll out dough to 1/4-in. thickness. Cut into 2-in. x 1-in. strips. Place 1 in. apart on greased baking sheets.

Bake at 325° for 12-14 minutes or until lightly browned. Remove to wire racks to cool.

For filling, combine caramels and milk in a large saucepan. Cook and stir over medium-low heat until caramels are melted and smooth. Remove from the heat; stir in the butter, sugar and pecans. Cool for 5 minutes. Spread 1 teaspoon over each cookie.

For icing, in a microwave, melt the chips and milk; stir until smooth. Stir in the butter, sugar and vanilla. Cool for 5 minutes. Spread 1 teaspoon icing on each cookie; top each with a pecan half. Let stand until set. Store in an airtight container.

Macadamia Fudge

PREP: 20 MIN. + CHILLING **YIELD:** ABOUT 2 POUNDS

There are few recipes I just have to pull out every holiday season, and this fudge is one. It couldn't be easier...or tastier!

Tina Jacobs ★ Wantage, New Jersey

  1-1/2 teaspoons butter, softened
      3 cups (18 ounces) semisweet chocolate chips
      1 can (14 ounces) sweetened condensed milk
Dash salt
      1 cup chopped macadamia nuts
  1-1/2 teaspoons vanilla extract

Line an 8-in. square pan with foil and grease the foil with butter; set aside.

In a heavy saucepan, combine the chocolate chips, milk and salt. Cook and stir over low heat until chips are melted. Remove from the heat; stir in nuts and vanilla. Pour into prepared pan. Chill for 2 hours or until firm.

Using foil, lift fudge out of pan. Gently peel off foil; cut fudge into 1-in. squares.

Keeping Homemade Candy Fresh

Properly storing homemade candy will help keep it fresh longer.

Most candy will keep for 2 to 3 weeks if stored in an airtight container in a cool, dry place. Fudge and caramels can be wrapped tightly and frozen for up to a year.

Only store one type of candy in a container. This will prevent candies from exchanging flavors. It will also stop hard candy from turning soft and soft candy from becoming hard.

Cranberry Bliss Cookies

PREP: 1 HOUR **BAKE:** 10 MIN./BATCH **YIELD:** 10 DOZEN

This delicious cookie was inspired by cranberry bars at a popular gourmet coffee shop. Every bite is loaded with cranberries, vanilla chips and macadamia nuts.

Joan Stanton ★ Ellensburg, Washington

  1-1/2 cups butter, softened
      1 cup sugar
      1 cup packed brown sugar
      3 eggs
      3 tablespoons grated orange peel
      1 teaspoon vanilla extract
    1/2 teaspoon orange extract
      4 cups all-purpose flour
      1 package (5.1 ounces) instant vanilla pudding mix
  1-1/2 teaspoons baking soda
    3/4 teaspoon salt
      2 cups dried cranberries
      1 package (10 to 12 ounces) vanilla *or* white chips
      1 cup coarsely chopped macadamia nuts

In a large bowl, cream butter and sugars until light and fluffy. Beat in the eggs, orange peel and extracts. Combine the flour, pudding mix, baking soda and salt; gradually add to creamed mixture and mix well. Stir in the cranberries, chips and nuts.

Drop by tablespoonfuls 2 in. apart onto ungreased baking sheets; flatten slightly. Bake at 375° for 8-10 minutes or until lightly browned. Remove to wire racks to cool. Store in an airtight container.

Editor's Note: The cookies may be frozen in airtight container for up to 2 months.

Coconut Cashew Brittle

PREP: 25 MIN. **BAKE:** 10 MIN. + COOLING
YIELD: ABOUT 3 POUNDS

*This rich, buttery brittle has always been part of our
Christmas candy collection. Lots of coconut and cashews
ensures it's extra scrumptious.*

Darlene Brenden ★ Salem, Oregon

2	tablespoons plus 1 cup butter, *divided*
2	cups cashew halves
2	cups flaked coconut
2	cups sugar
1	cup light corn syrup
1/2	cup plus 1 teaspoon water, *divided*
2	teaspoons vanilla extract
1-1/2	teaspoons baking soda

Grease two 15-in. x 10-in. x 1-in. pans each with
1 tablespoon butter; set aside.

Combine the cashews and coconut on another 15-in. x
10-in. x 1-in. baking pan. Bake at 350° for 8-10 minutes or
until golden brown, stirring occasionally.

In a large heavy saucepan, combine the sugar, corn syrup
and 1/2 cup water. Cook and stir over medium heat until
the mixture comes to a boil. Add the remaining butter;
cook and stir until butter is melted. Continue cooking,
without stirring, until a candy thermometer reads
300° (hard-crack stage).

Meanwhile, combine the vanilla, baking soda and
remaining water. Remove saucepan from the heat; add
cashews and coconut. Stir in baking soda mixture. Quickly
pour into prepared baking pans. Spread with a buttered
metal spatula to 1/4-in. thickness. Cool before breaking
into pieces. Store in an airtight container.

Editor's Note: We recommend that you test your candy thermometer
before each use by bringing water to a boil; the thermometer should read
212°. Adjust your recipe temperature up or down based on your test.

Marshmallow Pecan Fudge

PREP: 15 MIN. + CHILLING   **YIELD:** 2 POUNDS

Creamy chocolate covers chewy marshmallows and crunchy nuts in this fantastic fudge. It disappears quickly from my holiday candy tray, but because it's prepared in 15 minutes, I can easily make more!

Jan Lutz ★ Stevens Point, Wisconsin

1   teaspoon plus 1 cup butter, *divided*
2   cups miniature marshmallows
1   cup chopped pecans
8   squares (1 ounce *each*) milk chocolate, chopped
2   packages (4 ounces *each*) German sweet chocolate, chopped

Line a 9-in. square pan with foil and grease the foil with 1 teaspoon butter. Sprinkle the marshmallows and pecans into the pan.

In a large heavy saucepan, combine the milk chocolate, German chocolate and remaining butter. Cook over low heat until smooth, stirring frequently. Pour over the marshmallows and pecans. Refrigerate for about 1 hour or until firm.

Using foil, lift the candy out of the pan. Discard foil; cut the candy into 1-in. squares. Store in an airtight container in the refrigerator.

Cherry-Pretzel Almond Bark

PREP: 15 MIN. + CHILLING   **YIELD:** 2-1/4 POUNDS

I love the contrast of sweet and salty flavors in candy, and this pretty bark is no exception. The dried cranberries add tangy taste as well as a festive color.

Margaret Goodrich ★ Sparta, Missouri

1-1/2   pounds white candy coating, chopped
1   cup slivered almonds
1   cup crushed pretzels
1   cup dried cherries

In a large microwave-safe bowl, melt candy coating; stir until smooth. Stir in the almonds, pretzels and cherries.

Spread mixture onto a waxed paper-lined baking sheet. Refrigerate for 30 minutes or until firm. Break into pieces. Store in an airtight container.

Reindeer Kibble

Don't let Santa be the only one who gets a sweet treat on Christmas Eve. Start a new family tradition by making something special for his reindeer, too!

When baking cookies during the holiday season, save any broken cookies and the crumbs from baking sheets. Combine them with some of the following foods—cereal, broken pretzels, birdseed and peanuts. Store in an airtight jar. On Christmas Eve, mix in dried or fresh cranberries. Have your kids sprinkle Reindeer Kibble in the backyard, away from the house. Not only will Santa's reindeers enjoy the treat, but the birds, squirrels and raccoons will be delighted with the holiday feast!

Oatmeal Gingersnaps

PREP: 20 MIN.   **BAKE:** 10 MIN./BATCH
YIELD: ABOUT 3-1/2 DOZEN

I always get compliments on these delicious chewy cookies. The spicy aroma fills my kitchen when they're baking and never fails to set a warm holiday mood.

Sherry Harke ★ South Bend, Indiana

- 1/2 cup shortening
- 1 cup sugar
- 1 egg
- 1/4 cup molasses
- 1-1/2 cups all-purpose flour
- 3/4 cup quick-cooking oats
- 1 teaspoon baking soda
- 1 teaspoon ground ginger
- 1/4 teaspoon salt
- 1/4 teaspoon ground cloves

Additional sugar

In a large bowl, cream the shortening and sugar until light and fluffy. Beat in the egg and molasses. Combine the dry ingredients; gradually add to creamed mixture and mix well. Roll into 1-in. balls; roll in additional sugar.

Place 2 in. apart on greased baking sheets. Flatten with a glass dipped in sugar. Bake at 350° for 10 minutes or until set (do not overbake). Remove to wire racks to cool.

Poppy Seed Thumbprints

PREP: 15 MIN. **BAKE:** 10 MIN./BATCH **YIELD:** 5 DOZEN

This crisp little cookie has the fantastic flavor of shortbread. A dollop of raspberry preserves on top makes them look especially festive for the holidays.

Kelly Pember ★ Wheeler, Wisconsin

1/2	cup butter, softened
1	cup confectioners' sugar
1/2	cup canola oil
1	egg
1	teaspoon vanilla extract
2-2/3	cups all-purpose flour
1/2	teaspoon salt
2	tablespoons poppy seeds
1	teaspoon grated lemon peel
1/3	cup seedless raspberry preserves

In a large bowl, cream butter and confectioners' sugar until light and fluffy. Beat in the oil, egg and vanilla. Combine flour and salt; gradually add to creamed mixture and mix well. Beat in poppy seeds and lemon peel.

Shape into 1-in. balls. Place 1 in. apart on ungreased baking sheets. Using a wooden spoon handle, make an indentation in the center of each cookie. Spoon 1/4 teaspoon preserves into each cookie.

Bake at 325° for 10-12 minutes or until bottoms are lightly browned. Remove to wire racks to cool.

Buttery Bow Cookies

PREP: 1 HOUR + CHILLING   **BAKE:** 10 MIN./BATCH
YIELD: 6 DOZEN

I was thrilled when my aunt passed this European-style cookie recipe onto me many years ago. Family and friends look for the tasty, edible bows on my cookie trays each Christmas.

Diana Mangelsen ★ Frederic, Wisconsin

    3   cups all-purpose flour
    1   teaspoon baking powder
  1/4   teaspoon salt
    1   cup cold butter
    1   egg, beaten
  1/2   cup heavy whipping cream
    3   tablespoons butter, melted
        Red and green colored sugar

In a large bowl, combine the flour, baking powder and salt; cut in butter until crumbly. Combine the egg and cream; gradually beat into crumb mixture until a ball forms. Cover and refrigerate for 30 minutes or until easy to handle.

Divide dough into three portions. On a lightly floured surface, roll each portion into an 8-in. x 6-in. rectangle. Brush with melted butter; sprinkle with colored sugar. Cut into 8-in.-long x 1/4-in.-wide strips. Place 2 in. apart on ungreased baking sheets; form into bows.

Bake at 350° for 10-12 minutes or until bottoms are lightly browned. Remove from pans to wire racks to cool.

Chocolate Mint Surprises

PREP: 30 MIN. + CHILLING
BAKE: 5 MIN./BATCH + FREEZING
YIELD: ABOUT 6 DOZEN

I came up with this recipe a few years ago and have shared it with many people. I would often snack on these treats after my baby's middle-of-the-night feeding.

Sheila Kerr ★ Revelstoke, British Columbia

  3/4   cup butter, softened
    1   cup sugar
    1   egg
    1   teaspoon vanilla extract
    3   squares (1 ounce *each*) unsweetened chocolate, melted
        and cooled
  2-1/2 cups all-purpose flour
  1-1/2 teaspoons baking powder
  1/2   teaspoon salt

MINT FILLING:

    4   cups confectioners' sugar
    3   tablespoons butter, softened
  1/4   cup evaporated milk
    2   to 3 teaspoons peppermint extract
  1/2   teaspoon vanilla extract
    2   pounds dark chocolate candy coating, melted

In a large bowl, cream butter and sugar until light and fluffy. Beat in egg and vanilla. Add the melted chocolate. Combine the flour, baking powder and salt; gradually add to chocolate mixture and mix well. Shape in two 10-in. rolls; wrap each in plastic wrap. Refrigerate for 4 hours or until firm.

Unwrap dough and cut into 1/4-in. slices. Place 2 in. apart on ungreased baking sheets. Bake at 375° for 5-7 minutes or until the edges are firm. Remove to wire racks to cool.

For filling, in a small bowl, combine the confectioners' sugar, butter, milk and extracts until smooth. Shape into 1/2-in. balls. Place a ball in the center of each cookie; flatten. Freeze for 30 minutes.

Dip cookies in melted candy coating to completely cover; allow excess to drip off. Place on waxed paper; let stand until set.

Snow-Covered Cookies

PREP: 45 MIN. + CHILLING
BAKE: 15 MIN./BATCH + COOLING
YIELD: 3-1/2 DOZEN

A tender chocolate cookie is topped with a slightly sweet, snow white frosting in this classic recipe. Tight on time? Make the dough one day and bake the next.

Marsha Rider ★ Hephzibah, Georgia

1	cup butter, softened
1/2	cup confectioners' sugar
2	teaspoons vanilla extract
1-1/2	cups all-purpose flour
1	cup ground pecans
1/2	cup grated German sweet chocolate (1-3/4 ounces)
3/4	teaspoon ground cinnamon
1/2	teaspoon salt
6	ounces white candy coating, melted

In a large bowl, cream butter and confectioners' sugar until light and fluffy. Beat in vanilla. Combine the flour, pecans, chocolate, cinnamon and salt; gradually add to creamed mixture and mix well. Cover and refrigerate for 1 hour or until easy to handle.

Shape the dough into 1-in. balls. Place 2 in. apart on ungreased baking sheets. Bake at 350° for 12-14 minutes or until the edges are lightly browned. Remove to wire racks to cool.

Drizzle or spread the melted candy coating over cookies; let stand until set.

Ginger Creme Sandwich Cookies

PREP: 25 MIN. + CHILLING
BAKE: 10 MIN./BATCH + COOLING
YIELD: 2-1/2 DOZEN

With a lemony filling, these spiced cookies go over big because they have old-fashioned, comfort-food appeal.

Carol Walston ★ Granbury, Texas

3/4   cup shortening
1   cup packed light brown sugar
1   egg
1/4   cup molasses
2-1/4   cups all-purpose flour
3   teaspoons ground ginger
2   teaspoons baking soda
1   teaspoon ground cinnamon
1/2   teaspoon salt
1/4   cup sugar

FILLING:

1   package (3 ounces) cream cheese, softened
1/3   cup butter, softened
2   teaspoons lemon extract
2   cups confectioners' sugar
1   teaspoon vanilla extract

In a large bowl, cream the shortening and brown sugar until light and fluffy. Beat in egg and molasses. Combine the flour, ginger, baking soda, cinnamon and salt; gradually add to the creamed mixture and mix well. Cover and refrigerate overnight.

Shape into 1-in. balls; roll in sugar. Place 2 in. apart on ungreased baking sheets. Flatten with a fork, forming a crisscross pattern. Bake at 375° for 8-10 minutes or until set (do not overbake). Remove to wire racks to cool.

In a small bowl, combine the filling ingredients until smooth. Spread over the bottoms of half of the cookies; top with remaining cookies. Store in the refrigerator.

Pistachio Chip Cookies

PREP: 15 MIN. + CHILLING   **BAKE:** 10 MIN./BATCH
YIELD: ABOUT 6 DOZEN

Of all the cookies I prepare at Christmas, these are the most popular. My husband and sons gobble them up so fast, I make at least three batches!

Lynne Ogg ★ Cedar, Minnesota

1	cup butter, softened
1	package (8 ounces) cream cheese, softened
1	cup sugar
1	egg
1	teaspoon vanilla extract
2-1/4	cups all-purpose flour
1	package (3.4 ounces) instant pistachio pudding mix
1	teaspoon baking powder
1	cup dark chocolate chips

In a large bowl, cream the butter, cream cheese and sugar until light and fluffy. Beat in egg and vanilla. Combine the flour, pudding mix and baking powder; gradually add to creamed mixture and mix well. Stir in chocolate chips. Refrigerate for 1 hour or until easy to handle.

Roll dough into 1-in. balls. Place 2 in. apart on greased baking sheets; flatten slightly with the bottom of a glass.

Bake at 350° for 10-12 minutes or until bottoms are lightly browned. Remove to wire racks to cool.

Brazil Nut Meringues

PREP: 20 MIN.   **BAKE:** 30 MIN./BATCH + COOLING
YIELD: 3-1/2 DOZEN

These crisp meringues simply melt in your mouth. No one would guess that a mere four ingredients could create such a fantastic treat!

Margaret Reinhardt ★ Muskego, Wisconsin

1-1/2	cups Brazil nuts
2	egg whites
1/8	teaspoon cream of tartar
1/2	cup sugar

Using the slicing blade of a food processor, slice Brazil nuts; set aside.

In a small bowl, beat egg whites and cream of tartar on medium speed until soft peaks form. Gradually add sugar, 1 tablespoon at a time, beating on high until stiff glossy peaks form and sugar is dissolved, about 6 minutes. Gently fold in nuts.

Drop by teaspoonfuls 2 in. apart onto parchment paper-lined baking sheets. Bake at 275° for 30-35 minutes or until firm to the touch. Cool completely on pans on wire racks. Store in an airtight container.

Rich Peanut Clusters

PREP: 20 MIN. + CHILLING **YIELD:** ABOUT 15 DOZEN

It's cheaper to make these bite-size morsels than it is to buy them in the store. Best of all, family and friends agree they taste better!

Janice Garvert ★ Plainville, Kansas

- 2 packages (12 ounces *each*) semisweet chocolate chips
- 2 packages (10 to 12 ounces *each*) vanilla *or* white chips
- 1 tablespoon shortening
- 1 teaspoon vanilla extract
- 1/2 teaspoon butter, softened
- 2 cans (12 ounces *each*) salted peanuts

In a microwave, melt the chips and shortening; stir until smooth. Stir in vanilla and butter. Add peanuts; mix well.

Drop by teaspoonfuls onto waxed paper-lined pans. Refrigerate until set. Store in an airtight container.

Honey Cream Taffy

PREP: 1-3/4 HOURS + COOLING **YIELD:** ABOUT 5 DOZEN

An old-fashioned favorite, this golden taffy gets my whole family pulling together in a special way! We wrap the melt-in-your-mouth confections in twists of waxed paper and give them out to our holiday visitors.

Iliene Taylor ★ Kearns, Utah

- 1 tablespoon butter, softened
- 1 cup heavy whipping cream
- 2 cups honey
- 1 cup sugar

Grease a 15-in. x 10-in. x 1-in. pan with butter; place in the refrigerator. In a large deep heavy saucepan, combine cream and honey. Add sugar; cook over medium heat and stir with a wooden spoon until sugar is melted and mixture comes to a boil.

Cover pan with a tight-fitting lid and boil for 1 minute. Uncover; cook, without stirring, until a candy thermometer reads 290° (soft-crack stage). Remove from the heat and pour into prepared pan (do not scrape sides of saucepan). Cool for 5 minutes. Using a wooden spoon, bring edges of honey mixture into center of pan. Cool 5-10 minutes longer or until cool enough to handle.

Using buttered hands, pull and stretch taffy until ridges form. (Taffy will lose its gloss and become light tan in color.) Pull into ropes about 1/2 in. thick. With a buttered kitchen scissors, cut into 1-in. pieces. Wrap individually in plastic wrap or waxed paper.

Editor's Note: We recommend that you test your candy thermometer before each use by bringing water to a boil; the thermometer should read 212°. Adjust your recipe temperature up or down based on your test.

Cran-Orange Cookies

PREP: 30 MIN. **BAKE:** 15 MIN./BATCH + COOLING
YIELD: 6 DOZEN

A sweet orange frosting pairs well with the tart cranberry flavor in these soft, cake-like cookies.

Crystal Jo Bruns ★ Iliff, Colorado

- 1 cup butter, softened
- 1 cup sugar
- 1/2 cup packed brown sugar
- 1 egg
- 2 tablespoons orange juice
- 1 teaspoon grated orange peel
- 2-1/2 cups all-purpose flour
- 1/2 teaspoon salt
- 1/2 teaspoon baking soda
- 2 cups chopped fresh *or* frozen cranberries
- 1/2 cup chopped walnuts

ICING:
- 1-1/2 cups confectioners' sugar
- 2 tablespoons orange juice
- 1/2 teaspoon grated orange peel

In a large bowl, cream butter and sugars until light and fluffy. Beat in the egg, orange juice and peel. Combine the flour, salt and baking soda; gradually add to creamed mixture and mix well. Stir in cranberries and walnuts.

Drop by tablespoonfuls 2 in. apart onto greased baking sheets. Bake at 375° for 12-14 minutes or until edges are lightly browned. Remove to wire racks to cool.

Combine icing ingredients; spread over cooled cookies.

Pecan Pie Cookies

PREP: 45 MIN. **BAKE:** 10 MIN./BATCH + COOLING
YIELD: 3 DOZEN

My family loves pecans. In fact, we have pecan pie at Thanksgiving and these pecan cookies at Christmas.

Julie McQuiston ★ Bradenton, Florida

- 3/4 cup shortening
- 1 cup packed brown sugar
- 1 egg
- 1 teaspoon vanilla extract
- 2 cups all-purpose flour
- 1 teaspoon baking powder
- 1/2 teaspoon salt

FILLING:
- 1 cup finely chopped pecans
- 1/2 cup packed brown sugar
- 1/4 cup heavy whipping cream
- 1 teaspoon vanilla extract

In a large bowl, cream shortening and brown sugar until light and fluffy. Beat in egg and vanilla. Combine the flour, baking powder and salt; gradually add to creamed mixture and mix well.

Shape into 1-in. balls. Place 2 in. apart on ungreased baking sheets. Using the end of a wooden spoon handle, make a 1/2-in.-deep indentation in the center of each ball. Combine filling ingredients; spoon into cookies.

Bake at 350° for 9-11 minutes or until lightly browned. Cool for 1 minute before removing from pans to wire racks.

Chocolate Almond Wafers

PREP: 20 MIN. + CHILLING
BAKE: 10 MIN./BATCH
YIELD: ABOUT 4-1/2 DOZEN

When my children were younger, we would make dozens of different cookies and candies. These mouth-watering wafers were always a favorite.

Phyl Broich-Wessling ★ Garner, Iowa

- 3/4 cup butter, softened
- 3/4 cup sugar
- 1 egg
- 1 teaspoon vanilla extract
- 1-1/4 cups all-purpose flour
- 2/3 cup baking cocoa
- 1 teaspoon baking powder
- 3/4 cup sliced almonds
- 2/3 cup ground almonds

In a large bowl, cream the butter and sugar until light and fluffy. Beat in egg and vanilla. Combine the flour, cocoa and baking powder; gradually add to creamed mixture and mix well. Stir in sliced almonds.

Shape dough into a 14-in. log. Roll in ground almonds. Wrap in plastic wrap. Refrigerate for 2 hours or until firm.

Unwrap and cut into 1/4-in. slices. Place 1 in. apart on ungreased baking sheets. Bake at 375° for 9-11 minutes or until set. Remove to wire racks to cool.

Coating Cookie Edges

To coat Chocolate Almond Wafers in ground almonds, spread the ground almonds lengthwise down a piece of waxed paper. Place the cookie log on top of the almonds; roll gently, pressing the almonds onto the dough.

Toffee Meringue Drops

PREP: 25 MIN.　**BAKE:** 25 MIN. + COOLING
YIELD: 3 DOZEN

The original recipe called for mini chocolate chips and crushed peppermint candy. I didn't have those ingredients on hand so I substituted toffee bits. Everyone loved the tasty results!

Bette Richards ★ Caledonia, Ontario

- 2　egg whites
- 1/8　teaspoon cream of tartar
- 1/2　cup sugar
- 1/2　cup milk chocolate English toffee bits
- 1/2　cup finely chopped pecans

In a large bowl, beat egg whites and cream of tartar on medium speed until soft peaks form. Gradually add sugar, 1 tablespoon at a time, beating on high until stiff glossy peaks form and sugar is dissolved, about 6 minutes. Fold in toffee bits and pecans.

Drop by tablespoonfuls 2 in. apart onto parchment paper-lined baking sheets. Bake at 250° for 25-30 minutes or until set and dry. Turn oven off; leave the cookies in oven for 1 hour.

Cool completely on pans on wire racks. Store in an airtight container.

Chocolate Mexican Wedding Cakes

PREP: 20 MIN.　**BAKE:** 10 MIN./BATCH + COOLING
YIELD: ABOUT 4 DOZEN

Bits of unsweetened chocolate add a delicious twist to typical Mexican Wedding Cakes. It wouldn't be Christmas without these delectable morsels!

bethany ★ Taste of Home Online Community

- 3/4　cup butter, softened
- 3/4　cup packed brown sugar
- 3　squares (1 ounce *each*) unsweetened chocolate, melted
- 1　teaspoon vanilla extract
- 2　cups all-purpose flour
- 1/2　teaspoon salt
- 1　cup finely chopped pecans
- 1/2　cup confectioners' sugar

In a large bowl, cream butter and brown sugar until light and fluffy. Beat in chocolate and vanilla. Combine the flour and salt; gradually add to the creamed mixture and mix well. Stir in the pecans.

Shape into 1-in. balls. Place 2 in. apart on ungreased baking sheets. Bake at 350° for 8-12 minutes or until set.

Roll warm cookies in confectioners' sugar; cool on wire racks. When completely cool, roll again in sugar.

Hint-of-Berry Bonbons

PREP: 1-1/2 HOURS + CHILLING
YIELD: ABOUT 4-1/2 DOZEN

You'll have a hard time eating just one of these heavenly sweets. Inside the rich milk chocolate coating is a fudgy center with a hint of strawberry. Their white chocolate drizzle makes these bonbons even more special.

Brenda Hoffman ★ Stanton, Michigan

1	package (8 ounces) cream cheese, softened
1	cup milk chocolate chips, melted and cooled
3/4	cup crushed vanilla wafers (about 25 wafers)
1/4	cup strawberry preserves
15	ounces milk chocolate candy coating, chopped
2	squares (1 ounce *each*) white baking chocolate

In a large bowl, beat cream cheese until fluffy. Beat in the melted chocolate chips. Stir in wafer crumbs and preserves. Cover and refrigerate for 2 hours or until easy to handle.

Divide mixture in half. Return one portion to the refrigerator. Shape remaining mixture into 1-in. balls. Place on a waxed paper-lined pan; refrigerate. Repeat with the remaining mixture.

In a microwave, melt milk chocolate candy coating at 70% power for 1 minute; stir. Microwave at additional 20-second intervals, stirring until smooth. Dip balls in coating; allow excess to drip off. Place on waxed paper-lined baking sheets. Refrigerate until set.

In a microwave, melt white chocolate at 70% power for 1 minute; stir. Microwave at additional 10- to 20-second intervals, stirring until smooth. Transfer to a heavy-duty resealable plastic bag; cut a small hole in a corner of bag. Decorate candies with white chocolate. Store in an airtight container in the refrigerator.

Cinnamon Lollipops

PREP: 15 MIN. **COOK:** 25 MIN. + STANDING
YIELD: 1 DOZEN

Fans of cinnamon will fall head over heels for these festive lollipops. Make them throughout the year using different cookie cutter shapes or heat-resistent lollipop molds.

Sheryl Salisbury ★ Weatherford, Oklahoma

1	cup sugar
1/2	cup light corn syrup

Dash salt

1/2	teaspoon cinnamon oil
3	to 4 drops red food coloring
12	lollipop sticks

Butter 12 assorted 3-in. metal cookie cutters. Place on a parchment paper-lined baking sheet; set aside.

In a large heavy saucepan, combine the sugar, corn syrup and salt. Cook and stir over medium heat until sugar is dissolved. Bring to a boil; cook, without stirring, until a candy thermometer reads 300° (hard-crack stage).

Remove from the heat; stir in oil and food coloring (keep face away from mixture as odor is very strong). Immediately pour sugar mixture into prepared cutters.

Remove cutters just before lollipops are set; firmly press a lollipop stick into each. Cool completely. Store in an airtight container.

Editor's Note: We recommend that you test your candy thermometer before each use by bringing water to a boil; the thermometer should read 212°. Adjust your recipe temperature up or down based on your test.

Chocolate-Hazelnut Crinkle Cookies

PREP: 30 MIN. + CHILLING **BAKE:** 10 MIN./BATCH
YIELD: ABOUT 7-1/2 DOZEN

Santa won't leave a crumb on the plate when you set out these confections. The hazelnut flavor shines through.

Mary Ann Dell ★ Phoenixville, Pennsylvania

2/3	cup hazelnuts
2	tablespoons sugar
1/2	cup butter, softened
1-1/2	cups packed brown sugar
2	eggs
6	squares (1 ounce *each*) bittersweet chocolate, melted
1/4	cup milk
1	teaspoon vanilla extract
2-3/4	cups all-purpose flour
2	tablespoons baking cocoa
2	teaspoons baking powder
3/4	teaspoon salt
1	cup confectioners' sugar

In a food processor, process hazelnuts and sugar until ground; set aside.

In a large bowl, cream butter and brown sugar until light and fluffy. Beat in the eggs, chocolate, milk and vanilla. Combine the flour, cocoa, baking powder and salt; gradually add to creamed mixture and mix well. Stir in the reserved hazelnut mixture. Refrigerate for 2 hours or until firm.

Shape into 1-in. balls. Roll in confectioners' sugar. Place 2 in. apart on greased baking sheets.

Bake at 350° for 10-12 minutes or until surface cracks. Remove to wire racks to cool. Store in an airtight container.

Wreath Cookies

PREP: 30 MIN.   **BAKE:** 10 MIN./BATCH + COOLING
YIELD: 4 DOZEN

Our home economists enhance crisp sugar cookies with white chocolate, coconut and red-hots. The wreath shape is so fun and festive.

1	cup butter, softened
1-1/2	cups sugar
6	squares (1 ounce *each*) white baking chocolate, melted
2	eggs
2	teaspoons vanilla extract
4	cups all-purpose flour
1/2	teaspoon salt
2-1/2	cups confectioners' sugar
1/4	cup plus 2 teaspoons water, *divided*
3	cups flaked coconut
6	to 8 drops green food coloring
1/4	cup red-hot candies

In a large bowl, cream butter and sugar until light and fluffy. Beat in the chocolate, eggs and vanilla. Combine the flour and salt; gradually add to the creamed mixture and mix well.

On a lightly floured surface, roll out dough to 1/4-in. thickness. Cut with a floured 3-in. scalloped cookie cutter. Place 1 in. apart on ungreased baking sheets; cut out centers using a floured 1-in. scalloped cookie cutter.

Bake at 350° for 10-14 minutes. Remove to wire racks to cool completely.

For glaze, in a small bowl, combine confectioners' sugar and 1/4 cup water. Place coconut in a resealable plastic bag; add food coloring and remaining water. Seal bag and toss until coconut is tinted. Spread cookies with glaze; sprinkle with coconut. Decorate with red-hots.

Fabulous DESSERTS

Pumpkin Fruitcake

(pictured on page 141)

PREP: 25 MIN.   **BAKE:** 50 MIN. + COOLING
YIELD: 12 SERVINGS

I make this dessert many times during the Thanksgiving and Christmas seasons. The moist cake has wonderful pumpkin flavor and is flecked with pecans, dates, raisins and cherries.

Janet Hradsky ★ Three Rivers, Michigan

3/4	cup butter, softened
1-1/2	cups sugar
3	eggs
1	cup canned pumpkin
2	cups all-purpose flour
2	teaspoons baking powder
1-1/2	teaspoons pumpkin pie spice
1/2	teaspoon salt
1/4	teaspoon baking soda
2/3	cup milk
1/2	cup chopped pecans
1/2	cup chopped dates
1/2	cup raisins
10	red candied cherries, chopped

GLAZE:

1-1/2	cups confectioners' sugar
1/4	teaspoon vanilla extract
2	to 3 tablespoons milk

Fresh raspberries, optional

In a large bowl, cream butter and sugar. Add eggs; mix well. Stir in the pumpkin. Combine the flour, baking powder, pumpkin pie spice, salt and baking soda; add to creamed mixture alternately with milk. Fold in the pecans, dates, raisins and cherries.

Spoon into a greased and floured 10-in. fluted tube pan. Bake at 350° for 50-60 minutes or until a toothpick inserted near the center comes out clean. Cool for 10 minutes before removing from pan to a wire rack to cool completely.

For glaze, combine the confectioners' sugar, vanilla and enough milk to achieve desired consistency. Drizzle over the cake. Garnish with fresh berries if desired.

Napkin Ring Party Favor

Ornaments can serve triple duty at Christmas. Not only do they adorn your tree, they can also be used as festive napkin rings and party favors (as shown here)! Thread a small Christmas ornament onto a length of double-sided satin ribbon, then tie the ribbon around a napkin. At the end of dinner, remind each guest to take the trinket home and place it on their tree as a merry memento.

Brownie-Peppermint Ice Cream Pie

PREP: 30 MIN. **BAKE:** 35 MIN. + FREEZING
YIELD: 8 SERVINGS

A rich, chocolaty brownie crust is a perfect partner to refreshing peppermint ice cream. Guests have come to expect this make-ahead dessert at my holiday meals.

Carol Gillespie ★ Chambersburg, Pennsylvania

1	package fudge brownie mix (8-inch square pan size)
1/2	cup vanilla *or* white chips
1/2	cup 60% cacao bittersweet chocolate baking chips
1/3	cup caramel ice cream topping
1	pint peppermint ice cream, softened
1	cup heavy whipping cream
1/4	cup confectioners' sugar
1/8	teaspoon peppermint extract
1/4	cup crushed peppermint candies

Prepare brownie batter according to package directions; stir in vanilla and bittersweet chips. Spread onto the bottom and up the sides of a greased 9-in. pie plate.

Bake at 350° for 35-40 minutes or until a toothpick inserted near the center comes out clean. Cool for 5 minutes. Gently press down center of crust if necessary. Cool completely on a wire rack.

Drizzle caramel topping over crust; spread evenly with ice cream. Cover and freeze for 4 hours or until firm.

Remove from the freezer 10 minutes before serving. Meanwhile, in a small bowl, beat cream, confectioners' sugar and extract until stiff peaks form. Spread over ice cream; sprinkle with crushed peppermints.

Berry Ice Cream Charlotte

PREP: 45 MIN. **BAKE:** 10 MIN. + FREEZING
YIELD: 14 SERVINGS

Cake slices, strawberry ice cream and ganache make this a special dessert. It takes some time to prepare, but it can be stored in the freezer for up to a week.

Suzette Jury ★ Keene, California

- 4 eggs, *separated*
- 1/2 cup sugar, *divided*
- 2 tablespoons canola oil
- 1 teaspoon vanilla extract
- 2/3 cup cake flour
- 1 teaspoon baking powder
- 1/4 teaspoon salt

Confectioners' sugar

- 1 cup seedless strawberry jam
- 18 squares (1 ounce *each*) semisweet chocolate, chopped
- 1 cup heavy whipping cream
- 6 cups strawberry ice cream, softened

Whipped cream and fresh strawberries

Place the egg whites in a small bowl; let stand at room temperature for 30 minutes. Line a greased 15-in. x 10-in. x 1-in. baking pan with waxed paper. Grease paper; set aside.

In a small bowl, beat the egg yolks on high speed for 5 minutes or until thick and lemon-colored. Gradually beat in 1/4 cup sugar. Beat in oil and vanilla. Sift the flour, baking powder and salt together; gradually add to the yolk mixture and mix well.

Beat egg whites on medium speed until soft peaks form. Gradually beat in remaining sugar, 1 tablespoon at a time, on high until stiff peaks form. Gradually fold into batter. Spread evenly into prepared pan.

Bake at 350° for 8-12 minutes or until cake springs back when lightly touched. Cool for 5 minutes. Invert onto a kitchen towel dusted with confectioners' sugar. Gently peel off waxed paper. Roll up cake in the towel jelly-roll style, starting with a short side. Cool completely on a wire rack.

Line a 4-qt. bowl with plastic wrap. Unroll cake; spread jam evenly over cake to within 1/2 in. of edges. Roll up again. Cut into 1/2-in. slices; place in the prepared bowl, completely covering the bottom and sides. Cover and freeze until cake is firm.

For ganache, place the chocolate in a bowl. In a small saucepan, bring the cream just to a boil. Pour over the chocolate; whisk until smooth. Cool to room temperature, stirring occasionally.

Spread 1 cup of ice cream into cake-lined bowl; top with 1/2 cup ganache. Repeat layers four times. Top with the remaining ice cream. Cover and freeze until firm.

Just before serving, remove from the freezer and invert onto a serving plate. Remove bowl and plastic wrap. Let stand for 15 minutes before cutting into wedges. Garnish with whipped cream and strawberries.

Brandy Snap Cannoli

PREP: 1-1/2 HOURS **BAKE:** 5 MIN./BATCH + COOLING
YIELD: ABOUT 2 DOZEN

For this recipe, our home economists combined two classic recipes...brandy snaps and cannoli. You can assemble and refrigerate them up to an hour before serving.

- 1/2 cup butter, cubed
- 1/2 cup sugar
- 3 tablespoons molasses
- 1 teaspoon ground ginger
- 1/4 teaspoon salt
- 1 cup all-purpose flour
- 2 tablespoons brandy

FILLING:

- 1-1/2 cups ricotta cheese
- 3 tablespoons grated orange peel
- 3 tablespoons sugar, *divided*
- 1-1/2 cups miniature semisweet chocolate chips, *divided*
- 1-1/2 cups heavy whipping cream

In a small saucepan, combine the first five ingredients. Cook and stir over medium heat until butter is melted. Remove from the heat. Stir in flour and brandy; keep warm.

Drop tablespoonfuls of batter onto a parchment paper-lined or well-greased baking sheet; spread each into a 4-in. circle. Bake at 350° for 5-6 minutes or until the edges begin to brown. Cool for about 1 minute or just until cookie starts to firm.

Working quickly, loosen each cookie and curl around a metal cannoli tube to shape. Remove cookies from tubes; cool on wire racks.

For filling, in a large bowl, combine the ricotta, orange peel and 1 tablespoon sugar; stir in 1/2 cup chocolate chips. In a small bowl, beat cream on medium speed until soft peaks form. Gradually add remaining sugar, beating on high until stiff peaks form. Fold into the ricotta mixture. Chill until serving.

Just before serving, pipe filling into cannoli shells. Dip ends in remaining chocolate chips.

About Ganache

Ganache is a rich, silky mixture made with heavy whipping cream and chocolate and sometimes flavored with extracts or liqueurs. It is used for frostings and fillings.

Chocolate Mallow Cake

PREP: 1 HOUR **BAKE:** 30 MIN. + CHILLING
YIELD: 15 SERVINGS

Nothing compares to homemade cake, especially when gathering with friends and family for a special occasion. Everyone will love the marshmallow frosting.

Edna Hoffman ★ Hebron, Indiana

- 1/3   cup shortening
- 1   cup sugar
- 1/2   cup packed brown sugar
- 2   eggs
- 2   squares (1 ounce *each*) unsweetened chocolate, melted and cooled
- 1   teaspoon vanilla extract
- 1   cup buttermilk
- 1/4   cup water
- 1-3/4   cups cake flour
- 1-1/2   teaspoons baking soda
- 3/4   teaspoon salt

FILLING:
- 1   cup packed brown sugar
- 3   tablespoons all-purpose flour
- 1   cup milk
- 2   egg yolks, beaten
- 2   tablespoons butter
- 1   teaspoon vanilla extract
- 1/2   cup chopped pecans

FROSTING:
- 1-1/2   cups sugar
- 2   egg whites
- 1/3   cup water
- 1   tablespoon light corn syrup
- 1/4   teaspoon cream of tartar
- 2   cups miniature marshmallows
- 1   square (1 ounce) unsweetened chocolate, melted

In a large bowl, cream shortening and sugars. Add eggs, one at a time, beating well after each. Beat in the chocolate and vanilla. Combine buttermilk and water. Combine the cake flour, baking soda and salt; add to the creamed mixture alternately with buttermilk mixture.

Pour into a greased and floured 13-in. x 9-in. baking pan. Bake at 350° for 30-35 minutes or until a toothpick inserted near the center comes out clean. Cool for 10 minutes before removing from pan to a wire rack.

For filling, in a small saucepan, combine brown sugar and all-purpose flour. Stir in milk until smooth. Cook and stir over medium-high heat until thickened and bubbly. Reduce heat; cook and stir 2 minutes longer. Remove from the heat. Stir a small amount of hot filling into egg yolks; return all to pan, stirring constantly. Bring to a gentle boil; cook and stir 2 minutes longer. Remove from the heat. Gently stir in butter and vanilla. Cool to room temperature without stirring.

Spread filling over the cake to within 1/2 in. of edges; sprinkle with the pecans. Refrigerate for 30 minutes or until set.

For frosting, in a heavy saucepan over low heat, combine the sugar, egg whites, water, corn syrup and cream of tartar. With a portable mixer, beat on low speed for 1 minute. Continue beating on low over low heat for 8-10 minutes or until frosting reaches 160°.

Pour into the large bowl of a heavy-duty stand mixer; add marshmallows. Beat on high for 7-9 minutes or until stiff peaks form. Carefully spread over cake. Pipe thin lines of melted chocolate over cake; gently pull a toothpick or sharp knife through lines in alternating directions. Store in the refrigerator.

Editor's Note: The unfilled and unfrosted cake can be frozen for up to 2 months. Thaw at room temperature, then fill and frost as directed.

Drizzle and Drag Design

This design adds a little glamour to any cake...and it's easy to do! First, spread the frosting over the cake, making it smooth and even. Place melted chocolate in a resealable plastic bag; cut a small hole in one corner of the bag. Pipe lines of melted chocolate lengthwise over cake at 1-in. intervals. Gently drag a bamboo skewer or toothpick widthwise across the frosting from right to left. About an inch down from this first mark, drag the toothpick across the frosting from left to right. Repeat, alternating directions, until the entire cake top has been decorated.

Cool Cranberry Pie

PREP: 20 MIN. + CHILLING   **YIELD:** 8 SERVINGS

This cool and creamy pie has real holiday appeal. Many folks prefer it to traditional cranberry pie.

Mary Relyea ★ Canastota, New York

- 1 package (3 ounces) raspberry gelatin
- 1/3 cup plus 1/4 cup sugar, *divided*
- 1 cup cranberry juice
- 1 package (3 ounces) cream cheese, softened
- 1 tablespoon milk
- 1 teaspoon vanilla extract
- 1 carton (12 ounces) frozen whipped topping, thawed
- 1 can (16 ounces) jellied cranberry sauce
- 1 extra-servings-size graham cracker crust (10 inches)

In a small bowl, combine gelatin and 1/3 cup sugar. In a small saucepan, bring cranberry juice to a boil. Add to the gelatin mixture; stir until dissolved. Cover and refrigerate until slightly thickened, about 1 hour.

In a small bowl, combine the cream cheese, milk, vanilla and remaining sugar until smooth. Whisk thickened gelatin mixture for 2-3 minutes or until smooth. Add to the cream cheese; beat until smooth. Remove 1/2 cup of the whipped topping for garnish; cover and refrigerate. Fold remaining topping into cream cheese mixture.

Place the cranberry sauce in a small bowl; mash with a fork until spreadable. Spread over bottom of crust. Spoon the cream cheese mixture over top. Cover and refrigerate for at least 3 hours or until firm. Garnish with the reserved whipped topping.

Cool for 5 minutes. Turn the cake onto a kitchen towel dusted with confectioners' sugar. Gently peel off waxed paper. Roll up cake in the towel jelly-roll style, starting with a short side. Cool completely on a wire rack.

Unroll cake and spread ice cream over cake to within 1/2 in. of edges. Roll up again. Cover and freeze until firm.

Cut into slices; drizzle with the hot fudge topping. If desired, garnish with the crushed candies and dust with confectioners' sugar.

White Chocolate Coconut Cake

PREP: 25 MIN. + CHILLING **BAKE:** 25 MIN. + COOLING
YIELD: 12 SLICES

This eye-catching cake is my very own creation. The white "snowball" look makes the cake a perfect choice for a Christmas celebration.

Greta Kirby ★ Carthage, Tennessee

- 1   package (18-1/4 ounces) white cake mix
- 1   cup water
- 1   can (15 ounces) cream of coconut, *divided*
- 3   egg whites
- 1   can (5 ounces) evaporated milk
- 2/3 cup vanilla *or* white chips
- 2   ounces cream cheese, softened
- 1   cup heavy whipping cream, *divided*
- 3-1/2 cups flaked coconut, *divided*
- 2   teaspoons vanilla extract
- 1/4 cup sugar

In a large bowl, combine cake mix, water, 3/4 cup cream of coconut and egg whites; beat on low speed for 30 seconds. Beat on medium for 2 minutes.

Pour into three greased and floured 9-in. round baking pans. Bake at 350° for 22-26 minutes or until a toothpick inserted near the center comes out clean. Cool for 10 minutes before removing from the pans to wire racks to cool completely.

For filling, in a small saucepan, combine the evaporated milk, chips, cream cheese, 3 tablespoons heavy cream and remaining cream of coconut; cook and stir over low heat until chips are melted.

Remove from the heat; stir in 1-1/2 cups coconut and 1 teaspoon vanilla. Transfer to a large bowl; cover and refrigerate until mixture reaches spreading consistency, stirring occasionally.

For frosting, in a large bowl, beat remaining cream until it begins to thicken. Add sugar and remaining vanilla; beat until stiff peaks form.

Place bottom cake layer on a serving plate; spread with half of the filling. Repeat layers. Top with remaining cake layer. Frost top and sides of cake; sprinkle with remaining coconut. Refrigerate leftovers.

Peppermint Angel Roll

PREP: 30 MIN. **BAKE:** 15 MIN. + FREEZING
YIELD: 10 SERVINGS

This is a very festive dessert for Christmas. The angel food cake makes it less heavy than many traditional holiday recipes. I love it because it's so simple and convenient during a hectic season!

Holly Dicke ★ Plain City, Ohio

- 1   package (16 ounces) angel food cake mix
- 1   tablespoon confectioners' sugar
- 1/2 gallon peppermint ice cream, softened
- 1   jar (11-3/4 ounces) hot fudge ice cream topping, warmed

Crushed peppermint candies and additional confectioners' sugar, optional

Prepare cake batter according to package directions. Line a greased 15-in. x 10-in. x 1-in. baking pan with waxed paper and grease the paper. Spread batter evenly into pan. Bake at 350° for 15-20 minutes or until cake springs back when lightly touched.

Walnut Mincemeat Pie

PREP: 15 MIN. **BAKE:** 50 MIN. **YIELD:** 6-8 SERVINGS

Here's a tasty twist on the more traditional mincemeat pie.
This one's sweeter, creamier, easier to make and so yummy!

Mary Reagan ★ Warsaw, New York

Pastry for single-crust pie (9 inches)
- 1 cup sugar
- 2 tablespoons all-purpose flour
- 1/8 teaspoon salt
- 3 eggs, lightly beaten
- 1/4 cup butter, melted
- 1 cup prepared mincemeat
- 1/2 cup chopped walnuts

Line a 9-in. pie plate with pastry; flute edges. Line pastry shell with a double thickness of heavy-duty foil. Bake at 450° for 5 minutes. Remove foil; bake 5 minutes longer. Cool on a wire rack. Reduce heat to 350°.

In a bowl, combine the sugar, flour and salt. Stir in the eggs, butter, mincemeat and walnuts until blended. Pour into crust. Bake for 40-45 minutes or until a knife inserted near center comes out clean (cover edges loosely with foil if necessary to prevent overbrowning). Cool on a wire rack.

Cherry Pear Pie

PREP: 30 MIN.   **BAKE:** 50 MIN. + COOLING
YIELD: 8 SERVINGS

Two of my family's favorite fruits appear in this splendid pie with a nutty streusel topping. I like to serve slices with cherry-vanilla frozen yogurt.

Trisha Kruse ★ Eagle, Idaho

Pastry for single-crust pie (9 inches)
- 6 cups sliced peeled fresh pears
- 1/2 cup dried cherries
- 4-1/2 teaspoons lemon juice
- 1/2 teaspoon almond extract
- 3/4 cup sugar
- 1/4 cup cornstarch

TOPPING:
- 3/4 cup all-purpose flour
- 1/3 cup sugar
- 1/3 cup cold butter
- 1/2 cup sliced almonds

Line a 9-in. pie plate with pastry; trim and flute edges.

In a large bowl, toss pears and cherries with lemon juice and extract. Combine sugar and cornstarch. Add to pear mixture; toss to coat. Spoon into crust. In a small bowl, combine flour and sugar; cut in butter until crumbly. Stir in almonds. Sprinkle over filling.

Bake at 375° for 50-60 minutes or until crust is golden brown and filling is bubbly. Cover edges with foil during the last 15 minutes to prevent overbrowning if necessary. Cool on a wire rack.

Orange Chocolate Torte

PREP: 35 MIN.   **BAKE:** 30 MIN. + COOLING
YIELD: 9 SERVINGS

This torte is doubly delicious with chocolate in both the batter and frosting. Orange marmalade adds a bit of tartness.

Nancy Mueller ★ Menomonee Falls, Wisconsin

- 1/4 cup butter, softened
- 1/2 cup plus 2 tablespoons sugar
- 2 eggs
- 1/2 teaspoon vanilla extract
- 2 tablespoons water
- 2 tablespoons orange liqueur
- 1/2 teaspoon grated orange peel
- 1/2 cup plus 2 tablespoons all-purpose flour
- 3 tablespoons baking cocoa
- 1/2 teaspoon baking soda
- 1/8 teaspoon salt
- 3/4 cup chocolate syrup

FILLING:
- 2 tablespoons orange liqueur
- 1/2 cup orange marmalade

FROSTING:
- 1/3 cup heavy whipping cream
- 1 tablespoon light corn syrup
- 1 cup (6 ounces) semisweet chocolate chips

Kumquats, optional

Line an 8-in. square baking dish with parchment paper; coat paper with cooking spray and set aside.

In a large bowl, cream butter and sugar until light and fluffy. Add eggs, one at a time, beating well after each addition. Stir in vanilla. In a small bowl, combine the water, orange liqueur and orange peel. Combine the flour, cocoa, baking soda and salt; add to creamed mixture alternately with water mixture.

Pour into prepared dish. Bake at 350° for 25-30 minutes or until a toothpick inserted near the center comes out clean. Cool for 10 minutes before removing from pan to a wire rack to cool completely.

Split cake in half horizontally; sprinkle cut sides with orange liqueur. Place bottom layer, cut side up, on a serving plate; spread with marmalade. Top with remaining layer, cut side down.

For frosting, in a heavy saucepan, combine cream and corn syrup. Bring to a boil, stirring constantly. Remove from the heat. Stir in chocolate chips until melted. Cool to room temperature; stir until smooth. Spread over top of cake. Garnish with kumquats if desired.

Eggnog Pie

PREP: 15 MIN. + CHILLING   **YIELD:** 8 SERVINGS

A dear friend always received rave reviews when she served this easy pie. So I knew I needed the recipe! It's great for busy people who still love to make homemade desserts.

Patty Adler ★ Wray, Colorado

2	cups eggnog
1	cup milk
1	package (4.6 ounces) cook-and-serve vanilla pudding mix
1	tablespoon rum *or* 1/2 teaspoon rum extract
1/8	teaspoon ground nutmeg
1	pastry shell (9 inches), baked

Whipped topping and additional ground nutmeg, optional

In a large saucepan, cook the eggnog, milk and pudding mix over medium heat until thickened and bubbly. Remove from the heat and cool slightly. Stir in rum and nutmeg. Pour pudding mixture into crust. Chill until set. Garnish with whipped topping and sprinkle with nutmeg if desired.

Editor's Note: This recipe was tested with commercially prepared eggnog.

Cranberry-Topped Cake

PREP: 30 MIN. + COOLING   **BAKE:** 1-1/4 HOURS + COOLING
YIELD: 10-12 SERVINGS

For me, part of the joy of Christmas is sharing tempting treats such as this special cake. I love trying new recipes, but I also rely on classics like this one.

Helen Vail ★ Glenside, Pennsylvania

1-1/3	cups sugar, *divided*
4	cups fresh *or* frozen cranberries, thawed

CAKE:

5	egg yolks
3/4	cup cold water
1/2	cup canola oil
2-1/2	teaspoons grated lemon peel
2-1/2	teaspoons vanilla extract
2	cups all-purpose flour
1-1/2	cups sugar
3	teaspoons baking powder
1	teaspoon salt
7	egg whites
1/2	teaspoon cream of tartar

FROSTING:

2	cups heavy whipping cream
2	tablespoons sugar
2	teaspoons vanilla extract

Grease bottoms of two 8-in. square baking dishes; sprinkle each with 1 tablespoon of the sugar. Sprinkle 2 cups of the cranberries in each pan; sprinkle with remaining sugar. Cover and bake at 325° for 30 minutes. Uncover; cool for 1 hour.

In a small bowl, beat the egg yolks, water, oil, lemon peel and vanilla until well blended. In a large bowl, combine the flour, sugar, baking powder and salt; gradually beat into egg mixture until blended.

In another large bowl, beat egg whites until foamy. Add cream of tartar; beat until stiff peaks form. Fold a fourth of the egg whites into batter. Fold in remaining whites. Spoon batter over cranberries.

Bake at 325° for 45-55 minutes or until cake springs back when lightly touched. Cool for 10 minutes before inverting on wire racks to cool completely.

For frosting, in a large bowl, beat cream until soft peaks form. Add the sugar and vanilla; beat until stiff peaks form. Place one cake on a serving plate; spread with some of the frosting. Top with remaining cake. Frost top and sides of cake. Cover and store in the refrigerator.

Chocolate-Raspberry Cream Puff Ring

PREP: 70 MIN. **BAKE:** 35 MIN. + COOLING
YIELD: 12 SERVINGS

This recipe began as a basic cream puff ring. I decided to make it more special by adding a hot fudge topping and raspberry sauce.

Mitzi Babb ★ Boulder, Colorado

1/2	cup fresh raspberries
2	tablespoons red currant jelly
2	tablespoons sugar
1/4	teaspoon cornstarch

Dash salt

PASTRY:

3/4	cup water
6	tablespoons butter, cubed
1/2	teaspoon salt
3/4	cup all-purpose flour
3	eggs

FILLING:

2	cups heavy whipping cream
1/2	cup confectioners' sugar
1	teaspoon vanilla extract
1/2	cup plus 3 tablespoons hot fudge ice cream topping, warmed, *divided*
1/2	cup miniature semisweet chocolate chips
1/2	cup chopped pecans

Mash raspberries, reserving juice; strain and discard seeds. In a heavy saucepan, combine jelly and reserved juice. Bring to a boil over medium heat. Combine the sugar, cornstarch and salt; stir into berry mixture until dissolved. Cook over medium heat until sauce is clear and begins to thicken. Transfer to a bowl; refrigerate until chilled.

Cover a baking sheet with foil; grease the foil. Trace a 6-in. circle onto foil; set aside. In a large saucepan, bring water, butter and salt to a boil. Add flour all at once and stir until a smooth ball forms. Remove from the heat; let stand for 5 minutes. Add eggs, one at a time, beating well after each addition. Continue beating until mixture is smooth and shiny.

Drop batter by rounded tablespoonfuls onto prepared pan, along the inside of the circle (mounds should be slightly touching). Bake at 400° for 35-40 minutes or until golden brown.

Lift foil and transfer to a wire rack. Immediately cut a slit in the side of each puff to allow steam to escape; cool. Carefully cut ring in half horizontally and set top aside; remove soft dough from inside with a fork. Place ring bottom on a serving plate.

For filling, in a large bowl, beat cream until it begins to thicken. Add confectioners' sugar and vanilla; beat until soft peaks form. Stir in 1/2 cup of the fudge topping until combined. Fold in chocolate chips and pecans.

Spread filling over bottom of cream puff ring; replace top. Drizzle with chilled raspberry sauce and the remaining fudge topping. Refrigerate until serving.

Cheesecake with Raspberry Sauce

PREP: 1 HOUR **BAKE:** 50 MIN. + CHILLING
YIELD: 16 SERVINGS

It is a family tradition to have this for our Christmas dinner. And when my daughter was away from home, I made this for her birthday—I shipped it with candles on dry ice.

Jeanette Volker ★ Walton, Nebraska

1-3/4   cups graham cracker crumbs
1/4   cup sugar
1/3   cup butter, melted

FILLING:
5   packages (8 ounces *each*) cream cheese, softened
1   cup sugar
1   cup (8 ounces) sour cream
1/2   cup heavy whipping cream
2   teaspoons vanilla extract
7   eggs, lightly beaten

SAUCE/TOPPING:
1   package (12 ounces) frozen unsweetened raspberries, thawed

1/2   cup sugar
2   cups heavy whipping cream
1/2   cup confectioners' sugar
1   teaspoon vanilla extract

In a small bowl, combine cracker crumbs and sugar; stir in butter. Press onto the bottom and 1 in. up the sides of a greased 10-in. springform pan. Place on a baking sheet. Bake at 350° for 5-8 minutes. Cool on a wire rack.

In a large bowl, beat cream cheese and sugar until smooth. Beat in the sour cream, heavy cream and vanilla. Add eggs; beat on low speed just until combined. Pour into crust. Place pan on a double thickness of heavy-duty foil (about 17 in. square); securely wrap foil around pan.

Place in a large baking pan; add 1 in. of hot water to larger pan. Bake at 350° for 50-60 minutes or until center is almost set. Remove pan from water bath. Cool on a wire rack for 10 minutes. Carefully run a knife around edge of pan to loosen. Cool 1 hour longer. Refrigerate overnight.

For sauce, place the raspberries and sugar in a food processor; cover and process until blended. For topping, in a small bowl, beat heavy cream until it begins to thicken. Add confectioners' sugar and vanilla; beat until soft peaks form. Serve cheesecake with raspberry sauce and topping.

Dissolve the coffee granules in hot water. Cool to room temperature; set aside.

Meanwhile, line the bottom and sides of a 9-in. springform pan with ladyfingers. Set aside 1/4 cup crushed candy for topping. Stir the coffee mixture and remaining crushed candy into ice cream. Spoon into prepared pan. Freeze for 30 minutes.

In a large bowl, beat cream until it begins to thicken. Add confectioners' sugar; beat until stiff peaks form. Fold in creme de cacao if desired. Spread over the ice cream. Sprinkle with reserved candy. Cover and freeze until firm. Remove from the freezer 30 minutes before serving. Remove sides of pan.

Peppermint Ribbon Cake

PREP: 20 MIN.   BAKE: 35 MIN. + COOLING
YIELD: 12 SERVINGS

With its pretty pink layer and fabulous mint flavor, this is a great holiday dessert. Because I work full-time, I like the fact that it calls for a convenient cake mix.

Lisa Varner ★ Greenville, South Carolina

    1   package (18-1/4 ounces) white cake mix
  1/2   teaspoon peppermint extract
  1/2   teaspoon red food coloring
  1/2   cup plus 2 tablespoons crushed peppermint candies, *divided*
    1   cup confectioners' sugar
    1   tablespoon milk

Prepare the cake batter according to package directions. Transfer 1 cup to a small bowl; stir in the extract, food coloring and 1/2 cup crushed candies.

Spoon 2 cups of remaining batter into a greased and floured 10-in. fluted tube pan. Carefully top with the peppermint batter; do not swirl. Top with the remaining plain batter.

Bake at 350° for 35-45 minutes or until a toothpick inserted near the center comes out clean. Cool for 10 minutes before removing from the pan to a wire rack to cool completely.

Combine confectioners' sugar and milk; drizzle over cake. Sprinkle with remaining crushed candies.

Frozen Tiramisu Dessert

PREP: 30 MIN. + FREEZING   YIELD: 12 SERVINGS

Our daughter-in-law loves tiramisu so I knew I had to try this recipe. Not only is it easy to prepare, it's absolutely delicious. Get ready to dole out seconds!

Joan Hallford ★ North Richland Hills, Texas

    1   tablespoon instant coffee granules
    1   tablespoon hot water
    2   packages (3 ounces *each*) ladyfingers, split
    5   Heath candy bars (1.4 ounces *each*), crushed and *divided*
    1   quart vanilla ice cream, softened
    1   cup heavy whipping cream
    3   tablespoons confectioners' sugar
    2   tablespoons creme de cacao, optional

Mini Chocolate Raspberry Cakes

PREP: 25 MIN. **BAKE:** 25 MIN. + COOLING
YIELD: 4 SERVINGS

Instead of making individual hot fudge sundaes for guests, prepare these cute little cakes! Raspberry and chocolate always pair well. I like to stir 1/2 cup raspberries directly into the sauce, but you can also use them as a garnish.

Pamela Shank ★ Parkersburg, West Virginia

2	eggs
1	cup sugar
1/2	cup water
1/2	cup canola oil

1/2	teaspoon raspberry extract
1/4	teaspoon vanilla extract
1	cup all-purpose flour
1/2	cup baking cocoa
1-1/2	teaspoons baking soda
1/4	teaspoon salt

RASPBERRY SAUCE:

1/4	cup sugar
1	tablespoon cornstarch
2	cups fresh raspberries
1/4	cup water

TOPPING:

1	cup vanilla ice cream
1	cup hot fudge ice cream topping, warmed

Chopped pecans and additional fresh raspberries, optional

In a bowl, beat the eggs, sugar, water, oil and extracts until well blended. In another bowl, combine the flour, cocoa, baking soda and salt. Gradually beat into sugar mixture until blended.

Pour into four 4-in. fluted tube pans or 6-oz. ramekins coated with cooking spray. Bake at 350° for 25-30 minutes or until a toothpick inserted near the center comes out clean. Cool for 5 minutes before removing from pans to a wire rack to cool completely.

For raspberry sauce, in a saucepan, combine sugar and cornstarch. Stir in raspberries and water; bring to a boil. Cook and stir for 1-2 minutes or until thickened. Remove from the heat; cool slightly. Press through a sieve; discard the seeds.

To serve, scoop ice cream into cake centers. Drizzle with ice cream topping and raspberry sauce; sprinkle with pecans and additional raspberries if desired.

Plate Painting

Add a touch of elegance to a dessert plate by painting the plate with two sauces.

We put the hot fudge ice cream topping and the strained raspberry sauce from Mini Chocolate-Raspberry Cakes into two clean plastic condiment squeeze bottles. Pipe three alternating 2-in. strips of each sauce onto a dessert plate. Drag a bamboo skewer through the sauces to create a curved trail. Continue with the design at about 1/2-in. intervals.

Cranberry-Apricot Bread Pudding

PREP: 25 MIN.   **BAKE:** 35 MIN.   **YIELD:** 8 SERVINGS

I adjusted a favorite bread pudding recipe to make it a little healthier. My version calls for 2 egg whites and only 1 whole egg. Dried fruits add texture and sweetness to a heartwarming dessert.

Lillian Julow ★ Gainesville, Florida

1	cup chopped dried apricots
1/2	cup unsweetened apple juice
1/4	cup dried cranberries
1-1/4	cups milk
2	egg whites
1	egg, lightly beaten
1/2	cup packed brown sugar
1	teaspoon ground cinnamon
1	teaspoon vanilla extract
1/2	teaspoon ground nutmeg
1/4	teaspoon ground cardamom
6	cups cubed day-old bread
8	tablespoons whipped topping
1/4	cup chopped walnuts, toasted

In a small saucepan, combine apricots and apple juice. Bring to a boil. Reduce heat; simmer, uncovered, for 5-8 minutes or until liquid is almost absorbed. Stir in the cranberries; set aside.

In a large bowl, combine the milk, egg whites, egg, brown sugar, cinnamon, vanilla, nutmeg and cardamom. Add bread cubes; toss to coat. Let stand for 15 minutes. Stir in apricot mixture.

Transfer to an 8-in. square baking dish coated with cooking spray. Bake, uncovered, at 350° for 35-40 minutes or until a knife inserted near the center comes out clean. Let stand for 5 minutes before serving. Top each serving with 1 tablespoon whipped topping and 1-1/2 teaspoons chopped walnuts.

In a large bowl, cream the butter and sugars. Add eggs, one at a time, mixing well after each addition. Combine the buttermilk and vanilla. Combine the flour, baking soda and salt; add to creamed mixture alternately with the buttermilk mixture, beating well after each addition. Beat in melted peanut butter chips.

Pour 2 cups batter into a small bowl; stir in the melted chocolate chips. Pour half of the plain batter into a greased and floured 10-in. fluted tube pan. Cover with chocolate batter. Top with remaining plain batter; swirl with a knife.

Bake at 350° for 60-65 minutes or until a toothpick inserted near the center comes out clean. Cool for 10 minutes before removing from pan to a wire rack to cool completely.

For glaze, in a small bowl, combine chips. In a small saucepan, bring cream to a boil. Remove from the heat and pour over chips. Let stand for 5 minutes; stir until smooth. Cool for 2 minutes; drizzle over cake.

Gingered Pear Crisp

PREP: 25 MIN. + STANDING **BAKE:** 50 MIN.
YIELD: 8 SERVINGS

Here's a delicious variation on a classic apple crisp. The spark provided by the ginger complements the delicate flavor of pears. It's awesome served a la mode.

Helen Conwell ★ Fairhope, Alabama

4	pounds pears, peeled and cut into 1/2-inch slices
1	tablespoon cornstarch
1/2	cup pear nectar
2	tablespoons sugar
1	tablespoon lemon juice

TOPPING:

1	cup all-purpose flour
2/3	cup packed brown sugar
2/3	cup blanched almonds, toasted and chopped
3	tablespoons crushed vanilla wafers
4	teaspoons candied *or* crystallized ginger, chopped
1	teaspoon ground cinnamon
1/4	teaspoon salt
1/2	cup cold butter
1	pint caramel and vanilla ice cream

Place pears in a large bowl; sprinkle with cornstarch and toss to coat. Combine the pear nectar, sugar and lemon juice; pour over pears and toss to coat. Let stand for 15 minutes. Transfer to a greased 11-in. x 7-in. baking dish.

For topping, in a large bowl, combine the flour, brown sugar, almonds, vanilla wafers, ginger, cinnamon and salt. Cut in butter until crumbly. Sprinkle over pear mixture.

Bake at 375° for 50-60 minutes or until fruit is bubbly and topping is golden brown. Serve warm with ice cream.

Marbled Pound Cake

PREP: 45 MIN. **BAKE:** 1 HOUR + COOLING
YIELD: 16 SERVINGS

This rich pound cake features the classic combination of chocolate and peanut butter. Buttermilk in the batter lends to its moist texture.

Kelly McDonald ★ Edinburg, Texas

1	cup butter, softened
1-1/4	cups sugar
1	cup packed brown sugar
5	eggs
1	cup buttermilk
2	teaspoons vanilla extract
3	cups cake flour
1	teaspoon baking soda
1/4	teaspoon salt
1-1/2	cups peanut butter chips, melted
1-1/4	cups semisweet chocolate chips, melted

GLAZE:

1	cup semisweet chocolate chips
1/3	cup peanut butter chips
1/2	cup heavy whipping cream

Cherry Chocolate Coconut Cupcakes

PREP: 35 MIN. + CHILLING **BAKE:** 20 MIN. + COOLING
YIELD: 2 DOZEN

Chocolate-covered coconut candy is tucked inside each of these morsels. The cream cheese frosting is complemented by chocolate-covered cherries.

Sandy Ploy ★ Whitefish Bay, Wisconsin

1	package (10 to 12 ounces) vanilla *or* white chips
1/2	cup butter, cubed
1	cup heavy whipping cream
1	teaspoon coconut extract
1	can (21 ounces) cherry pie filling
1	cup buttermilk
2	eggs
2	cups all-purpose flour
2	cups sugar
3/4	cup baking cocoa
2	teaspoons baking soda
1	teaspoon baking powder
1/2	teaspoon salt
6	packages (1.9 ounces *each*) chocolate-covered coconut candy bars
1/2	cup semisweet chocolate chips
1	teaspoon shortening
24	maraschino cherries, well drained
3-1/4	cups confectioners' sugar
2	tablespoons coarse sugar

For ganache, in a small saucepan, melt the vanilla chips and butter with the heavy cream over low heat; stir until blended. Transfer to a large bowl; stir in the extract. Cover and refrigerate for at least 4 hours, stirring occasionally.

In a large bowl, beat the pie filling, buttermilk and eggs until well blended. Combine the flour, sugar, cocoa, baking soda, baking powder and salt; gradually beat into pie filling mixture until blended.

Fill paper-lined muffin cups one-third full. Cut candy bars in half; place half of a candy bar in the center of each cupcake. Cover each with 2 tablespoonfuls batter. Bake at 375° for 16-20 minutes or until a toothpick comes out clean. Cool for 10 minutes before removing from pans to wire racks to cool completely.

Meanwhile, in a small microwave-safe bowl, melt the chocolate chips and shortening; stir until smooth. Dip the cherries in chocolate mixture; place on a waxed paper-lined baking sheet. Refrigerate until set.

Remove ganache from refrigerator; gradually beat in the confectioners' sugar until frosting is light and fluffy. Pipe over cupcakes; sprinkle with coarse sugar. Garnish with chocolate-dipped cherries.

Melting Chocolate in the Microwave

Place chocolate in a microwave-safe bowl. Melt semisweet chocolate on high (100% power) for 1 minute; stir. Microwave at additional 10- to 20-second intervals, stirring after each interval. Melt milk chocolate and vanilla or white chocolate at 70% power. Stir frequently until the chocolate is melted; do not overheat.

Mint Chocolate Torte

PREP: 30 MIN. + CHILLING **BAKE:** 15 MIN. + COOLING
YIELD: 14 SERVINGS

This recipe is a combination of two different ones...the chocolate cake from my childhood and the filling from a pie I saw in a cookbook. The flavor is reminiscent of an after-dinner chocolate mint.

Nadine Taylor ★ Durham, North Carolina

  3/4 cup baking cocoa
  1/2 cup hot water
    2 cups sugar
1-3/4 cups all-purpose flour
    1 teaspoon baking soda
    1 teaspoon salt
  1/4 teaspoon baking powder
    1 cup milk
  1/2 cup mayonnaise
    2 eggs
    2 teaspoons vanilla extract

FILLING:
    2 cups miniature marshmallows
  1/4 cup milk
Dash salt
  1/8 to 1/4 teaspoon peppermint extract
    2 to 3 drops green food coloring, optional
    1 cup heavy whipping cream, whipped

TOPPING:
    1 cup (6 ounces) semisweet chocolate chips
  1/3 cup heavy whipping cream

In a small bowl, combine the cocoa and water until smooth; set aside. In a large bowl, combine the sugar, flour, baking soda, salt and baking powder. Add the milk, mayonnaise, eggs, vanilla and cocoa mixture; beat on medium speed for 2 minutes.

Pour into three greased and floured 9-in. round baking pans. Bake at 350° for 15-20 minutes or until a toothpick inserted near the center comes out clean. Cool for 10 minutes; remove from pans to wire racks to cool completely.

For filling, combine the marshmallows, milk and salt in a small saucepan; cook and stir over low heat until the marshmallows are melted. Remove from the heat; stir in the peppermint extract and food coloring if desired. Transfer to a bowl; refrigerate until chilled.

Fold in the whipped cream. Place bottom cake layer on a serving plate; spread with a third of the filling. Repeat the layers twice.

For topping, combine chocolate chips and cream in a small saucepan; cook and stir over low heat until chips are melted. Drizzle over top and down sides of cake. Store in the refrigerator.

Editor's Note: Reduced-fat or fat-free mayonnaise is not recommended for this recipe.

Pecan Pound Cake

PREP: 15 MIN. **BAKE:** 1-1/4 HOURS + COOLING
YIELD: 12-16 SERVINGS

This tender cake has been a family favorite for years. It has a rich, buttery taste, a crispy crust—and makes a wonderful substitute for fruitcake at Christmas! Delicious with coffee or tea, this cake freezes very well.

Joan Ferguson ★ Elkhorn, Nebraska

    2 cups butter, softened
    2 cups sugar
    9 eggs
    1 tablespoon lemon juice
    3 teaspoons vanilla extract
    1 teaspoon grated lemon peel
    3 cups all-purpose flour
    1 teaspoon baking powder
  1/4 teaspoon salt
    4 cups chopped pecans
1-1/2 cups golden raisins
Confectioners' sugar, optional

In a large bowl, cream butter and sugar until light and fluffy. Add eggs, one at a time, beating well after each addition. Beat in the lemon juice, vanilla and lemon peel. Combine the flour, baking powder and salt; gradually add to creamed mixture just until combined. Fold in pecans and raisins.

Pour into a greased and floured 10-in. fluted tube pan. Bake at 350° for 1-1/4 to 1-1/2 hours or until a toothpick inserted near the center comes out clean. Cool for 10 minutes; remove from the pan to a wire rack to cool completely. Dust with confectioners' sugar if desired.

In a large bowl, beat the cheeses, sugar, cornstarch, orange juice and extract until smooth. Add the eggs; beat on low speed just until combined. Pour half of the batter over the crust.

Place the cranberry sauce, cranberries and water in a food processor; cover and process until blended. Spoon over batter; cut through with a knife to swirl. Carefully spread remaining batter over top.

Place springform pan in a large baking pan; add 1 in. of hot water to larger pan. Bake at 325° for 60-70 minutes or until center is just set and top appears dull.

Remove pan from water bath. Cool on a wire rack for 10 minutes. Carefully run a knife around the edge of the pan to loosen; cool 1 hour longer. Refrigerate overnight. Just before serving, drizzle with chocolate topping.

Cherry-Almond Pound Cake

PREP: 25 MIN. **BAKE:** 65 MIN. + COOLING
YIELD: 15 SERVINGS

This recipe uses dried cherries, which adds lots of chewy texture. To play up the almond flavor even more, use amaretto instead of the orange juice.

Myrna Tycholaz ★ Winnipeg, Manitoba

1	cup dried cherries
1/4	cup orange juice
1-1/4	cups butter, softened
1/2	cup (4 ounces) almond paste
2-1/2	cups sugar
6	eggs
1/2	teaspoon almond extract
3	cups all-purpose flour
1	teaspoon baking powder
1/2	teaspoon baking soda
1/2	teaspoon salt
1	cup (8 ounces) sour cream

GLAZE:
1-1/2	cups confectioners' sugar
2	to 3 tablespoons orange juice

In a small saucepan, bring the cherries and orange juice to a boil. Remove from the heat; cool to room temperature.

In a large bowl, cream the butter, almond paste and sugar until light and fluffy. Add the eggs, one at a time, beating well after each addition. Beat in extract. Combine the flour, baking powder, baking soda and salt; add to the creamed mixture alternately with sour cream. Stir in the cherry mixture.

Spoon into a greased and floured 10-in. fluted tube pan. Bake at 325° for 65-75 minutes or until a toothpick inserted near the center comes out clean. Cool 10 minutes before removing from pan to a wire rack.

Combine glaze ingredients; drizzle over warm cake. Cool completely.

Cranberry Orange Cheesecake

PREP: 45 MIN. **BAKE:** 1 HOUR + CHILLING
YIELD: 12 SERVINGS

I can't go to any Christmas gathering without this show-stopping dessert in tow. The combination of cranberries, chocolate and orange is a winner.

Laura Lufkin ★ Essex, Massachusetts

1	cup finely chopped pecans
2/3	cup chocolate wafer crumbs
1/4	cup butter, melted
3	tablespoons brown sugar
2	packages (8 ounces *each*) cream cheese, softened
2	cartons (8 ounces *each*) Mascarpone cheese
1-1/4	cups sugar
2	tablespoons cornstarch
2	teaspoons orange juice
1	teaspoon orange extract
4	eggs, lightly beaten
3/4	cup whole-berry cranberry sauce
1/4	cup orange-flavored dried cranberries
1	tablespoon water
1/4	cup chocolate ice cream topping, warmed

Place a greased 9-in. springform pan on a double thickness of heavy-duty foil (about 18 in. square); securely wrap around pan.

Combine the pecans, wafer crumbs, butter and brown sugar. Press onto the bottom and 1 in. up the sides of prepared pan. Place on a baking sheet. Bake at 325° for 8-10 minutes or until lightly browned. Cool on a wire rack.

Line a 9-in. pie plate with bottom pastry; trim even with edge of plate. Arrange apples in crust; set aside.

In a small saucepan, combine the corn syrup, sugar, butter, cornstarch, cinnamon and salt. Cook and stir over low heat until butter is melted and sugar is dissolved. Pour over apples.

Roll out remaining pastry to fit top of pie; place over filling. Trim, seal and flute edges; cut slits in top.

Bake at 425° for 15 minutes. Reduce heat to 325°. Bake for 40-50 minutes or until crust is golden brown and filling is bubbly. Cover edges with foil during the last 15 minutes to prevent overbrowning if necessary.

Meanwhile, in a small saucepan, combine the topping ingredients. Cook and stir over low heat until butter is melted and sugar is dissolved.

Place pie on a baking sheet. Pour topping over top crust. Bake for 3-4 minutes or until bubbly. Cool on a wire rack.

Apple Peel Swirls

When making an apple dessert, use the fruit's peel to fashion a fun garnish. Starting at the top of the apple, peel off the skin with a citrus zester. Work around the apple in a circular pattern. Place the peels in ice water and refrigerate for at least 20 minutes. (When you have enough peels for a garnish, you can finish peeling the apples with a vegetable peeler.) When ready to use, drain and pat dry.

Walnut Apple Pie

PREP: 25 MIN.   **BAKE:** 1 HOUR + COOLING
YIELD: 8 SERVINGS

Loaded with lots of tender apples and adorned with a nutty caramel topping, this pleasing pie is always a hit with old and young alike.

Winifred Eckerle ★ Gering, Nebraska

Pastry for double-crust pie (9 inches)
6	cups thinly sliced peeled tart apples
1/3	cup light corn syrup
1/4	cup sugar
2	tablespoons butter
1	tablespoon cornstarch
1	teaspoon ground cinnamon
1/4	teaspoon salt

TOPPING:
1/4	cup finely chopped walnuts
1/4	cup packed brown sugar
3	tablespoons dark corn syrup
2	tablespoons butter

Eve Pudding

PREP: 35 MIN.   **COOK:** 1-1/2 HOURS + COOLING
YIELD: 12 SERVINGS

Mom served this as our traditional Christmas Day dessert. My kids are puzzled as to why we don't eat this steamed pudding on Christmas Eve!

Lois Herman ★ Watertown, New York

1/2	cup butter, softened
1	cup sugar
2	eggs
1-1/2	cups all-purpose flour
1	teaspoon baking soda
1/4	teaspoon salt
1/4	teaspoon ground nutmeg
3	cups chopped peeled tart apples
1	cup chopped dates

SAUCE:
2	eggs
1/2	cup sugar
2	tablespoons butter
1	cup heavy whipping cream
1	teaspoon vanilla extract

In a large bowl, cream the butter and sugar until light and fluffy. Add the eggs, one at a time, beating well after each addition. Combine the flour, baking soda, salt and nutmeg; add to creamed mixture. Fold in apples and dates.

Transfer to a well-greased 8-cup pudding mold; cover. Place the mold on a rack in a deep pot; add 1 in. of hot water to the pot.

Bring to a gentle boil; cover and steam for 1-1/2 to 1-3/4 hours or until a toothpick inserted near the center comes out clean, adding more water as needed. Remove the mold from the pot; let stand for 10 minutes.

In a small heavy saucepan, combine the eggs, sugar and butter. Heat over low heat, whisking constantly, until the mixture thickens and reaches 160°, about 4 minutes. Remove from the heat; cool to room temperature.

In a small bowl, beat cream until it begins to thicken. Add the vanilla; beat until stiff peaks form. Fold into the egg mixture.

Unmold pudding onto a serving plate; cut into wedges. Serve with sauce.

Holiday Cheesecake Pie

PREP: 30 MIN. **BAKE:** 45 MIN. + CHILLING
YIELD: 2 PIES (8 SERVINGS EACH)

This unique recipe showcases easy-to-prepare pumpkin cheesecake and a cool, creamy topping.

Cami Rosenberg-Dews ★ Bristol, Connecticut

1	can (15 ounces) solid-pack pumpkin
1	can (12 ounces) evaporated milk
3/4	cup sugar
4	ounces cream cheese, softened
1/2	teaspoon pumpkin pie spice
1/4	teaspoon salt
2	eggs, lightly beaten
2	graham cracker crusts (9 inches)
1-1/2	cups cold eggnog
1	package (3.4 ounces) instant vanilla pudding mix
1	cup whipped topping

Additional whipped topping, optional

In a large bowl, beat pumpkin, milk, sugar, cream cheese, pumpkin pie spice and salt until smooth. Add the eggs; beat on low speed just until combined. Divide evenly between the graham cracker crusts.

Bake at 350° for 45-55 minutes or until a knife inserted near the center comes out clean. Cool on a wire rack.

In a small bowl, whisk the eggnog and pudding mix for 2 minutes. Fold in whipped topping. Spread over pies. Cover and refrigerate for 1 hour. Garnish with additional whipped topping if desired.

Editor's Note: This recipe was tested with commercially prepared eggnog.

Peanut Cake Bars

PREP: 1-3/4 HOURS **BAKE:** 30 MIN. + STANDING
YIELD: 20 BARS

A bakery favorite inspired the Taste of Home Test Kitchen to create this recipe. Individual pieces of white cake are coated with a crunchy peanut coating.

1/2	cup butter, softened
1-1/2	cups sugar
4	egg whites
2	teaspoons vanilla extract
2	cups all-purpose flour
1	teaspoon baking powder
1/2	teaspoon baking soda
1/4	teaspoon salt
1-1/3	cups buttermilk

GLAZE:

7-1/2	cups confectioners' sugar, *divided*
1	cup milk, *divided*
1	teaspoon vanilla extract, *divided*
2	cans (12 ounces *each*) salted peanuts, chopped, *divided*

In a large bowl, cream the butter and sugar until light and fluffy. Add egg whites, one at a time, beating well after each addition. Beat in the vanilla. Combine the flour, baking powder, baking soda and salt; add to the creamed mixture alternately with the buttermilk, beating well after each addition.

Pour into a greased 13-in. x 9-in. baking pan. Bake at 350° for 30-35 minutes or until a toothpick inserted near the center comes out clean. Cool on a wire rack.

For glaze, in a shallow bowl, mix 3-3/4 cups confectioners' sugar, 1/2 cup milk and 1/2 teaspoon vanilla until smooth. Place one can of peanuts in another shallow bowl.

Cut cake into 20 bars. Coat the top and sides of each square with glaze, then roll in nuts. Place on wire racks over waxed paper; let dry completely.

Make a second batch of glaze with remaining confectioners' sugar, milk and vanilla. Coat cake squares a second time, then roll in remaining nuts. Let dry completely.

Ambrosia Pecan Pie

PREP: 10 MIN. **BAKE:** 50 MIN. + COOLING
YIELD: 8 SERVINGS

Orange peel and coconut combine with pecans to make this rich-tasting dessert. It always wins compliments at Christmas dinner.

Bernadine Stine ★ Roanoke, Indiana

3 eggs
3/4 cup light corn syrup
1/2 cup sugar
3 tablespoons brown sugar
3 tablespoons orange juice
2 tablespoons butter, melted
1 teaspoon grated orange peel
1/8 teaspoon salt
1-1/2 cups chopped pecans
2/3 cup flaked coconut
1 unbaked pastry shell (9 inches)

In a large bowl, beat the eggs, corn syrup, sugars, orange juice, butter, orange peel and salt until well blended. Stir in pecans and coconut.

Pour into the pastry shell. Bake at 350° for 50-60 minutes or until a knife inserted near the center comes out clean. Cover edges with foil during the last 15 minutes to prevent overbrowning if necessary. Cool on a wire rack.

thick and lemon-colored. Stir in water and vanilla. Combine the flour, baking powder and salt; add to egg mixture and beat until smooth.

Spread batter evenly into prepared pan. Bake at 350° for 12-15 minutes or until the cake springs back when lightly touched. Cool for 5 minutes.

Invert the cake onto a kitchen towel dusted with confectioners' sugar. Gently peel off parchment paper. Roll up cake in the towel jelly-roll style, starting with a short side. Cool completely on a wire rack.

Unroll cake; spread ice cream evenly over cake to within 1/2 in. of edges. Roll up again. Place seam side down on a serving platter. Cover and freeze for at least 1 hour.

Melt four squares of chocolate; spread over a parchment paper-lined baking sheet. Refrigerate for 30 minutes.

Break chilled chocolate into 3-in. x 1-in. pieces. Melt remaining chocolate; spread over top, sides and ends of cake. Working quickly, place chocolate pieces on cake to resemble bark. Freeze until serving. Remove from the freezer 10 minutes before cutting. Dust with confectioners' sugar.

Making Chocolate Bark

Chocolate bark adds a unique texture to this Yule Log. Here's how to make it. Spread melted chocolate on a parchment paper-lined baking sheet. Chill for 30 minutes. Use your hands to break into pieces (about 3 in. x 1 in.). Press chocolate pieces into the chocolate icing on the cake, arranging them to resemble bark.

Yule Log

PREP: 35 MIN.   **BAKE:** 15 MIN. + FREEZING
YIELD: 10 SERVINGS

I enjoy making something extra special for dessert on Christmas Eve, when we host my husband's family. The pistachio ice cream in this treat is a unique filling.

Valerie Gee ★ West Seneca, New York

3 eggs
1 cup sugar
1/3 cup water
1 teaspoon vanilla extract
3/4 cup all-purpose flour
1 teaspoon baking powder
1/4 teaspoon salt
1/4 cup confectioners' sugar
3 cups pistachio ice cream, softened
12 squares (1 ounce *each*) bittersweet chocolate, *divided*

Additional confectioners' sugar

Line a greased 15-in. x 10-in. x 1-in. baking pan with parchment paper; grease the paper and set aside.

In a large bowl, beat eggs for 3 minutes. Gradually add the sugar, beating for 2 minutes or until mixture becomes

Snowball Cake

PREP: 25 MIN.   **BAKE:** 40 MIN. + CHILLING
YIELD: 20 SERVINGS

I couldn't pry this family secret recipe from my sister-in-law, but I could from her mother! The old-fashioned flavor of toasted coconut and cherries never goes out of style.

Norma Wehrung ★ Getzville, New York

- 1 package (16 ounces) angel food cake mix
- 2 envelopes unflavored gelatin
- 1/4 cup cold water
- 1 cup boiling water
- 1 can (20 ounces) crushed pineapple, undrained
- 1 cup sugar
- 3 tablespoons lemon juice
- 1/4 teaspoon salt
- 4 envelopes whipped topping mix
- 2 cups milk

Toasted flaked coconut and maraschino cherries

Prepare and bake cake according to package directions, using an ungreased 10-in. tube pan. Immediately invert cake onto a wire rack; cool completely, about 1 hour.

Meanwhile, in a large bowl, sprinkle gelatin over cold water; let stand for 1 minute. Stir in the boiling water until gelatin is dissolved. Add the pineapple, sugar, lemon juice and salt. Refrigerate until partially thickened, about 40 minutes.

In a large bowl, beat whipped topping mixes and milk until stiff. Fold into pineapple mixture.

Run a knife around sides and center tube of cake pan; remove cake from pan and cut into 1-in. cubes. Place half of the cake cubes in a 13-in. x 9-in. dish; top with half of the filling. Repeat layers. Refrigerate for at least 1 hour.

Sprinkle with the coconut. Cut into squares; top each with a cherry.

Amaretto Ice Cream

PREP: 20 MIN. + FREEZING **YIELD:** 10 SERVINGS

Ordinary ice cream just won't do for the holidays. So I make this cool and creamy treat featuring Amaretto, almonds and chocolate chips. Guests can't resist it!

Nancy Paul ★ Lakeview, Ohio

- 2 cups heavy whipping cream
- 1 can (14 ounces) sweetened condensed milk
- 2 egg yolks
- 1/4 cup Amaretto
- 1/4 teaspoon almond extract
- 1/2 cup sliced almonds, toasted
- 1/4 cup semisweet chocolate chips
- 1/4 cup sliced almonds

In a large bowl, beat cream until stiff peaks form; set aside. In a small saucepan, heat milk to 175°, stirring constantly. Whisk a small amount of the hot mixture into egg yolks. Return all to the pan, whisking constantly. Cook and stir over low heat until mixture reaches at least 160° and coats the back of a metal spoon. Remove from the heat.

Cool quickly by placing pan in a bowl of ice water; stir for 2 minutes. Stir in the Amaretto and extract. Fold in the whipped cream and toasted almonds. Pour into a 9-in. square pan; cover and freeze for 4 hours or until firm.

In a microwave, melt chocolate chips; stir until smooth. Cut ice cream into squares. Drizzle each serving with the chocolate; sprinkle with almonds.

Gingerbread with Crunchy Topping

PREP: 30 MIN. **BAKE:** 40 MIN. + COOLING
YIELD: 12 SERVINGS

I credit my mom with instilling in me a love of baking. Tried-and-true recipes like this make holidays with my family extra special. It wouldn't be Christmas without gingerbread!

Pat Habiger ★ Spearville, Kansas

- 1/2 cup shortening
- 1/2 cup sugar
- 1 egg
- 1 cup molasses
- 2-1/2 cups cake flour
- 1 teaspoon baking powder
- 1 teaspoon ground ginger
- 1 teaspoon ground cinnamon
- 1/2 teaspoon baking soda
- 1/2 teaspoon salt
- 1/2 teaspoon ground cloves
- 1 cup water

TOPPING:
- 1 cup packed dark brown sugar
- 1/2 cup all-purpose flour
- 1 teaspoon ground cinnamon
- 1/2 teaspoon ground ginger
- 1/2 cup cold butter
- 1 cup chopped pecans
- 1 teaspoon grated lemon peel

Whipped cream, optional

In a large bowl, cream shortening and sugar. Beat in egg and molasses. Combine the flour, baking powder, ginger, cinnamon, baking soda, salt and cloves; add to creamed mixture alternately with water.

Pour into a greased 13-in. x 9-in. baking dish. Bake at 350° for 30 minutes.

For topping, in a small bowl, combine the brown sugar, flour, cinnamon and ginger. Cut in butter until mixture resembles coarse crumbs. Stir in pecans and lemon peel. Sprinkle over gingerbread.

Bake 10 minutes longer or until a toothpick inserted near the center of cake comes out clean. Cool on a wire rack. Serve with whipped cream if desired.

Almond Coconut Flans

PREP: 40 MIN. **BAKE:** 30 MIN. + CHILLING
YIELD: 8 SERVINGS

Individual desserts always make an impression at special occasion suppers, and these flans are no exception. The almond and coconut flavor is awesome.

Melinda Winner ★ Gulfport, Mississippi

2	cups sugar, *divided*
3-1/2	cups milk
6	eggs
1/2	teaspoon salt
1	teaspoon almond extract
1/2	teaspoon coconut extract
2	squares (1 ounce *each*) semisweet chocolate
1/4	cup slivered almonds, toasted
3	tablespoons flaked coconut

In a heavy saucepan over medium-low heat, cook 1 cup sugar until melted, about 20 minutes. Do not stir. Reduce heat to low; cook for 5 minutes or until the syrup is golden brown, stirring occasionally. Quickly pour into eight ungreased 6-oz. ramekins or custard cups, tilting to coat bottom of dish. Let stand for 10 minutes.

Meanwhile, in a large saucepan, heat milk until bubbles form around sides of saucepan. Remove from the heat. In a large bowl, whisk the eggs, salt and remaining sugar. Stir 1 cup warm milk into egg mixture; return all to the pan and mix well. Add extracts. Slowly pour into prepared dishes.

Place ramekins in a baking pan; fill pan with boiling water to a depth of 3/4 in. Bake, uncovered, at 325° for 30-35 minutes or until the centers are just set (mixture will jiggle). Remove ramekins from water bath; cool for 1 hour. Cover and refrigerate overnight.

Carefully run a knife around edge of dishes to loosen; invert each dish onto a rimmed serving dish. Melt the chocolate; drizzle over flans. Sprinkle with almonds and coconut. Serve immediately.

Deck
THE HALLS

MATERIALS:

Divided container such as a cutlery tray or serving piece to coordinate with your tableware and linens

Candles of various sizes and shapes

Wire-edge ribbon for trim on candles

Assorted greens and Christmas trims as shown

DIRECTIONS:

1. Place candles into compartments as desired, varying the height for added interest. (If needed, place smaller candles on a sturdy base to add height.)

2. Tie ribbon around the larger candles if desired.

3. Fill remaining compartments with assorted greens and Christmas trims.

Glowing Christmas Centerpiece

CRAFT LEVEL: QUICK & EASY

FINISHED SIZE: Size will vary depending on size of tray or divided container used.

There's no need to call your local florist and order a centerpiece for a holiday gathering. With a few easy-to-find and inexpensive items—like a simple divided container, holiday candles and seasonal materials—you can quickly create your own festive table decoration that captures the warm and cheery feel of Christmas.

Taste of Home Craft Editor

Making the Glowing Christmas Centerpiece

1. Place candles of different shapes and heights into selected compartments of a divided container.

2. Fill the remaining compartments with assorted greens and Christmas trims.

No-Sew Wreath

CRAFT LEVEL: QUICK & EASY

FINISHED SIZE: Wreath measures about 12 inches across.

I was knitting one day and looked up at the TV. My eyesight was fuzzy because of the close work I was doing. I thought I saw a wreath with round shapes in it. It turned out that the television program was showing a wreath made out of leaves. But I decided to fashion the one I had seen instead!

   Darleen Crosgrove ★ Lawrenceville, Georgia

MATERIALS:

44-inch length of kitchen plastic wrap

Eight 3-inch Styrofoam balls

1/3 yard of 44-inch-wide gold fabric

Two 1-inch gold ornaments

1/8-inch gold cord

2-1/2 yards of 2-1/2-inch-wide gold wire-edge ribbon

Heavy thread or string

Fabric glue

6-inch length of craft wire for hanger

Ruler

Scissors

DIRECTIONS:

Wreath:

1. Lay kitchen plastic wrap on a flat surface.

2. Place Styrofoam balls in a row down the center of the plastic wrap.

3. Wrap plastic wrap around balls creating a long tube with the balls inside.

4. Wrap a length of heavy thread around the tube between the two center balls. Pull ends tight and knot thread. Trim the ends close to knot.

5. Keeping the balls close together and working outward from center point, tie a length of heavy thread between each set of balls as before. (Check at intervals to make sure the tube can be formed into a circle.) Then tie each end closed next to the balls. Trim excess plastic wrap at each end.

6. Lay fabric wrong side up on a flat surface.

7. Place plastic-covered tube of balls down the center of the fabric.

8. Wrap the fabric around the balls, creating a long tube with the foam balls inside. Trim excess fabric from long edge. Glue along long edge as needed to hold. Let dry.

9. Trim excess fabric from ends, leaving about 1 in. of fabric at each end of tube.

10. Overlap the ends of the fabric tube, forming a wreath shape. Tie overlapped ends together with heavy thread, making the join as unnoticeable in front as possible.

11. Cut a 10-in. length of gold cord. Tie opposite ends to a gold ornament.

12. From wire-edge ribbon, cut seven 10-in. lengths and one 18-in. length for the center top.

13. Slip gold cord with ornaments attached over the 18-in. length of ribbon and tie ribbon in an overhand knot around the overlapped ends so ornaments hang from the top of the wreath. Shape ends in a bow as shown in the photo above.

14. Tie remaining pieces of ribbon in an overhand knot between remaining balls. Fold ends of ribbon to back to make bow shapes as shown.

Finishing:

1. Fold the wire for hanger in half to form a loop.

2. Attach wire ends to ribbon on center back to secure hanging loop.

Crafter's Note: Simply use different fabric and ribbon to turn this Yuletide wreath into one for another occasion. You can also tie on other trinkets in place of the ornaments. To adjust the size of the wreath, attach more or fewer Styrofoam balls—or use balls of different sizes.

Mini Gingerbread House

PREP: 4 HOURS   **BAKE:** 15 MIN. + STANDING
YIELD: 1 HOUSE

Gingerbread houses always bring joy to the faces of the young and young at heart! Prepare several batches of dough (one batch at a time) and decorate a number of houses in different ways to create a gingerbread village.

DOUGH:
- 1/2 cup shortening
- 1/2 cup packed dark brown sugar
- 1/2 cup dark corn syrup
- 1/2 cup molasses
- 1 tablespoon ground ginger
- 1 tablespoon ground cinnamon
- 4 cups all-purpose flour

ICING AND ASSEMBLY:
- 2 egg whites
- 2-2/3 cups confectioners' sugar
- 1/4 teaspoon cream of tartar
- 2 Pirouette cookies
- 42 Tootsie Roll Midgees
- Edible glitter
- 16 snowflake-shaped sprinkles
- 3 *each* vanilla and chocolate chewy pudding snack bites
- 9 miniature semisweet chocolate nonpareils
- 1 milk chocolate candy bar (1.55 ounces)
- 6 ice cream sugar cones

Making a Gingerbread House

1. On sturdy paper, cut out the patterns for the gingerbread house. Roll out one portion of dough; position one pattern on top and cut out. Repeat with remaining dough and patterns. Continue with the recipe as directed.

2. Align the walls at right angles to each other. Prop with small spice bottles for stability. Let dry before removing bottles.

Special Equipment:
Pastry or heavy-duty resealable plastic bag
Pastry tip—#5 round tip
Small bottles or jars for propping
Covered board (12 inches x 7 inches)

Using light cardboard or poster board, make gingerbread house pattern pieces according to the diagram below; set aside. In a heavy saucepan, cook and stir the shortening, brown sugar, corn syrup and molasses over medium heat until sugar is dissolved. Remove from the heat; stir in ginger and cinnamon. Stir in flour, 1 cup at a time, until dough can be formed into a ball. With a lightly floured rolling pin, roll out dough directly onto a greased baking sheet to 1/4-in. thickness.

Position patterns on dough. Using a sharp knife, cut around the patterns. Remove patterns, then remove dough scraps; cover and save scraps to reroll if necessary. Bake at 350° for 10-15 minutes or until gingerbread springs back when lightly touched. Immediately place patterns over the gingerbread; cut around edges to trim. Cool on baking sheet for 3-4 minutes or until gingerbread begins to harden. Carefully remove to a wire rack; cool.

For icing and assembly: In a large bowl, beat the egg whites, confectioners' sugar and cream of tartar on low speed for 1 minute. Beat on high for 6-8 minutes or until stiff. Place a damp cloth over bowl and cover tightly between uses.

Cut a small hole in the corner of a pastry or plastic bag; insert #5 round tip. Place some icing in bag. Pipe icing along base and sides of front wall and one side wall. Position at right angles to each other and place on covered board; prop with small bottles or jars. Repeat with second side section and back. Let dry; remove bottles. For side supports, carefully cut Pirouette cookies widthwise in half. Pipe icing along one side of each; position at corners of the house.

For roof: Pipe icing along peak of roof. Position roof pieces; let dry. For roof tiles, cut Tootsie Rolls widthwise in half. Flatten with a rolling pin; cut each flattened piece in half. Pipe an icing line 1/2 in. from bottom of one side of roof. Curve Tootsie Roll pieces around your finger or a wooden spoon handle. Press along icing; repeat until one horizontal row is finished. Repeat six times, slightly overlapping each row until one roof piece is covered.

Repeat on other side. Pipe a thick line of icing along top, front and back roof seams. Using the same technique, place a row of Tootsie Roll pieces at a right angle to direction of roof tiles along the top, front and back seams; let dry. Pipe a few thick clusters of icing onto front roof tiles to resemble snow. Sprinkle with the edible glitter.

For finishing touches: In a bead pattern, pipe icing around front door. Pipe 1-in. squares on both sides of door and on each side of house for windows. Pipe windowpanes. Decorate the corners with snowflake-shaped sprinkles.

For wreath over door, attach pudding bites and nonpareils to front of house using icing. On covered board, spread icing into a 1-in. curved strip from the front door to the edge of the board for path. Cut the candy bar into small rectangles; press side by side into icing. Let dry.

Using scissors, cut the sugar cones to varying heights. If desired, pipe a thick circle of icing around open end of each cone to help hold in place. Position cones around house.

Editor's Note: Icing is for decorative purposes only because of the uncooked egg whites. If gingerbread house will be eaten, substitute a royal icing recipe using meringue powder. Edible glitter and meringue powder are available from Wilton Industries. Call 1-800/794-5866 or visit www.wilton.com. Use of coupler ring will allow you to easily change pastry tips between decorating steps.

ROOF ←5 7/16"→   ↕ 4 1/4"

FRONT & BACK ←5"→   ↕ 5 13/16"

SIDES ←4 1/4"→   ↕ 3 1/4"

Tudor Gingerbread House

Practice—and patience—make perfect. Just ask Johanna Rosson of Macomb, Illinois! Through the years, this creative wife and mother has honed her skills for designing and decorating gingerbread houses. Her masterpieces have ranged from humble, homey cottages to magnificent mansions (like the awe-inspiring Tudor shown below).

You, too, can create your own holiday house. First, start with your favorite gingerbread house recipe (like Mini Gingerbread House on page 176). If you want to add brickwork your house, read the instructions on the next page before baking.

Then try some of Johanna's design techniques detailed here. Friends and family will be impressed with your Christmas creation!

Johanna says to preserve your gingerbread house from year to year, completely cover it with plastic; store in a cool, dry place. You may need to do some refurbishing before the house is displayed each year.

Brickwork (1)

The house shown here has two brick patterns—standard row bricks above and decorative herringbone bricks by the front door. Before baking your gingerbread house, use a knife to score the dough and create a brick pattern. Bake and cool as directed.

To create red bricks, tint one tablespoon of water with red food coloring. Brush the mixture over the bricks with a new, clean paint brush. Blot gently with paper towels; let dry.

For the mortar, pipe a small amount of Royal Icing over the bricks with your fingertip. Immediately wipe gently with paper towels to remove excess.

Window Shutters (1)

Tint icing if desired with food color paste or gel. Using a basket weave tip, pipe shutters in a straight line on the sides of the windows.

Evergreen Garland and Wreath (1)

Tint icing green. To create a garland, pipe petals around windows or the roofline with a small petal tip. Pipe icing in a circle to make a wreath. Before the icing dries, use a tweezers to arrange pearlized dragees on the garland and wreath. For bows, use a small red tip to pipe red tinted frosting on the dried garland and wreath.

Log Pile (2)

Cut or break pretzel rods into pieces. The length of the logs should be in proportion to the size of the house. Stack the logs to create a pyramid shape, using white icing to hold the logs in place.

Cobblestone Path (3)

Break thin cookies, such as almond, gingersnaps or chocolate wafers, into pieces. Spread white icing along path. Arrange broken cookie pieces in icing to create a cobblestone look.

Fence (3)

With white icing, anchor miniature pretzel twists to the display base all around the house. Use icing to secure pretzel twists upside down on the pretzel base, allowing the sides of the pretzels to touch. For the garland, tint icing green. Pipe along the tops of the pretzels with a small open star tip (such as #17). Use red tinted icing and a small round tip to add bows.

Ornamental Timber Design

Spread a thin layer of white icing on the house to resemble stucco; allow to dry. Tint icing brown with food coloring gel or paste. With a basket weave tip (such as #45), pipe timbers onto the house.

Porch Roof And Pillars

Johanna makes gingerbread and cuts out a rectangular front piece and two side triangles. After baking and cooling, she glues the pieces together with white icing. (You may need to hold in place until dry.) Once dried, attach the porch to the house front with icing; let dry. Cut green candy canes to desired length with a serrated knife. Using white icing, attach the candy cane pillars to the porch roof and floor.

Evergreen Trees

Upside-down ice cream sugar cones are an easy way to create evergreen trees. If the cones are too tall, use scissors or a serrated knife to cut them to the desired height. If you want taller trees, stack two cones. (For another tree base idea, see below for what Johanna uses to make snowmen.)

Tint the frosting green. With a closed star tip or a large ruffle tip, pipe icing on the lower one-third or one-fourth of the cone. Then pipe on the next one-third or one-fourth, continuing until you reach the top. This allows the top branches to hang over the bottom branches. Place on waxed paper to set. If desired, pipe white icing over trees for a snowy effect.

Snowman (4)

Johanna uses a soft Rice Krispie Treat mixture to create the base for snowmen (and sometimes for evergreen trees). Cover the snowman with white icing and decorate as desired. The scarf and hat are made from Airhead Candy.

Quilter's ruler

Rotary cutting tools (optional)

Standard sewing supplies

DIRECTIONS:

Cutting:

Either use quilter's marking pen or pencil to mark the fabrics before cutting them with a scissors or use rotary cutting tools to cut the pieces as directed in the instructions that follow. Cut strips crosswise from selvage to selvage.

1. Trim each of the eight different fabrics into 4-in.-wide strips. From each strip, cut four 4-in. squares, creating a total of thirty-two 4-in. squares.

2. From the fabric for the inner border, cut two 1-in.-wide x 11-in.-long strips and two 1-in.-wide x 36-1/2-in.-long strips.

3. From the fabric for the outer border, cut two 3-in.-wide x 36-1/2-in.-wide strips and two 3-in.-wide x 17-in.-long strips.

4. From binding fabric, cut three 2-1/4-in.-wide strips.

Piecing:

Do all stitching with right sides of fabrics together, edges even, matching or neutral thread and an accurate 1/4-in. seam. Press seams as directed.

1. Lay out 30 of the 4-in. squares randomly in three rows with 10 squares in each row (there will be two extra squares).

2. Sew the blocks in each row together in planned order.

3. Press seams in each row in opposite directions.

4. Sew the rows together.

5. Press seams in opposite directions.

Applique:

1. Trace the star patterns separately onto tracing paper with pencil.

2. Trace each star twice onto paper side of fusible web, leaving at least 1/2 in. between shapes. Cut shapes apart, leaving a margin of paper around each.

3. Fuse stars onto wrong side of gold applique fabric following the manufacturer's instructions. When cool, cut out stars along outline of patterns. Remove paper backing.

Star Table Runner

CRAFT LEVEL: BEGINNER

FINISHED SIZE: Runner is about 17 inches wide x 41 inches long.

In a twinkling, this quilted covering can turn an everyday table into a seasonal showpiece. This appliqued project is easy enough for beginners.

Mary Cain ★ Sun Prairie, Wisconsin

MATERIALS:

Patterns on page 181

Paper-backed fusible web

Tracing paper and pencil

44-inch-wide 100% cotton fabrics—1/8 yard each of eight different coordinating print fabrics for pieced squares, 1/8 yard of coordinating small print for inner border, 1/4 yard of dark print for outer border, 1/4 yard of dark print for binding, 1/6 yard of small gold print for star appliques and 5/8 yard for backing

20-inch x 44-inch piece of lightweight quilt batting

All-purpose thread—neutral or colors to match fabrics

Rayon or decorative thread in color to coordinate with star applique fabric

Tear-away stabilizer

Quilter's marking pen or pencil (optional)

 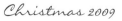

4. Fuse stars to right side of pieced runner where desired.

5. Place tear-away stabilizer behind stars.

6. Using rayon or decorative thread, blanket-stitch around each star. Bring all loose threads to the back and secure.

7. Remove stabilizer.

Inner Border:

1. Sew short inner border strips to opposite short edges of pieced top. Press seam toward inner border.

2. In the same way, sew the long inner border strips to the opposite long edges of the pieced top. Press as before.

Outer Border:

1. Sew long outer border strips to opposite long edges of the inner border. Press seam toward outer border.

2. In the same way, sew the short outer border strips to the opposite short edges of the inner border. Press as before.

Quilting:

1. Place backing fabric wrong side up on a flat surface.

2. Center batting on top of backing.

3. Center pieced runner right side up on top of batting. Smooth out all wrinkles.

4. Baste layers together as needed to hold.

5. Quilt as desired.

6. Trim excess batting and backing even with outer edges.

Star Runner Patterns

LARGE STAR
TRACE 1–TRACING PAPER
CUT 2–FUSED GOLD PRINT

MEDIUM STAR
TRACE 1–TRACING PAPER
CUT 2–FUSED GOLD PRINT

SMALL STAR
TRACE 1–TRACING PAPER
CUT 2–FUSED GOLD PRINT

Binding:

1. Sew narrow ends of binding strips together diagonally to make one long strip.

2. Trim one short end of binding strip diagonally and press 1/4 in. to the wrong side.

3. Fold and press binding strip in half lengthwise with wrong sides facing.

4. Sew binding to front of runner with a 1/4-in. seam, mitering corners and overlapping ends. Trim excess binding.

5. Fold binding to back of runner, encasing raw edges and mitering the corners.

6. With matching or neutral thread, either sew binding in place using a long zigzag stitch or hand-sew fold of binding to backing. Remove basting.

Through the Grapevine

Intertwined in this tree stand idea is a rustic, outdoor look. Place purchased grapevine wreaths of different sizes around the tree stand, using smaller ones toward the top. (If needed, cut a slit in one side of each wreath to fit around the tree trunk.) For color, tuck berry springs among the vines.

Acrylic craft paints (Delta Ceramcoat paints shown)—Black, Cardinal Red (or color to match your fabric), Dolphin Grey, Lisa Pink, Hunter Green, Ivory, Medium Flesh, Straw and Metallic Gold

Paintbrushes—small and medium flat, fine liner, 1/2-inch angle brush and rake brush (optional)

Toothpick

Textured snow medium

Satin spray sealer

DIRECTIONS:

1. Trace pattern below onto folded tracing paper. Turn tracing paper over and retrace design on opposite side of the fold.

2. Unfold paper for a complete pattern.

Cutting:

1. Lay pattern on 1 x 8 pine and slip graphite paper between the pattern and wood.

2. Trace outline of star with a stylus or dry ballpoint pen to transfer the pattern to the wood.

3. Cut out shape with scroll or band saw.

Painted Santa Star

CRAFT LEVEL: INTERMEDIATE

FINISHED SIZE: Santa star measures about 7 inches high x 5-3/4 inches wide.

I love designing holiday ornaments that feature Santa Claus. He's always a cheery way to say, "Merry Christmas." And with this project Kris Kringle has a starring role. To make this project, I tried a variation on my preferred technique of decorative painting. Using both fabric and paint added extra eye appeal without a lot of extra time.

Bobbie Traxinger ★ Rapid City, South Dakota

MATERIALS:

Pattern at right

Tracing paper and pencil

Scissors

Graphite paper

Stylus or dry ballpoint pen

Purchased 1-inch high wooden star

8-inch length of 1 x 8 pine (real dimensions are 3/4 x 7-1/4 inches)

Scroll or band saw

Sandpaper

Drill with 1/16-inch bit

20-inch length of 19-gauge wire

6-inch square of red Christmas print fabric

Fabric stiffener

Craft knife

Water container

Paper towels

Palette or foam plate

Painted Santa Star Pattern

Drill 1/16-in. hole

SANTA STAR
TRACE 1—TRACING PAPER
CUT 1—1 x 8 PINE

Foldline

Preparation:

1. Drill holes through large star where shown on pattern.

2. Drill another hole through top point of 1-in. star.

3. Sand stars as needed and wipe with a damp paper towel to remove sanding dust.

4. Place fabric wrong side up on a flat surface.

5. Center large star on fabric and trace around the shape with pencil. Cut out shape carefully.

6. Use the medium flat brush to coat one side of large star and both sides of fabric with fabric stiffener. Position fabric, right side up, on wooden star so edges line up; then, working from the center out, smooth out any bubbles or wrinkles with your fingers. The edges should be close, but need not be perfect. Let dry.

7. Use craft knife to rim off any fabric that extends beyond edges of star.

8. Following manufacturer's instructions, spray all sides of large star with sealer, including fabric. Let dry.

Painting:

Keep paper towels and container of water handy to clean brushes. Place small amounts of paint as needed onto foam plate or palette. Let paint dry after every application. Refer to pattern and photo as a guide while painting as directed in the instructions that follow.

1. Use graphite paper to transfer main design lines to fabric side of star as before, omitting facial details.

2. Using medium flat paintbrush, paint the sides and back of Santa Cardinal Red or a color to match fabric.

3. Using small flat paintbrush, paint Santa's face Medium Flesh, beard Dolphin Grey, mittens Hunter Green and boots and belt Black. Paint the front, back and sides of 1-in. star Straw.

4. Replace pattern and slip graphite paper between pattern and wood. Transfer the facial features as before.

5. Use small flat brush and Black to paint eyes.

6. For cheeks and nose, dip angle brush into water. Touch brush to paper towel just until shine disappears. Touch Lisa Pink along the long side of brush and blend by brushing several times on palette or foam plate. The color should be intense on long side of brush and fade gradually to clear. Pull the loaded edge of brush along transferred lines for cheeks and nose, making small upside down C-strokes. Let dry and reapply if needed.

7. In the same way, use Lisa Pink to shade the outer edges of Santa's face.

8. Use fine liner and Ivory to paint eyebrows.

9. Use toothpick and Ivory to add a tiny dot to each eye.

10. Use liner or rake brush to add fine lines of Ivory over the Dolphin Grey beard, varying the direction and length of strokes and letting some extend onto Santa's suit. Define the mustache by the direction of the strokes.

11. Shade under the bottom edge of the mustache with Dolphin Grey.

12. For fur trim, apply snow texture medium according to manufacturer's instructions.

13. Use liner and Metallic Gold to paint belt buckle.

Finishing:

1. Spray each wood piece with sealer. Let dry.

2. Insert one end of 19-gauge wire through one of Santa's hands. Pull through and twist ends to secure.

3. Wrap craft wire around pencil once to coil, add the star and make one or two more coils.

4. Insert other wire end through Santa's other hand and twist the end to secure.

Crafter's Note: Choose a variety of plaids, checks or any small print fabrics for Santa's suit to make a whole set of stars. Instead of using wire, drill one hole through the top point of the star. Then pull a length of ribbon or thread through and tie in a loop to hang.

Sparkling Water

To set this festive arrangement afloat, place three tall, narrow glass vases inside a footed glass bowl. (Place floral adhesive on the bottom of the vases if needed to secure them in place.) Partially fill the vases with water and place a tea light inside each. Form a purchased seasonal garland into a circle and arrange it on top of the bowl around the vases.

Caring for Christmas Plants

With their bright splashes of color, live plants add a festive flair to holiday decorating. Here are some general points about these plants.

- It is best to keep Christmas plants way from young children and pets.
- Place them away from fireplaces, heating vents, radiators, outside doors or windows. Avoid temperature extremes.
- Keep in a room where the daytime temps will be between 60° to 70°.
- Place in a well-lit area out of direct sunlight.
- Make sure the pot has good drainage. Don't overwater or allow the pots to sit in standing water.
- Check water daily.

Christmas Cactus

Amaryllis

Kalanchoe

Holly

Cyclamens

Poinsettias

Poinsettias are the most popular of the Yuletide plants and are available in white, pink, salmon and red, as well as marbled plants with pink and white. Contrary to popular belief, poinsettias are not poisonous. If ingested, they may cause a stomachache and nausea. The sap may cause skin irritation.

Poinsettias do not like cold weather or temperature extremes. If the temperature is below 50°, make sure it is protected from the cold as you take it from the store to your home. Don't leave it in the car while you continue to shop.

Christmas Cactus

Christmas cactus is different from the typical desert cactus, and in general requires a little more water. Their flowers come in white, pink, salmon, fuchsia and yellow. They can be kept as year-round houseplants and, in the summer months, will do well outside in a shady area.

Holly

Holly generally has green or variegated leaves with red berries. The spines on the leaves are sharp, so holly should be handled carefully. Cut holly will keep about two weeks. For floral arrangements, recut stems and place in water. If possible place centerpieces in a shallow dish of water.

Amaryllis

Amaryllis have long stems with large lily-shaped flowers and are available in white, pink, salmon and red and multicolored varieties.

An amaryllis can take from 7 to 10 weeks to flower, so plan accordingly when planting the bulb. These plants are top heavy once the flowers bloom and the stems can break. To prevent this, stake the plant, making sure not to damage the bulb.

Kalanchoe

Kalanchoe (ka-lən-chō) has tiny clusters of star-like flowers in many colors that can last for months. Let the soil dry between watering.

Cyclamens

Cyclamens (sī-klə-mən) prefer cooler temperatures from 60° to 65°. If given the right environment, its blooms can last for 2 to 3 months. The flowers come in white, pink or red. They like evenly moist soil...don't let it dry out.

Mistletoe

Mistletoe is generally hung on a doorframe and requires no special care. When purchased fresh, the poisonous berries have usually been replaced by plastic berries.

Kris Moose Ornaments

CRAFT LEVEL: QUICK & EASY

FINISHED SIZE: Moose ornament measures about 6 inches x 6 inches without hanger.

"They're so cute!" That's the typical reaction I hear about these plaid moose ornaments. They're a great way to use up fabric scraps or to recycle plaid clothing.

Nancy Rhodes ★ Piseco, New York

MATERIALS:

Patterns on page 187

Tracing paper and pencil

7-inch x 12-inch piece of plaid wool or flannel fabric for body and scarf

Felt—5-inch x 7-inch piece of brown for head and ears, and 2-inch x 5-inch piece of tan for antlers

All-purpose thread—brown and color to match plaid fabric

Black quilting thread or six-strand embroidery floss for nostrils

Two coordinating 1/2-inch four-hole buttons

Two 7mm black beads for eyes

Polyester stuffing

8-inch length of 2-ply jute string for hanger

Glue gun and glue sticks

Standard sewing supplies

DIRECTIONS:

1. Trace patterns onto folded tracing paper as directed. Cut out and open each for complete patterns.

2. Cut a 3/4-in.-wide x 12-in.-long piece of plaid fabric for scarf. Cut 3/4-in.-long fringe along each narrow edge of scarf.

3. Fold remaining plaid fabric in half with right sides facing. Pin body pattern to fabric with grain lines matching. Sew around outside edges of body pattern, leaving straight bottom edge open for turning. Trim excess fabric away, cutting 1/8 in. outside stitching.

4. Turn body inside out. Stuff body firmly. Turn raw edges in and hand-sew opening closed with matching thread.

5. Pin head pattern to a double layer of brown felt. Cut out head piece following pattern outline.

6. Pin ear pattern to a double layer of remaining brown felt. Cut out ears following outline of pattern. Fold each ear in half along fold line of pattern. With matching thread, stitch close to straight edge of each ear.

7. With edges matching and fold at the top, pin straight edge of each ear to right side of one head piece where shown on pattern.

8. Sew around outside edges of head with a 1/8-in. seam, catching the straight edge of each ear in stitching. Cut a 1-in.-long slit through one layer of felt only where shown on pattern.

9. Turn head inside out. Stuff head firmly. Hand-sew opening on back of head piece closed with matching thread.

10. Using black quilting thread or three strands of six-strand embroidery thread, stitch two French knots on front of moose's head where shown on pattern. See Fig. 1 for stitch illustration.

11. Using black thread or embroidery floss, hand-sew two beads to front of head where shown on pattern for eyes.

12. Pin antler pattern to tan felt. Cut out antlers following outline of pattern.

13. Fold jute string in half for hanger. Glue ends to center of antler piece.

14. Glue antler piece to back of moose's head.

15. Referring to photo for position, glue moose's head to front top edge of moose's body.

16. Hand-sew buttons to front of moose's body.

17. Wrap scarf around moose's neck and tie ends in an overhand knot.

18. Spot-glue scarf to moose as needed to hold.

Moose Ornament Patterns

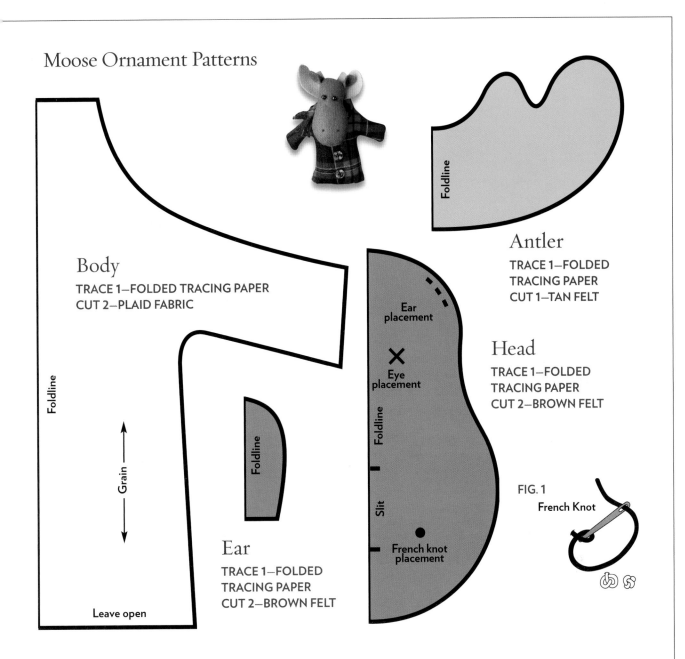

Body

TRACE 1—FOLDED TRACING PAPER
CUT 2—PLAID FABRIC

Foldline

Grain

Leave open

Ear

TRACE 1—FOLDED
TRACING PAPER
CUT 2—BROWN FELT

Foldline

Antler

TRACE 1—FOLDED
TRACING PAPER
CUT 1—TAN FELT

Foldline

Ear
placement

Eye
placement

Foldline

Slit

French knot
placement

Head

TRACE 1—FOLDED
TRACING PAPER
CUT 2—BROWN FELT

FIG. 1
French Knot

Fruit-Filled Wreath

CRAFT LEVEL: INTERMEDIATE

FINISHED SIZE: Wreath measures about 19 inches across.

This bountiful wreath bursts with colorful dried papayas, tangelos, quinces, kiwano and other fruits to create a beautiful arrangement for Christmastime. Feel free to experiment with different fruits or to substitute more of the apples or pears.

Taste of Home Craft Editor

MATERIALS:

Three each medium tangelos, lemons, limes, kiwano and star fruit

Three each medium apples, papayas, pears and quinces

Lemon, orange or pineapple juice

15-inch oasis floral foam wreath frame

30 to 50 floral greening pins

Sheet moss to cover wreath frame

20 to 25 pine boughs, arborvitae and lemon leaf stems (6 inches each)

Two medium pomegranates, halved

Five kumquats or key limes, halved

One bunch Concord or seedless red grapes

Five medium pinecones

30 to 50 wired floral wood picks

Food dehydrator

DIRECTIONS:

Preparation:

1. In a dehydrator, dehydrate the citrus fruits, kiwano and star fruit according to manufacturer's directions until almost crisp.

2. Cut the apples, papayas, pears and quinces into 1/8- to 1/4-in. slices. Soak in lemon, orange or pineapple juice for 10-20 minutes. Drain and pat dry. Dehydrate.

3. Store dried fruit in an airtight container.

Assembly:

1. Moisten sheet moss under running water; squeeze dry.

2. Using greening pins, attach moss to all sides of the wreath frame.

3. Cut pine boughs, arborvitae and lemon leaf stems at an angle.

4. Insert stems into sides and top of the foam frame.

5. Attach halved fresh fruits, grape clusters, pinecones and dehydrated fruits using floral wood picks or greening pins.

Lighted Wine Bottles

CRAFT LEVEL: QUICK & EASY

FINISHED SIZE: Size will vary depending on size of wine bottle used.

Decorating a basement bar or rec room can cost a fortune. But this fun idea turns wine bottles into inexpensive art!

Lewis Lehman ★ Muskego, Wisconsin

MATERIALS:

Empty wine bottles and corks (see Crafter's Notes)

Drill with 1/2-inch drill bit designed for drilling glass and 1/8-inch drill bit

Eye protection

Work gloves

Clear sealant (optional)

Single-plug strand of 20-25 white mini lights for each bottle

DIRECTIONS:

1. Wash the wine bottles inside and out with hot, soapy water, removing label and any glue residue. Let dry thoroughly.

2. Wearing eye protection and work gloves, slowly and carefully drill a hole 1 to 2 in. up from the bottom of each bottle using a 1/2-in. drill bit designed for glass.

3. Rinse bottles to remove any glass particles. Let dry.

4. Carefully feed the non-plug end of a light strand into the drilled hole of each bottle, leaving a length of cord extending from the openings.

5. If desired, apply clear sealant to drilled openings to hold and protect the cord.

6. Drill an 1/8-in. hole lengthwise through corks to make it easier to reinsert them.

7. Insert corks into bottle tops.

Crafter's Notes: If the glass has any defects, it may crack during drilling. So plan on having a few extra empty bottles on hand. Make a simple wooden V-shaped fixture to hold the bottle while drilling.

Holiday Luminarias

CRAFT LEVEL: QUICK & EASY

FINISHED SIZE: Each luminaria measures about 7 inches tall x 8 inches across

It's easy to light the way to your front door with these festive luminarias.

Taste of Home Craft Editor

MATERIALS (FOR EACH):

Clear glass quart jar

About 1 cup of sand

Long handled pastry brush

Tea light candle

About 1/2 cup red faceted plastic beads

13-inch length of artificial wired pine garland

DIRECTIONS:

1. Place sand in the bottom of each jar. Use a long-handled pastry brush to level the sand.

2. Place the tea light candle in center of sand.

3. Sprinkle beads around candle, using pastry brush to distribute them evenly.

4. Wrap garland around outside bottom of jar and twist ends together to hold.

Vintage St. Nick Mini Quilt

CRAFT LEVEL: BEGINNER

FINISHED SIZE: Santa wall hanging is 14 inches wide x 12 inches high.

Just in the nick of time! Here comes a weary St. Nicholas at the end of a busy night. He has one more stop to make, setting up this tree and placing the little sled under it. In the spirit of the season, I added a tiny lantern to this old-time appliqued wall hanging to help light the jolly old elf's way.

Marjorie Carano ★ West Orange, New Jersey

MATERIALS:

Patterns on pages 191 and 192

Tracing paper and pencil

44-inch-wide 100% cotton or cotton-blend fabrics—1/2 yard each of beige solid for background and dark green print for backing, tree and outer border; 1/8 yard or scraps each of red print for inner border and sled; dark gold print for Santa's sack; light gold print for star; burgundy print for Santa's robe; white solid for beard, mustache and lantern; flesh solid for face; and black solid for lantern

Scrap of off-white fleece for trim on robe

Scrap of beige suede or beige solid cotton fabric for hands

14-inch x 16-inch piece of muslin

14-inch x 16-inch piece of lightweight quilt batting

Black all-purpose thread and thread to match fabrics

Rotary cutter and mat

Quilter's marking pen or pencil

Quilter's ruler

Black six-strand embroidery floss

Embroidery needle

Yellow permanent marker

Two plastic curtain rings for hangers

Standard sewing supplies

DIRECTIONS:

Cutting:

1. Trace patterns onto tracing paper with pencil. With grain lines matching, pin patterns to right side of fabrics as indicated on patterns. Cut out each shape.

2. From beige solid, cut a 14- x 12-in. piece for appliqued background.

3. Place muslin piece on a flat surface. Center batting on top of muslin and beige solid background piece right side up on top of batting. Pin corners and edges as needed to hold.

4. Referring to photo at left as a guide, pin shapes to right side of beige background piece, overlapping the shapes as shown on patterns and leaving at least 1/2 in. around edges of background.

5. Use quilter's marking pen or pencil to draw runners under sled and to add inside design lines on Santa's robe freehand.

6. Using matching thread and narrow satin stitch, applique exposed edges of shapes to background in following order:

Face, robe, mustache, beard, robe trim pieces, white lantern piece, black lantern pieces, star, tree, Santa's sack and sled.

7. Using matching thread, satin-stitch over inside design lines of the robe, catching straight edge of Santa's left mitten in the stitching.

8. Using black thread and a narrow satin stitch, stitch runners below sled.

9. With design centered, trim appliqued background to an accurate 13-in.-wide x 11-in.-high piece.

10. From red print, cut two 3/4- x 11-in. strips and two 3/4- x 13-1/2-in. strips for inner border.

11. From dark green print, cut a 15- x 13-in. piece for backing. Also cut two 1- x 11-1/2-in. strips and two 1- x 14-1/2-in. strips for outer border.

Borders:

Do all stitching with right sides of fabrics together, edges even, matching thread and an accurate 1/4-in. seam allowance.

1. Sew an 11-in. red print border strip to opposite sides of the appliqued background. Open and press.

2. In the same way, sew a 13-1/2-in. red print border strip to the top and bottom of appliqued background.

3. Sew an 11-1/2-in. dark green print border strip to opposite sides of inner border. Open and press.

4. In the same way, sew a 14-1/2-in. green print border strip to top and bottom of inner border.

Finishing:

1. Thread embroidery needle with unseparated black floss. Insert needle into front of sled and then into Santa's left mitten and back again through the front of the sled to create a loop of floss. Knot floss on back. In the same way, attach a loop of floss between the top of lantern and Santa's other hand.

2. Separate six-strand embroidery floss and thread needle with three strands. Attach a length of floss to each side of Santa's sack where shown in photo. Tie ends together in the center of the sack. Trim ends of floss as desired.

3. Use yellow marker to add a small flame to lantern.

Assembly:

1. With right sides facing, center the green print backing piece on top of the appliqued background piece. Pin as needed to hold.

2. Sew around outside edges of outer border with a 1/4-in. seam, leaving an opening for turning along one straight edge.

3. Clip corners diagonally.

4. Turn right side out through opening. Turn raw edges of opening in. With matching thread, hand-sew opening closed.

5. Hand-sew a plastic curtain ring to the back of each upper corner of the wall hanging.

Mini Quilt Patterns
(continued on page 192)

TRACE 1 EACH PIECE—TRACING PAPER

CUT 1 EACH PIECE—COLOR OF FABRIC INDICATED ON PATTERN

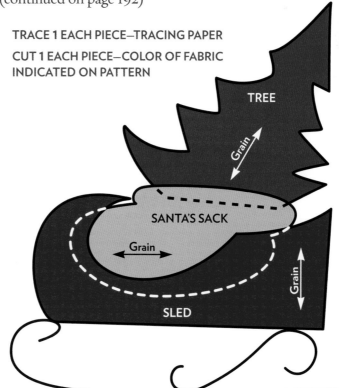

TREE

Grain

SANTA'S SACK

Grain

Grain

SLED

Mini Quilt Patterns
(continued)

TRACE 1 EACH PIECE—TRACING PAPER

CUT 1 EACH PIECE—COLOR OF FABRIC INDICATED ON PATTERN

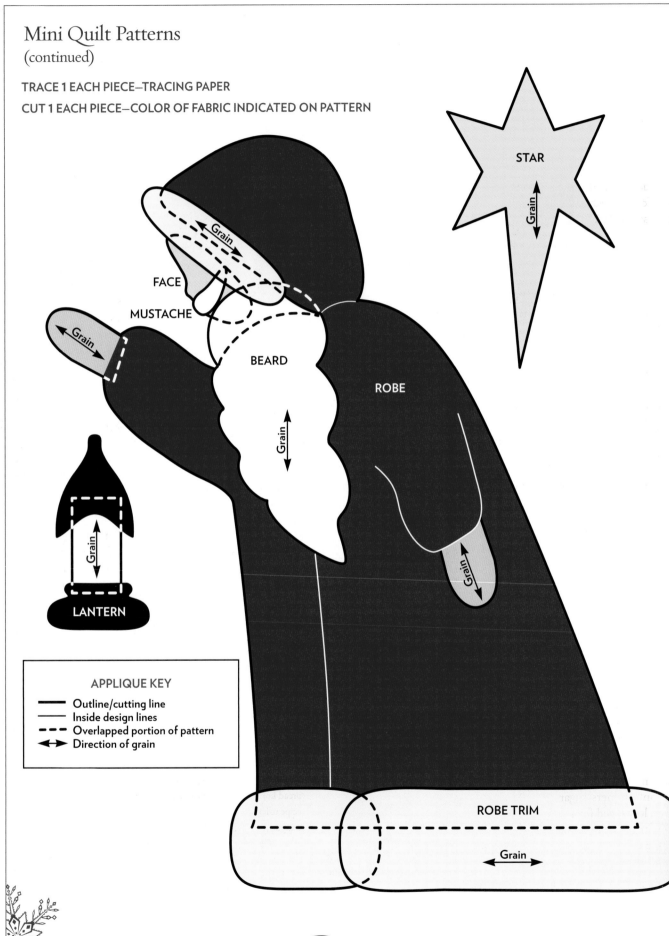

STAR

Grain

FACE

MUSTACHE

Grain

BEARD

ROBE

Grain

Grain

Grain

LANTERN

APPLIQUE KEY

— Outline/cutting line
— Inside design lines
--- Overlapped portion of pattern
◄—► Direction of grain

ROBE TRIM

Grain

Rustic Tabletop Trees

CRAFT LEVEL: BEGINNER

FINISHED SIZE: Size will vary depending on size of cones used.

For a rustic looking centerpiece, try your hand at these jute string and raffia Christmas trees. Tuck in a few branches from your evergreen, then add a little garland or some ornaments for a tabletop forest in a flash!

Taste of Home Craft Editor

MATERIALS:

Styrofoam cones in assorted sizes

Parchment paper

Straight pins

Three-ply natural jute string

Green raffia

Commercial stiffener

Large, medium and small 1/8-inch-thick natural wooden star cutouts

Gold metallic acrylic craft paint

Small flat paintbrush

Craft glue

DIRECTIONS:

1. Wrap each shape with parchment paper, using straight pins to secure the paper to the cone.

2. Soak jute string and raffia in stiffener as directed by manufacturer.

3. Wrap jute string around each cone in a spiral pattern. Add raffia in the same way. Continue to add jute and raffia alternately until desired look is achieved, making sure the bottom of the cone is level. Secure any loose ends with straight pins. Let dry.

4. Remove straight pins.

5. Carefully insert a table knife between the cone and the parchment paper to loosen.

6. Carefully remove parchment paper from the jute and raffia.

7. Paint all sides of each star gold. Let dry.

8. Glue a star to the top of each tree.

1. Wrap each cone with parchment paper, using straight pins to secure.

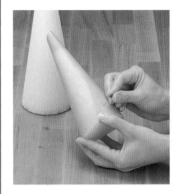

2. Wrap jute string and raffia around cone in a spiral pattern until desired look is achieved. Let dry.

3. With a table knife, remove parchment paper from the cone. Carefully separate the parchment paper from the jute and raffia.

Merry Mosaic Trees

CRAFT LEVEL: BEGINNER

FINISHED SIZE: Trees are about 10, 13, and 15 inches tall.

Instead of topping your table with evergreens, add a little more pizzazz by making these mirror mosaic trees! You can select tiles that work with your color scheme.

Taste of Home Craft Editor

MATERIALS:

1/2-inch and 1-inch x 1/4-inch rectangular mirror tiles in silver and different shades of blue (see Crafter's Note on page 195)

1/2-in. wide double-sided tape

9-, 12- and 15-in. tall Styrofoam tree shapes

Small silver ball ornaments for tree toppers

Craft glue

DIRECTIONS:

1. Wash mirror tiles in warm water and dishwashing detergent. Let dry.

2. Place a strip of double-sided tape around the bottom of one tree.

3. Adhere silver and blue 1/2-in. square mirror tiles onto the tape in a random order.

4. Place another strip of tape around the tree close to the top of the tiles you just attached. Adhere tiles onto the tape as before.

5. Continue to add tiles until all but about 1/2 in. at the top of the tree is covered with tiles.

6. Apply tape around the top of the tree as before.

7. Adhere 1- x 1/4-in. tiles vertically around the top of the tree.

8. Glue a silver ball ornament on top.

9. Repeat the process with the other two Styrofoam trees.

Crafter's Note: The number of tiles needed depends on the size of the trees used. To cover one 9-in., one 12-in. and one 15-in. tree, we used about 800 silver 1/2-in. tiles, 200 blue 1/2-in. tiles and 33 silver 1- x 1/4-in. tiles.

Dazzling Ornament Wreath

CRAFT LEVEL: QUICK & EASY

FINISHED SIZE: Wreath measures about 15 inches across.

With their vibrant colors and eye-catching shimmer, simple ball ornaments can create a stunning wreath for the holiday season. Choose a variety of wine and champagne hues as shown or try experimenting with different color combinations, such as turquoise, green and silver.

Taste of Home Craft Editor

MATERIALS:

12-inch wire wreath form and same-size circle of coordinating color stiff felt

Assorted colors and sizes of small ball ornaments with attached wires

Floral tape

Glue gun and glue stick

Craft wire

Wire cutters to cut wires

Ruler

Scissors

DIRECTIONS:

1. Hold a group of five to seven ornaments in your hand, positioning the ornaments in a tight bunch. Twist all of the wires together to hold the ornaments in place.

2. Repeat with more ornaments to create enough bunches to cover the front and sides of the wire wreath form.

3. Wrap the twisted wires on each bunch of ball ornaments with floral tape.

4. Wire bunches of ball ornaments to the wire wreath form, positioning them as close as possible to each other and covering the entire front and sides of wire wreath form.

5. Glue the circle of felt to the back of wreath to help conceal the wire ends. Let dry.

6. Use scissors to cut out the center of the felt circle, cutting as close as possible to the wire form.

7. Cut a 6-in. length of craft wire. Thread wire piece around the wire wreath form at the back of the wreath. Twist ends together to form a hanging loop.

Scrappy Yultide Stocking

CRAFT LEVEL: BEGINNER

FINISHED SIZE: Stocking measures about 10-1/2 inches wide x 17 inches long without hanging loop.

Piece together leftover fabric, and you can create this seasonal sock with time to spare. I like that it works with a variety of different prints or solids. The boa at the top easily adds flair.

Mary Ayres ✶ Boyce, Virginia

MATERIALS:

Pattern on page 197

Tracing paper and pencil

44-inch-wide 100% cotton or cotton-blend fabrics—1/8 yard each of four different coordinating red prints and three different coordinating green prints for piecing

Two 12-inch x 20-inch pieces of white solid 100% cotton or cotton-blend fabric for lining

All-purpose thread to match fabrics

Quilter's ruler (optional)

Rotary cutter and mat (optional)

7-inch length of 5/8-inch-wide green grosgrain ribbon for hanging loop

14-inch length of white feather boa or feather trim

Fabric glue (optional)

Standard sewing supplies

DIRECTIONS:

1. Either use photocopier to enlarge pattern 200% or draw a 1-in. grid on tracing paper and draw pattern as shown onto tracing paper with pencil.

2. Cut out pattern.

Cutting:

1. From two red print fabrics, cut two 3-in.-wide x 7-1/2-in.-long strips for A and C.

2. From two green print fabrics, cut two 3-in.-wide x 7-1/2-in.-long strips for B and D.

3. From one remaining red print fabric, cut two 3-in.-wide x 9-1/2-in.-long strips for E.

4. From each remaining red and green print fabric, cut two 3-in.-wide x 11-1/2-in.-long strips for F and G.

Piecing:

Do all piecing with matching thread, right sides of fabrics facing and an accurate 1/4-in. seam.

1. Referring to photo at left, sew strips A through G together for the front of the stocking.

2. Repeat to make a mirror image for the back of the stocking.

3. Press all seams on front down and all seams on back up.

Assembly:

1. Place a lining fabric piece on a flat surface with right side down.

2. Place a pieced fabric piece on top of lining with right side up. Pin or baste around edges to hold the layers together.

3. Repeat with remaining lining and pieced fabric pieces.

4. Place pieced fabric pieces together with right sides facing and with the strips and seams matching.

5. Pin pattern to layered fabrics with grain lines matching.

6. Sew sides and bottom of the stocking pieces together following outline of pattern. Remove pattern.

7. Trim away excess fabric, leaving a 1/4-in. seam allowance outside of stitching. Clip curves. Turn stocking right side out.

8. Turn 1/4-in. along top raw edge of stocking to wrong side for hem. With matching thread, stitch close to the first fold.

9. Pin narrow ends of ribbon piece together for hanging loop. Pin raw edges to inside of back seam of the stocking. Sew ends in place to secure hanging loop.

10. Glue or hand-sew feather boa or feather trim along top edge of stocking.

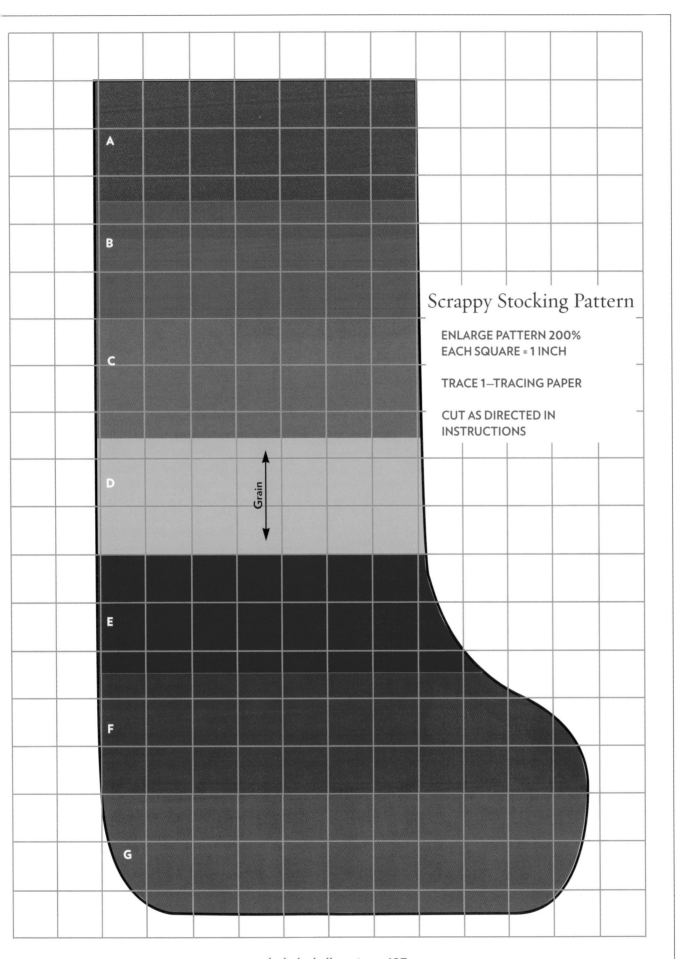

Scrappy Stocking Pattern

ENLARGE PATTERN 200%
EACH SQUARE = 1 INCH

TRACE 1–TRACING PAPER

CUT AS DIRECTED IN INSTRUCTIONS

Grain

A

B

C

D

E

F

G

Beaded Napkin Rings

CRAFT LEVEL: BEGINNER

FINISHED SIZE: Napkin ring measures about 5/8 inch wide x 2 inches across.

It's a cinch to create beautiful beaded napkin rings for your Christmastime table. Just follow these simple instructions.

    Nancy Valentine ★ Paupack, Pennsylvania

MATERIALS (FOR ONE NAPKIN RING):

Fifty-six 3mm round gold beads

Twenty-eight 6mm round gold beads

Fourteen 8mm green faceted beads

Fourteen 4mm red faceted beads

30-inch length of 24-gauge green craft wire

1 yard of clear monofilament nylon cord

Needle-nose pliers

Wire cutters

Two large-eye hand-sewing needles (optional)

DIRECTIONS:

Row 1:

1. Center one green faceted bead on the 30-in. length of green craft wire. Add a 6mm gold bead to the opposite ends of the wire.

2. Keeping beads centered, insert both ends of the wire through opposite sides of another green faceted bead. Pull the wire ends taut to draw the beads together, keeping the wire ends of equal length. See Fig. 1 below left.

3. Add another 6mm gold bead to each wire end.

4. Cross the ends of the wire through one 8mm green faceted bead the same as before.

5. Continue to add green and gold beads in the same way until the beaded strip is 14 center beads long. See Fig. 2 below.

6. Add two more 6mm gold beads (one on each wire end) and curl the beaded strip into a ring shape.

7. Thread one wire end through the first green bead and pull the ends tightly so all beads touch. See Fig. 3 on page 199.

8. Twist the wire ends together to secure.

9. Use wire cutters to clip excess wire.

10. Use needle-nose pliers to bend the twisted wire ends to the inside of the ring.

Row 2:

1. Thread one end of the clear nylon monofilament cord through any green bead of Row 1 and center the cord.

If desired, thread each end of the cord with a large-eye needle. Making sure the cord ends are of equal length, add 3mm gold round bead to each end.

2. Insert both cord ends through the opposite sides of a red bead. Pull the cords tightly to bring the beads close together.

3. Add another 3mm gold round bead to each end of the cord.

4. Insert the cord ends through the next green bead in Row 1 as before. Pull the cord ends tightly, making sure that the red bead comes to rest between two green beads in Row 1. See Fig. 4 on page 199.

5. Continue to add beads in this way until beginning of row is reached.

6. Thread one end of monofilament cord through the first green bead and pull ends tightly so all beads touch.

7. Knot the ends several times to secure.

8. Use wire cutters to clip excess.

9. Shape as needed to form a ring.

FIG. 1
Starting Row 1

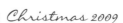

Side beads

Center beads

Side beads

FIG. 2
Completed Row 1

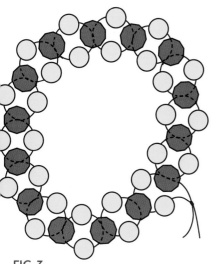

FIG. 3
Twist wire ends
to secure, forming the ring

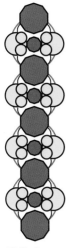

FIG. 4
Adding Row 2

Frosty the Place Card Holder

CRAFT LEVEL: BEGINNER

FINISHED SIZE: Lightbulb snowman place marker measures about 2-1/2 inches wide x 6-3/4 inches high without the place card.

Know why this snowy dining accent is glowing with cheer? A burned-out lightbulb was used to make it! Save those used bulbs and repurpose them at the holidays for delightful place card holders.

Nance Wilhite-Kueneman ★ Caldwell, Idaho

MATERIALS:

Standard lightbulb

Water container

Paper towels

Foam plate or palette

Acrylic craft paints—black, pink, orange and white

Iridescent glitter glaze (optional)

Paintbrushes—3/4-inch flat and small round

Black fine-line marker

15-inch length of black craft wire

Needle-nose pliers

Knit sock—red or desired color

24-inch length of heavy string

Glue gun and glue sticks

Scissors

Ruler

2-inch x 2-1/2-inch piece of white card stock

Medium black marker

DIRECTIONS:

Painting:

Keep paper towels and container of water handy to clean brushes. Place small amounts of paint as needed onto foam plate or palette. Add coats of paint as needed for complete coverage. Let paint dry after every application. Refer to photo at right as a guide while painting as directed in the instructions that follow.

1. Using flat brush and white, paint entire lightbulb.

2. If desired, apply glitter glaze to lightbulb following manufacturer's instructions. Let dry.

3. Use needle-nose pliers to carefully wrap one end of wire piece around socket end of lightbulb, securing the wire in place. Then shape the opposite end of wire in a flat spiral to hold place card.

4. From cuff end of sock, cut a 3-1/2-in.-wide circle-shaped band for snowman's hat and a 3/4-in.-wide circle-shaped band for scarf.

5. Glue 3/4-in.-wide band for scarf to bulb end of lightbulb so that lightbulb can stand upright.

6. Slip 3-1/2-in.-wide band over wire place card holder and socket end for hat.

7. Wrap heavy string around hat about 3/4 in. from cut end and tie ends in a small bow. Spot-glue bow to hat. Glue bottom edge of hat to lightbulb as needed to hold, leaving about 1-1/2 in. of lightbulb showing for snowman's face.

8. Dip end of paintbrush handle into black and dab on two small dots for eyes.

9. Using round brush and orange, paint a small circle for the nose.

10. Using round brush and pink, paint two larger circles for cheeks.

11. Use black fine-line marker to add a mouth.

12. Use medium black marker to write "For Santa" or a name on the card stock piece.

13. Slip card stock into spiraled wire.

Crochet Tabletop Tree Skirt

CRAFT LEVEL: INTERMEDIATE

FINISHED SIZE: Table tree skirt measures about 24 inches across.

Ringing in the holidays is easy with this old-fashioned crocheted tree skirt that is perfect for circling a table tree that I decorate for every holiday of the year. With this skirt, I can change the color of ribbons and bows to coordinate with seasonal celebrations—whether it's Christmas, Easter, Halloween or Thanksgiving!

Nanette Hankins ★ Old Fort, North Carolina

MATERIALS:

16-ounces of 4-ply (heavyweight) off-white cotton crochet thread

Size G/6 (4.25mm) crochet hook or size needed to obtain correct gauge

Yarn or tapestry needle

5-1/4 yards of 1/2-inch-wide red ribbon

Matching all-purpose thread

Hand-sewing needle

Small dressmaker snap

Measuring tape

Scissors

GAUGE: 4 dcs and 2 rows = 1 inch. Slight variations in gauge will change the finished size a bit.

DIRECTIONS:

Row 1: Ch 42, sc in second ch from hk and in each remaining ch across, turn: 41 scs.

Row 2: Ch 5 (counts as first tr and ch-1), sk next sc, tr in next sc, [ch 1, sk next sc, tr in next sc] across, turn: 20 ch-1 sps.

Row 3: Ch 1 for first sc, sc in each tr and in each ch-1 sp across, turn: 41 scs.

Row 4: Ch 3 (counts as first dc here and throughout), dc in next sc, [work 2 dcs in next sc, dc in next 2 scs] across, turn: 54 dcs.

Row 5: Ch 3, dc in next dc, * ch 2, sk next 2 dcs, [dc in next dc, work 2 dcs in next dc] twice; repeat from * across to last 4 dcs, ch 2, sk next 2 dcs, dc in last 2 dcs, turn: 9 ch-2 sps (eyelets) and 52 dcs.

Row 6: Ch 3, dc in next dc, * work 2 dcs in next ch-2 sp, [work 2 dcs in next dc, dc in next 2 dcs] twice; repeat from * across to last ch-2 sp, work 2 dcs in last ch-2 sp, dc in last 2 dcs, turn: 86 dcs.

Row 7: Ch 3, dc in next dc, ch 2, sk next 2 dcs, [dc in next 8 dcs, ch 2, sk 2 dcs] across to last 2 dcs, dc in last 2 dcs, turn: 9 ch-2 sps and 68 dcs.

Row 8: Ch 3, dc in next dc, * work 2 dcs in next ch-2 sp, [work 2 dcs in next dc, dc in next 3 dcs] twice; repeat from * across to last ch-2 sp, work 2 dcs in last ch-2 sp, dc in last 2 dcs, turn: 102 dcs.

Row 9: Ch 3, dc in next dc, ch 2, sk next 2 dcs, [dc in next 10 dcs, ch 2, sk 2 dcs] across to last 2 dcs, dc in last 2 dcs, turn: 9 ch-2 sps and 84 dcs.

Row 10: Ch 3, dc in next dc, * work 2 dcs in next ch-2 sp, [work 2 dcs in next dc, dc in next 4 dcs] twice; repeat from * across to last ch-2 sp, work 2 dcs in last ch-2 sp, dc in last 2 dcs, turn: 118 dcs.

Row 11: Ch 3, dc in next dc, ch 2, sk next 2 dcs, * [dc in next 5 dcs, work 2 dcs in next dc] twice, ch 2, sk 2 dcs; repeat from * across to last 2 dcs, dc in last 2 dcs, turn: 9 ch-2 sps and 116 dcs.

Row 12: Ch 3, dc in next dc, * work 2 dcs in next ch-2 sp, [dc in next 6 dcs, work 2 dcs in next dc] twice; repeat from * across to last ch-2 sp, work 2 dcs in last ch-2 sp, dc in last 2 dcs, turn: 150 dcs.

Row 13: Ch 3, dc in next dc, ch 2, sk next 2 dcs, * [dc in next 7 dcs, work 2 dcs in next st] twice, ch 2, sk 2 dcs; repeat from * across to last 2 dcs, dc in last 2 dcs, turn: 9 ch-2 sps and 148 dcs.

Row 14: Ch 3, dc in next dc, * work 2 dcs in next ch-2 sp, [dc in next 8 dcs, work 2 dcs in next dc] twice; repeat from * across to last ch-2 sp, work 2 dcs in last ch-2 sp, dc in last 2 dcs, turn: 182 dcs.

Row 15: Ch 3, dc in next dc, ch 2, sk next 2 dcs, * [dc in next 9 dcs, work 2 dcs in next st] twice, ch 2, sk 2 dcs; repeat from * across to last 2 dcs, dc in last 2 dcs, turn: 9 ch-2 sps and 180 dcs.

Row 16: Ch 3, dc in next dc, [work 2 dcs in next ch-2 sp, dc in each dc to next ch-2 sp] across to last 4 dcs, work 2 dcs in last ch-2 sp, dc in last 2 dcs, turn: 198 dcs.

Row 17: Ch 3, dc in next dc, ch 2, sk next 2 dcs, * [dc in next 10 dcs, work 2 dcs in next st] twice, ch 2, sk 2 dcs; repeat from * across to last 2 dcs, dc in last 2 dcs, turn: 9 ch-2 sps and 196 dcs.

Row 18: Ch 3, dc in next dc, * work 2 dcs in next ch-2 sp, [dc in next 11 dcs, work 2 dcs in next dc] twice; repeat from * across to last ch-2 sp, work 2 dcs in last ch-2 sp, dc in last 2 dcs, turn: 230 dcs.

Row 19: Ch 3, dc in next dc, ch 2, sk next 2 dcs, [dc in next 26 dcs, ch 2, sk next 2 dcs] across to last 2 dcs, dc in last 2 dcs, turn: 9 ch-2 sps and 212 dcs.

Row 20: Ch 3, dc in next dc, * work 2 dcs in next ch-2 sp, [dc in next 12 dcs, work 2 dcs in next dc] twice; repeat from * across to last ch-2 sp, work 2 dcs in last ch-2 sp, dc in last 2 dcs, turn: 246 dcs.

Row 21: Ch 3, dc in next dc, ch 2, sk next 2 dcs, [dc in next 28 dcs, ch 2, sk next 2 dcs] across to last 2 dcs, dc in last 2 dcs, turn: 9 ch-2 sps and 228 dcs.

Row 22: Ch 1, sl st in next dc, sl st in each of the chs of the ch-2 sp, sk next dc, * [work 5 dcs in next dc, sk next dc, sl st in next dc, sk next dc] seven times, sl st in each of the chs of the next ch-2 sp; repeat from * across to last 2 dcs, sl st in last 2 dcs. Fasten off.

Use yarn or tapestry needle to weave in all loose ends.

Finishing:

1. Cut eight 10-in. lengths of the red ribbon. Form each into a small bow as shown in Fig. 1 below and stitch across center with matching thread to hold.

2. Cut a 12-in. length of the red ribbon. Fold 1/2-in. twice to the wrong side and hand-tack a bow to the right side on one end. Hand-sew one half of the snap to the opposite end of the ribbon.

3. Place crocheted tree skirt right side up on a flat surface. Overlap straight edges of the tree skirt and align eyelets along straight edges. Starting at outer edge of the tree skirt and working toward the center, thread the snap end of the 12-in. length of a ribbon in and out of the overlapped eyelets. Fold excess to inside of tree skirt. Position the bow at the outer edge. Wrap snap-end of the ribbon to the inside of tree skirt. Sew other half of snap to the ribbon where needed to hold ribbon in place.

4. Cut seven 10-in. lengths of red ribbon. Starting at the outside edge, thread a length of ribbon through an inside row of eyelets. Wrap the end of the ribbon around the outside edge of the tree skirt. With matching thread, hand-tack the ribbon ends to the wrong side of the tree skirt at each end and sew a bow to the outer edge of each as shown in the photo at left.

Assembly:

1. To put tree skirt around tree, remove ribbon from the overlapped eyelets. Wrap tree skirt right side out around base of tree and overlap straight edges as before. Thread ribbon with bow through eyelets as before and snap to hold.

2. Cut a 36-in. length of red ribbon. Thread ribbon through eyelets at the center and tie ends in a bow.

ABBREVIATIONS	
ch(s)	chain(s)
dc(s)	double crochet(s)
hk	hook
sc(s)	single crochet(s)
sk	skip
sl st	slip stitch
sp(s)	space(s)
tr(s)	treble(s)
* [ ]	Instructions following asterisk or between brackets are repeated as directed.

FIG. 1

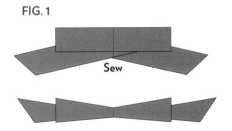

Sew

3. Roll the remaining length of the strip tightly between your thumb and forefinger, keeping strip's edges even. Slide pin/toothpick/tool out and glue end in place, or allow coil to open to desired size, then glue end in place. Strive for uniformity between like shapes.

4. When gluing quilled shapes together, use a straight pin or toothpick to place a drop of glue wherever the shapes touch.

Quilling Shapes (see Fig. 1 on page 203):

Marquise:

1. Roll a tight circle of paper around tool without gluing end.

2. Slip paper off the tool and let it expand to 1/4 in. Glue the end. Let dry.

3. Pinch the circle on opposite sides to points.

Closed V-scroll:

1. Crease strip at center.

2. Glue the paper strips together 1 in. from crease.

3. Roll remaining ends toward crease on outside of paper.

Making Snowflake:

1. Create the coils as directed in instructions that follow. Lengths given represent lengths of paper strips to tear, not lengths or widths of rolled shapes.

2. Tear twelve 6-in. lengths of paper. Form each into a marquise shape.

3. Tear six 3-in. lengths of paper. Form each into a closed V-scroll.

Assembly:

1. Place square of waxed paper on a flat surface.

2. Glue six marquise shapes together like spokes of a wheel as shown in Fig. 2. Let dry.

3. Glue a closed V-scroll between each marquise shape as shown in Fig. 3. Let dry.

4. Glue a marquise shape between the coils of each closed V-scroll as shown in Fig. 4. Let dry.

Quilled Snowflake

CRAFT LEVEL: INTERMEDIATE

FINISHED SIZE: Quilled snowflake ornament measures about 2-3/8 inches across without hanging loop.

Dreaming of a white Christmas? Then you'll want to whip up a flurry of these delicate quilled snowflakes to dangle in front of frosted windowpanes or tie on packages and the tree! Once you get the hang of rolling and shaping the paper strips, you'll want to curl up and make a snowy drift of these trims.

Cynthia Catto ★ Barre, Vermont

MATERIALS:

1/8-inch-wide white quilling paper or white construction paper cut into 1/8-inch-wide strips

Corsage pin, round toothpick or quilling tool for rolling paper

Ruler

Pencil

Straight pin or toothpick

Clear-drying craft glue

5-inch square of waxed paper

8-inch length of white thread for hanging loop

Scissors

DIRECTIONS:

Basic Quilling Instructions:

1. To roll paper coils, tear off a strip of 1/8-in.-wide quilling or construction paper to the length specified in the instructions.

2. Moisten one end of the strip slightly and press it onto the center of the corsage pin or toothpick. If using a quilling tool, place the paper end in the crevice.

Finishing:

1. Carefully remove snowflake ornament from waxed paper.

2. Insert one end of thread through center of one outer marquise shape. Tie ends of thread together in an overhand knot for hanger.

FIG. 1 Quilling shapes

Marquise

Closed V-scroll

FIG. 2 Gluing six marquise shapes together for center

FIG. 3 Adding closed V-scrolls

FIG. 4 Adding remaining marquise shapes

Very Merry View

Get a fresh outlook on Christmas cards with this wonderful window treatment. Drape a holly garland or other greenery over a curtain rod. Next, cut different lengths of narrow, red satin ribbon and tie one end of each piece to the curtain rod behind the garland. Glue or staple a Christmas card to the bottom end of each ribbon.

1. Zigzag or overcast edges of two 4- x 4-1/2-in. pieces of Aida cloth to prevent fraying. Fold each in half lengthwise and then in half crosswise to determine center and mark this point.

2. Draw lines across charts connecting arrows to find center of charts. Begin stitching each at this point so designs will be centered.

3. Working with 18-in. lengths of six-strand floss, separate strands and use two strands for cross-stitching and one strand for backstitching. Use four strands of blending filament for cross-stitching. See Fig. 1 below for stitch illustrations.

4. Each square on the chart is equal to one stitch worked over a set of fabric threads.

Musical Cherubs

CRAFT LEVEL: BEGINNER

FINISHED SIZE: Each tree trim is 3-1/2 inches wide x 3 inches high. The design area of each is 54 stitches wide x 43 stitches high.

Creating a happy harmonious atmosphere is what these musically inclined Christmas angels are designed to do—as they're enhancing branches, prettily wrapped presents and more! These cross-stitch cherubs are almost effortless to make. They work up quickly and you can choose any hues you like.

Penny Duff ★ Kennebunk, Maine

MATERIALS (FOR BOTH):

Charts on pages 204 and 205

Four 4-inch x 4-1/2-inch pieces of white 18-count Aida cloth

DMC six-strand embroidery floss in colors listed on color key

Kreinik metallic blending filament in color listed on color key

Small amount of polyester stuffing

Size 26 tapestry needle

White all-purpose thread

Standard sewing supplies

CROSS-STITCHED ANGELS	
COLOR KEY	**DMC**
☐ Ecru	
△ Light Pink	224
■ Red	304
◉ Dark Green	501
▣ Medium Green	502
▦ Light Tan	543
☒ Gold	680
● Dark Red	815
◎ Dark Blue	930
◹ Peach	951
BACKSTITCHING	
▬ Dark Green	501
▬ Medium Green	502
▬ Dark Red	815
▬ Dark Brown	938
BLENDING FILAMENT ..Kreinik	
☒ Gold Metallic	002

BELL ANGEL CHART

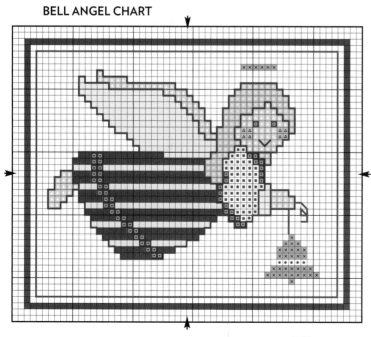

FIG. 1

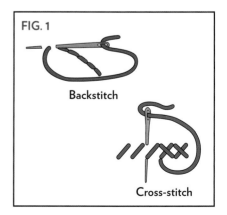

Backstitch

Cross-stitch

5. Use the colors indicated on the color key to complete cross-stitching, then backstitching.

6. Do not knot floss on back of work. Instead, leave a short tail of floss on back of work and hold it in place while working the first few stitches over it. To end a strand, run needle under a few neighboring stitches in back before cutting floss close to work.

7. When stitching is completed, and only if necessary, wash gently in lukewarm water. Press right side down on terry towel to dry.

Finishing:

1. Pin one unstitched piece of Aida cloth to the back of one stitched piece with edges matching.

2. Machine-stitch the two layers together, stitching one square outside border of stitched design and leaving a small opening for stuffing.

3. Stuff lightly and stitch the opening closed.

TRUMPET ANGEL CHART

4. Repeat for the other design.

5. Trim outside edges of each design five squares from stitching.

6. To fringe edges, remove threads from Aida cloth to one square from stitching.

7. Sew a 7-in. length of gold blending filament to back at top corners of each trim to make a hanging loop.

Sparkle Stuffed Santa

CRAFT LEVEL: BEGINNER

FINISHED SIZE: Santa is about 8-1/2 inches tall x 5 inches wide.

Invite St. Nick to stay awhile with this cute creation.

Irene Wegener ★ Corning, New York

MATERIALS:

Patterns on page 206

Tracing paper and pencil

Scissors

12-inch square of 100% cotton red print flannel

Red all-purpose thread

4-inch x 5-inch piece of unbleached muslin for face

2 cups of plastic doll pellets

Polyester stuffing

Purchased wood pieces—1/4-inch wooden domed furniture plug for nose and 1-inch-wide x 1/4-inch-thick star

9-inch length of white curly doll hair or textured bulky-weight white craft yarn for hair

3 yards of white sparkle yarn for beard (see Crafter's Note on page 206)

Water container

Paper towels

Palette or foam plate

Acrylic craft paints—black, dusty rose, gold and white

Toothpick

Small flat paintbrush

Powdered cosmetic blush

Cotton swab

Ultra-fine black permanent marker

Craft glue

Low-temperature glue gun and glue sticks

1/4-inch gold jingle bell

1-inch x 10-inch strip of white 100% cotton quilt batting or white felt for hat trim

2-inch-long artificial wired pine sprig with tiny holly berries for hat decoration

Three 5-inch-long stems of artificial wired pine garland

3-inch-long sprig of artificial frosted red berries

Standard sewing supplies

DIRECTIONS:

1. Trace enlarged body and face patterns on page 206 separately onto tracing paper.

2. Fold the 12-in. square of red print flannel in half with right sides together to make a 6- x 12-in. piece.

3. Pin body pattern to folded fabric with grain lines matching.

4. Sew around entire body pattern on traced lines. For opening, cut through only one layer of flannel on the dashed cutting line of pattern. Remove pattern.

5. Cut out the body, leaving a 1/4-in. seam allowance outside the stitching. Clip curves and trim corners diagonally. Turn body right side out.

6. Fill bottom of body with doll pellets.

7. Stuff body, leaving the top 2-1/2 in. unstuffed so top of hat can fold over.

8. Whipstitch opening closed. See Fig. 1 below for stitch illustration.

9. Hand-sew jingle bell to tip of hat.

10. Fold the 4- x 5-in. piece of muslin in half to make a 4- x 2-1/2-in. piece.

11. Pin the face pattern to folded fabric and cut out face, cutting through both layers on traced lines.

12. Apply a thin bead of tacky glue around the edge of one muslin face piece and place the second face piece on top with right side up and edges matching. Let dry.

13. Referring to pattern for position, use craft glue to attach muslin face to body piece, covering stitched opening on body. Let dry.

14. Apply a thin bead of tacky glue around the edge of the face. Place the 9-in. length of textured white yarn or curly doll hair over the glue, covering the edges of the muslin. Overlap the ends of the yarn or hair at the bottom of the face and trim excess. Let dry.

Painting:

Keep paper towels and container of water handy to clean brushes. Place small amounts of paint as needed onto foam plate or palette. Let paint dry after every application. Refer to photo as a guide while painting as directed in the instructions that follow.

1. Dip the end of the paintbrush handle into black and dab two dots onto face for eyes.

2. Use black permanent marker to add the eyebrows.

3. Dip toothpick into white and dab a tiny dot in each painted eye.

4. Paint the wooden screw-hole button dusty rose for nose.

5. Use glue gun to attach nose below the eyes.

6. Use cotton swab and a circular motion to apply powdered cosmetic blush to each cheek.

7. Paint the wooden star gold.

8. Use black marker to add a dashed border around the front edge of star.

Beard:

1. Cut one 5-in. piece of sparkle yarn and set aside. Wrap remaining yarn around your fingers. Carefully remove wrapped yarn from your fingers.

2. Tie the 5-in. piece across the center of wrapped yarn.

3. Cut the loops or yarn open.

4. Spread and shape the cut ends into a half circle for the beard.

5. Glue beard below nose.

Finishing:

1. Apply a bead of craft glue along one side of the strip of quilt batting or felt for hat trim.

2. Glue strip around the head above the face, covering the top edge of hair and overlapping the ends of the strip in back. Trim excess. Let dry.

3. Shape the 2-in.-long pine sprig into a circle for a wreath. Use glue gun to attach the wreath to front of the white hat trim. Let dry.

4. Lay the remaining three pine sprigs next to one another on a flat surface, staggering them so the ends are uneven. Use glue gun to hold the center of the sprigs together. Let dry.

5. Use glue gun to attach the pine sprigs to side of Santa's body. Let dry.

6. In same way, glue the frosted red berry sprig and wooden star to the pine sprigs. Let dry.

7. Tuck bottom corners of Santa's body in slightly to make a flatter bottom and stand Santa upright.

Crafter's Note: The white sparkle yarn (item #196457) is available from Factory Direct Craft Supply, 1-800-252-5223.

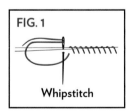

FIG. 1

Whipstitch

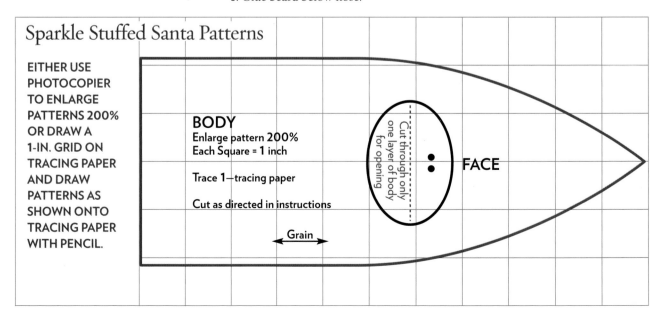

Sparkle Stuffed Santa Patterns

EITHER USE PHOTOCOPIER TO ENLARGE PATTERNS 200% OR DRAW A 1-IN. GRID ON TRACING PAPER AND DRAW PATTERNS AS SHOWN ONTO TRACING PAPER WITH PENCIL.

BODY
Enlarge pattern 200%
Each Square = 1 inch

Trace 1—tracing paper

Cut as directed in instructions

Grain

Cut through only one layer of body for opening

FACE

Happy Holidays

Gifts
TO GIVE

All Wrapped Up Card

CRAFT LEVEL: QUICK & EASY

FINISHED SIZE: Card measures 5-1/2 inches wide x 4-1/4 inches high.

Even a beginner can quickly assemble this surprisingly simple design. Save time by stamping an entire sheet of white card stock with your background image, then cutting it to make the front piece for multiple cards.

Jen Olski ★ Milwaukee, Wisconsin

MATERIALS:

8-1/2-inch x 5-1/2-inch red card stock rectangle

3-3/4-inch x 5-inch green card stock rectangle

3-1/2-inch x 4-1/4-inch white card stock rectangle

"Merry Christmas" background stamp (DeNami Design background stamp shown)

Red dye-based ink pad

Green dye-based ink pad

Three 6-inch lengths of coordinating 1/2-inch-wide ribbon

Double-sided tape or paper glue

Glue dots

DIRECTIONS:

1. Place the background stamp on table with the image side up.

2. Randomly ink background stamp with red ink pad, leaving uninked areas.

3. Using green ink pad, fill in the uninked areas of background stamp.

4. Lift background stamp and gently breathe on image side to moisten ink. Stamp image on the white card stock.

5. Adhere two lengths of ribbon to front of card, crossing the pieces. Adhere ends to back.

6. Center and adhere the stamped white card stock to the green card stock.

7. Fold red card stock rectangle in half crosswise for card.

8. With fold at the top, center and adhere green card stock to front of card.

9. Tie remaining ribbon in a bow. Trim ends. Adhere bow to front of card where the two ribbon pieces intersect.

Crafter's Note: If you don't have a large background stamp, simply use individual word or small image stamps to fill in your white card stock. Think of it as creating your own gift wrap. Instead of using two separate ink pads on your stamp, use a multicolored pad for a similar effect.

Angelic Wishes Card

CRAFT LEVEL: QUICK & EASY

FINISHED SIZE: Card measures 4-1/4 inches wide x 5-1/2 inches high.

Want to add special touches to cards? Embellish the mailing envelope with a stamped image or greeting that coordinates with the card. The envelope will stand out in a pile of mail, and your recipient will know there's something extra special inside.

Jen Olski ★ Milwaukee, Wisconsin

MATERIALS:

8-1/2-inch x 5-1/2-inch navy blue card stock rectangle

2-1/2-inch x 3-inch rectangle of white watercolor paper

2 feet of silver cording

Two blue beads

Angel stamp to fit size of white paper (Stampin' Up! stamp shown)

Star background stamp or star wheel with handle and navy blue ink cartridge (Stampin' Up! stamp shown)

Navy blue dye-based ink pad

Watercolor brush or blender pen

Glitter

Glue pen

Scissors

Double-sided tape or paper glue

DIRECTIONS:

1. Fold navy blue card stock rectangle in half crosswise for card.

2. Using either a stamp wheel with handle and navy ink cartridge or a background stamp with navy stamp pad, stamp star background pattern on front of card.

3. Use glue pen either to highlight portions of the stamped star background image or to randomly dot background. Sprinkle glitter on the background and tap off excess. Let dry.

4. With navy ink, stamp angel on white watercolor paper.

5. Using a moistened watercolor brush or a blender pen, trace outline of stamped angel, carefully drawing out

ink to create shadows and highlights or coloring in select areas of the image. Let dry.

6. String the beads on the silver cord. Wrap the cord twice around the front half of the folded navy card stock, positioning beads on the front of card. Secure ends of cord on the front of card so the stamped watercolor paper will cover the ends.

7. Using the blade of a scissors, distress the edges of the watercolor paper to create a frayed effect.

8. With fold of card on the left, adhere watercolor paper to front of card, covering the ends of cord.

Crafter's Note: It's important to use a dye-based ink pad for the water-coloring technique. A permanent ink or pigment ink will not create the same effect. Any outlined image stamp will work beautifully with this watercolor technique. Just cut your paper to fit the size. For variety and visual appeal, set your main image off center on the front of the card.

Oh, Christmas Tree! Card

CRAFT LEVEL: QUICK & EASY

FINISHED SIZE: Card measures 4-1/4 inches wide x 5-1/2 inches high.

What a way to make merry during the holiday season—and to save money at the same time! Use your creativity to make your own holiday cards. This one is a great way to use up scraps of paper, card stock, ribbon and cording.

Jen Olski ★ Milwaukee, Wisconsin

MATERIALS:

8-1/2-inch x 5-1/2-inch white card stock rectangle

4-1/4-inch x 4-1/4-inch x 3-inch green card stock triangle

1/2-inch x 1-inch brown card stock rectangle

1 foot of gold cording

Buttons of assorted colors

Seed beads of assorted colors

4-inch length of 1/4-inch-wide ribbon

"Happy Holidays" stamp and small star stamp (Stampin' Up! stamps shown)

Red dye-based ink pad

Yellow dye-based ink pad

Double-sided tape or paper glue

Glue dots

DIRECTIONS:

1. Fold white card stock rectangle in half crosswise for card.

2. With fold at the left, stamp "Happy Holidays" in red ink in upper right corner of the front of the card.

3. With yellow ink, stamp stars around words.

4. For the Christmas tree, fold green triangle in half widthwise. Crumple the green triangle slightly. Unfold and set aside.

5. Thread beads on cord. Adhere one end of cord to top back of triangle. Wrap around to front, sliding beads to the front. Continue wrapping cord and spacing beads in the same way. Adhere other end of cord to bottom back of tree. Trim off excess cord.

6. Wrap ribbon around brown rectangle and knot. Trim ends.

7. Adhere brown rectangle to bottom back of tree.

8. Adhere the tree to front of the card, overlapping the stamped image if necessary.

9. Adhere buttons to tree.

Crafter's Note: Use leftover beads and buttons of different shapes and sizes for a more eclectic look. Get creative with color! Your Christmas tree can be any hue, and unusual background papers will create a whimsical look for a holiday tree.

Little Soft Snowman

CRAFT LEVEL: BEGINNER

FINISHED SIZE: Snowman measures about 3-1/2 inches wide x 6-1/2 inches high.

This cute, little snowman makes an adorable tabletop decoration during the winter months. I like to use different fabrics for the hat and scarf so that each snowman is unique.

Bette Veinot ★ Bridgewater, Nova Scotia

MATERIALS:

Pattern on page 211

Tracing paper and pencil

Two 5-inch x 7-inch pieces of white knit (sweatshirt) fabric

4-inch-wide x 5-1/2-inch-high piece of blue knit ribbing for stocking cap

All-purpose thread—blue and white

1-inch-wide x 12-inch-long piece of blue print Polarfleece for scarf

1/2 cup of plastic doll pellets

Polyester stuffing

Acrylic craft paints—black, gold metallic and orange

Small flat paintbrush

Cosmetic blush and cotton swab

Textured snow medium

Iridescent glitter

Glue gun and glue sticks

Standard sewing supplies

DIRECTIONS:

Snowman:

1. Trace snowman pattern on page 211 onto tracing paper with pencil.

2. Pin the white knit fabric pieces together with right sides facing and edges matching. With grain lines matching, pin snowman pattern to the white knit fabric.

3. Sew around the outside edge of snowman pattern with a short straight stitch, leaving top open for turning where shown on pattern.

4. Cut snowman out, cutting 1/8 in. outside stitching. Clip curves. Turn snowman right side out.

5. Pour doll pellets into snowman. Stuff snowman firmly. Turn raw edges of opening in and hand-sew opening closed with matching thread.

Painting:

Refer to pattern and photo at left as a guide while painting as directed in the instructions that follow.

1. Dip handle end of paintbrush into black and dab two small dots onto snowman's head for the eyes. In the same way, add five tiny dots for the mouth.

2. Use small flat brush and orange paint to add a carrot-shaped nose.

3. Apply cosmetic blush to a cotton swab. With a circular motion, add snowman's cheeks.

4. Referring to photo for placement, paint a small gold metallic heart on the front of snowman as follows: Use handle end of paintbrush to dab on two small dots of gold metallic paint as shown in Fig. 1 on page 211. While the paint is still wet, use flat brush to pull the paint down from each dot to form point of heart.

Stocking Cap:

1. Fold blue knit ribbing piece in half crosswise to make a 5-1/2-in.-high x 2-in.-wide piece. Sew the long edges together with a narrow seam to make a tube. Turn tube right side out.

2. Roll up one raw edge of the blue knit tube twice to form cuff of stocking cap.

3. Place stocking cap on the snowman's head with seam in back and pull the cap down around sides of the snowman's head as shown in photo.

4. Hand-gather top of stocking cap together and tie a length of blue thread about 3/4 in. from top to hold.

5. Spot-glue stocking cap in place as needed to hold.

Scarf:

1. Wrap the scarf around the snowman's neck and tie ends in an overhand knot.

2. Spot-glue ends of the scarf to front of the snowman.

Finishing:

1. Apply textured snow to top and cuff of hat. While still wet, sprinkle the snow with iridescent glitter. Shake off the excess glitter. Let dry.

2. Spread a bit of glue on ends of the scarf. While glue is still wet, sprinkle the glue with iridescent glitter. Shake off excess the glitter. Let dry.

Make a Snowman Family

Want a snowman family to accent your home? Use a photocopier to enlarge the snowman pattern at top right to 170% and 225% to make snowmen 9- and 12-in.- high. Add twig arms and group the trio together to complete the scene.

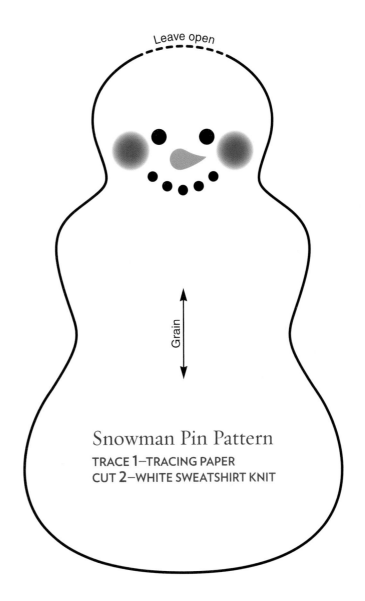

Leave open

Snowman Pin Pattern
TRACE 1–TRACING PAPER
CUT 2–WHITE SWEATSHIRT KNIT

Grain

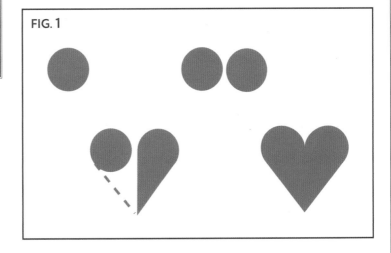

FIG. 1

Santa Tag Card

CRAFT LEVEL: BEGINNER

FINISHED SIZE: Card measures 4-1/4 inches across x 5-1/2 inches high.

This is a great craft to do ahead before the rush of the Christmas season. A "happy holidays" stamp makes quick work of the background, but you can use any seasonal greeting you happen to have on hand. If you're pressed for time and don't wish to create the Santa tag, glue a wallet-size photo of your family on the front.

Nina Gutierrez ★ Greendale, Wisconsin

MATERIALS:

Card stock—8-1/2-inch x 5-1/2-inch piece and 2-1/2-inch x 4-1/4-inch piece of green, 4-inch x 5-1/4-inch piece of red, 2-inch x 2-1/4-inch piece of white

Stamps—Happy Holidays and Santa (Stampin' Up Happy Holidays stamp Holiday Woodcuts stamps shown)

Black stamp pad

White pigment ink pad

Versa Mark Pad

Yellow and red markers

Black embossing powder

Heat gun

Double-sided tape

Pop dots

White Liquid Applique

White diamond glitter

1/4-inch round hole punch

Several 8-inch lengths of assorted novelty yarns

Scissors

DIRECTIONS:

1. Fold 8-1/2-in. x 5-1/2-in. piece of white card stock in half crosswise.

2. Use the Happy Holidays stamp and black, white and Versa Mark Pad to randomly stamp front of 4-in. x 5-1/4-in. red card stock piece. Let dry.

3. Place folded card on a flat surface with fold at the left. Glue stamped red card stock piece right side up to center front of green card.

4. Stamp white card stock piece with Santa stamp using the Versa Mark Pad. Sprinkle the stamped piece with black embossing powder. Shake off the excess powder and set with heat gun.

5. Color Santa's suit and hat with red marker and stars with yellow marker.

6. Apply the Liquid Applique to Santa's beard, mustache and hat trim. Sprinkle areas with diamond glitter and heat with heat gun until bubbles form. Let cool.

7. Cut opposite corners off of one short edge of the 2-1/2-in. x 4-1/4-in. piece of the green card stock, leaving a 3- x 2-1/2-in. rectangular-shaped tag.

8. Glue the stamped Santa piece to the rectangular space on green tag as shown in photo at left.

9. Tear a narrow strip off bottom edge of green piece to form an irregular edge.

10. Use hole punch to punch a hole through the top of the green tag.

11. Working with all yarn pieces as one, fold yarn in half. Thread fold of yarn through hole in tag and yarn ends through loop. Pull ends to tighten yarn on tag. Trim yarn ends as desired.

12. Use pop-dots to adhere tag to front of card.

DIRECTIONS:

Cast on 99 sts.

Row 1: K 1, p 1, k across row to last 2 sts, p 1, k 1: 99 sts.

Row 2: K 1, p 1, k 1, p across row to last 3 sts, k 1, p 1, k 1: 99 sts.

Repeat Rows 1 and 2 until about 10 yds. of yarn remain, attaching new skeins of yarn at the ends of the rows and ending with Row 1.

Next Row: K 1, p 1, k 1, p 1, p 1 and attach a small safety pin to last st worked, * p 5, p 1 and attach a small safety pin to last st worked; repeat from * across to last four sts, p 1, k 1, p 1, k 1: 99 sts. Each st with a safety pin will be dropped when binding off.

Binding Off:

Working in established pattern, bind off first 4 sts, draw yarn end through single st on working needle, drop marked st, * leaving about 1/2 in. of yarn over the dropped st, bind off next 5 sts and draw yarn end through single st on working needle, drop marked st; repeat from * across to last marked st, drop marked st, leaving about 1/2 in. of yarn over the dropped st, bind off remaining sts in pattern. Fasten off.

Finishing:

1. Use yarn or tapestry needle to weave in all loose ends.

2. Remove each small safety pin and drop each marked st down the entire length of the shawl to create pattern.

Knitted Wrap

CRAFT LEVEL: BEGINNER

FINISHED SIZE: Shawl is about 28 inches wide x 70 inches long.

As an added layer of warmth on a cold winter's night or a light covering for a summer's night stroll, this knit shawl is great for any season! The casually chic wrap is fashioned of silky-soft microspun sport-weight acrylic yarn. The lovely ladder design is such a simple pattern to stitch up...all it takes are dropped stitches.

Taste of Home Craft Editor

MATERIALS:

Six 2.5-ounce balls sport-weight yarn in color of choice (Lion Brand Microspun #144 Lilac yarn shown)

Size 7 (4.5mm) knitting needles or size needed to obtain correct gauge

16 small safety pins

Yarn or tapestry needle

Scissors

GAUGE: 20 sts and 28 rows = 4 inches in St st (k on RS, p on WS). Slight variation in gauge will change the finished size a bit.

ABBREVIATIONS	
k	knit
p	purl
RS	right side
st(s)	stitch(es)
WS	wrong side
*	Instructions following asterisk are repeated as directed.

Foam Christmas Package Tags

CRAFT LEVEL: BEGINNER

FINISHED SIZE: Tree gift tag measures about 3-3/4 inches across x 5-1/4 inches high. Santa gift tag measures about 3-3/4 inches wide x 5-1/2 inches high.

Personalize your gifts with fun and easy-to-make package tags. It takes only a few minutes to make one. You can even use it as an art craft with your children.

Sandy Rollinger ★ Apollo, Pennsylvania

MATERIALS:

Patterns on page 215

Tracing paper and pencil

Craft foam—one sheet each or scraps of blue, flesh, green, purple, red, yellow and white

Dimensional paint—blue, gold metallic, green and white

Permanent markers—black and red

Two 8-inch lengths of green satin ribbon

1/4-inch round hole punch

Craft glue

Scissors

DIRECTIONS:

Tree Gift Tag:

1. Trace patterns on page 215 onto tracing paper.

2. Trace shapes onto craft foam as directed on patterns.

3. Cut out each shape following outlines of patterns.

4. Use black marker to write "TO:" and "FROM:" and names on the front of the white tree stand piece.

5. Referring to photo above for position, glue star to top of tree and tree stand to bottom of tree. Let dry.

6. Use green dimensional paint to add zigzag pattern to front of tree. Let dry.

7. Use white dimensional paint to add small dots to front of tree. Let dry.

8. Punch round holes from blue, purple and red craft foam and glue them randomly to front of tree. Let dry.

9. Fold a length of ribbon in half to form a loop and glue ends to back of top of tree. Let dry.

Santa Gift Tag:

1. Trace patterns on page 215 onto tracing paper.

2. Trace shapes onto craft foam as directed on patterns.

3. Cut out each shape following outlines of patterns.

4. Use white dimensional paint to add a random swirl pattern to front of all white pieces. Let dry.

5. Use gold dimensional paint to outline blue rectangle, red piece and all white pieces except mustache. Let dry.

6. Use black marker to write "TO:" and "FROM:" and names on the front of the blue rectangle.

7. Use green dimensional paint to outline green mitten pieces. Let dry.

8. Referring to photo at left and pattern for position, glue white beard/hat trim piece centered on red piece and hat pom-pom to top of red piece.

9. Glue blue rectangle below beard.

10. Glue face piece to center of white beard piece and mustache to face.

11. Glue white coat trim pieces at an angle to corners of blue piece.

12. Glue green mittens to white coat trim pieces. Let dry.

13. Use white dimensional paint to add eyebrows and blue dimensional paint to add two small dots for eyes. Let dry.

14. Use red marker to add mouth.

15. Fold a length of green ribbon in half to form a loop and glue ends to back of top of Santa. Let dry.

Gift Tag Patterns

KEY	
———	Cutting/stitching line
- - - -	Overlapped portion of pattern

Santa Gift Tag

TRACE 1—TRACING PAPER CUT 1 EACH PIECE— COLOR OF CRAFT FOAM SHOWN ON PATTERN PIECES

Tree Gift Tag

TRACE 1—TRACING PAPER CUT 1 EACH PIECE— COLOR OF CRAFT FOAM SHOWN ON PATTERN PIECES

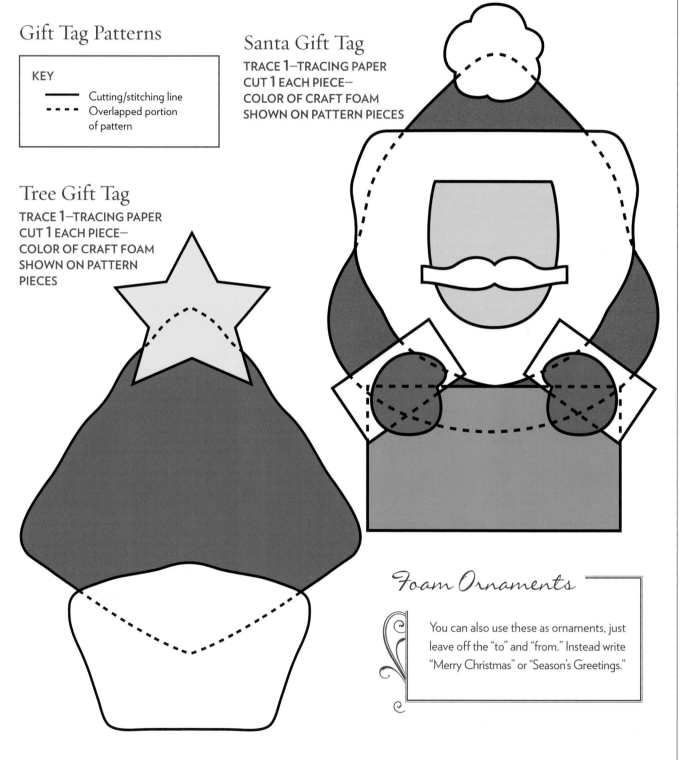

Foam Ornaments

You can also use these as ornaments, just leave off the "to" and "from." Instead write "Merry Christmas" or "Season's Greetings."

GAUGE: Working in St st, 16 sts and 24 rows = 4 inches.

STITCHES USED/GENERAL INSTRUCTIONS:

St st = stockinette stitch:

Row 1 (RS): K across row.

Row 2 (WS): P across row.

Repeat rows 1 and 2 as directed, changing colors as instructed and leaving a 10-in. tail of yarn at the end of each color change to use later to sew seam of cap.

DIRECTIONS:

Stocking Cap:

1. Make a provisional cast-on by using crochet hook and white yarn to make 91 chains (loop on hook does not count as a chain).

2. Cut yarn and pull a tail of yarn through the final loop on hook.

3. With green yarn and knitting needle, pick up 90 sts in back loop only of each chain, starting with back loop of first chain made and leaving last chain made unused.

4. Work in St st for 6-1/2 in., ending with a WS row. Fasten off, leaving a 15-in. tail of yarn.

5. Change to white yarn and work in St st for 2 in., ending with a RS row. Fasten off. Fold cast-on edge to WS for hem, bringing provisional cast-on row to needle.

6. Change to green yarn. Pull back loop of final chain of cast-on to ravel cast-on chain, leaving a green loop free. Pick up and purl free loop and first loop of row on needle as one. Continue in this way across row, forming the hem.

7. Work in St st for 1-1/2 in., ending with a WS row. Fasten off.

8. In same way, work a band of white yarn, green yarn and then white yarn. Fasten off.

9. Change to green yarn. * K 1, k 2 tog; repeat from * across row. Work in St st for 1-1/2 in., ending with a WS row. Fasten off.

10. Repeat step 9, working a band of white yarn, green yarn, white yarn and then green yarn. Fasten off.

11. Change to white yarn. Work in St st for 2 in.

Striped Stocking Cap

CRAFT LEVEL: BEGINNER

FINISHED SIZE: Stocking cap is about 27 inches long with pom-pom.

Folks of all ages will appreciate this head warmer! The cap is nice and stretchy, which makes it suitable for almost any size. And, thanks to the seam that runs up the back, I've taken it in to make the cap smaller, too. The design is especially nice for crafters who are learning to knit.

Amy Albert Bloom ★ Shillington, Pennsylvania

MATERIALS:

4-ply worsted-weight yarn—two 3-ounce skeins each of green and white

Size 8 (5mm) knitting needles or size needed to obtain correct gauge

Size H (5mm) crochet hook

Yarn or tapestry needle

6-inch square of cardboard for winding pom-pom

Scissors

12. Run yarn through sts remaining on needle. Draw up yarn tightly.

13. Fold stocking cap with right sides together, matching ends of rows. Thread needle with white yarn and sew seam of last white band. Sew remainder of back seam, using matching tails of yarn. Tuck seam to inside of hem and stitch seam with green yarn.

Pom-pom:

1. Working with a green strand and a white strand of yarn as one, wind yarn around 6-in. piece of cardboard 50 times.

2. Cut yarn at opposite edges of cardboard to make yarn pieces 6 in. long.

3. Tie a 24-in. piece of yarn tightly around center of stack.

4. Make another stack of yarn in the same way.

5. Place second stack of yarn on top of first stack. Tie the two stacks of yarn together tightly.

6. Holding long ends of yarn, shake the pom-pom to fluff yarns.

7. Use scissors to trim ends and make a ball measuring about 5 in. across. Do not cut long yarn ends.

8. Thread long yarn ends onto yarn or tapestry needle and sew pom-pom to tip of hat.

9. Fasten off and trim excess yarn.

ABBREVIATIONS	
k	knit
p	purl
RS	right side
st(s)	stitch(es)
tog	together
WS	wrong side
*	Instructions following asterisk are repeated as directed.

Charming Bookmark

CRAFT LEVEL: **QUICK AND EASY**

Whether you've had them for many years or only a few months, friends play an important role in every chapter of your life. So when you gather with your girlfriends over the holidays, let them know just how special they are by giving them a handcrafted bookmark.

Taste of Home Craft Editor

MATERIALS:

24-inch length of black cotton cording

Two 2-inch-long eye pins

Beads (green cube beads, round beads and three seed beads shown)

Needle-nose pliers

Wire cutters

Jump ring

Star charm

Glue or clear fingernail polish

Scissors

DIRECTIONS:

1. Thread an eye pin onto one end of length of black cording.

2. Add colored beads to the eye pin and use needle-nose pliers to form the end of the eye pin into a loop. Trim excess with wire cutters.

3. Add a jump ring and star charm onto the end of the eye pin.

4. Fold cording back and tie both strands in an overhand knot close to eye pin to secure.

5. Thread remaining eye pin onto opposite end of black cording.

6. Add colored bead or beads to the eye pin and form a small loop as before.

7. Fold the cording back, making bookmark as long as desired and knot as before.

8. Trim ends of cording close to the knots.

9. Add a drop of glue or clear nail polish to the cut ends of the cording to prevent fraying. Let dry.

DIRECTIONS:

Preparation:

1. Wash and dry the sweatshirt following the manufacturer's instructions.

2. Carefully cut off ribbing from each sleeve and from the bottom of the sweatshirt.

3. Measure sweatshirt from each underarm to bottom edge. Trim the bottom of the sweatshirt evenly if needed.

4. Measure your desired sleeve length and trim excess from the end of sleeves if needed. If the width of the sleeve is too big, taper the sleeve up to the underarm.

5. Cut up the center front of the sweatshirt from the bottom to the top to create a cardigan.

6. Turn the bottom edge of each sleeve 1/2 in. to the wrong side. Machine-sew hems in place with matching thread and a wide zigzag or long blanket stitch.

7. In the same way, hem the bottom edge of the sweatshirt and then the left and right front edges of the sweatshirt.

8. Thread hand-sewing needle with black pearl cotton and blanket-stitch around each hem. See Fig. 1 on page 219 for stitch illustration.

Appliques:

1. Fuse a slightly smaller piece of paper-backed fusible web to the wrong side of each fabric square for the background of the appliques. Trim each to an accurate 4-in. square. Do not remove paper backing.

2. Trace patterns onto paper side of fusible web as directed on patterns, leaving at least 1/2 in. between the shapes. Cut shapes apart, leaving a margin of paper around each.

3. Fuse shapes to wrong side of fabrics as directed. Let cool.

4. Cut out shapes along pattern lines.

5. Remove paper backing and position shapes on fused squares of fabric. Fuse shapes to fabric squares.

6. Applique around all shapes except star with matching thread and a narrow satin stitch. Blanket-stitch around star with red thread. Pull threads to back and fasten off loose ends.

continued on page...220

Merry Holiday Cardigan

CRAFT LEVEL: BEGINNER

FINISHED SIZE: Finished size will vary depending on the size of the sweatshirt. Each appliqued square measures 4 inches wide x 4 inches high.

Wear your creativity on your sleeve with this comfy cardigan. Appliques were stitched onto a plain red sweatshirt to fashion this Christmas cover-up.

Elaine Pfeifer ★ Norfolk, Nebraska

MATERIALS:

Purchased sweatshirt—red or desired color

Eight 5-inch squares of coordinating 100% cotton or cotton-blend fabrics for background of appliques (Elaine used four coordinating check and plaid fabrics)

100% cotton or cotton-blend fabrics—scraps each of black solid, red solid flannel, green solid, green mottled print, tan solid and white-on-white print for appliques

Patterns on page 219

Paper-backed fusible web

Pencil

All-purpose thread to match sweatshirt and fabrics

Quilter's ruler (optional)

Rotary cutter and mat (optional)

Twenty-one two-hole or four-hole buttons in assorted sizes and coordinating colors

Pearl cotton—black and white

Dimensional craft/fabric paint—black and orange

Black fine-line permanent marker

Standard sewing supplies

Cardigan Patterns

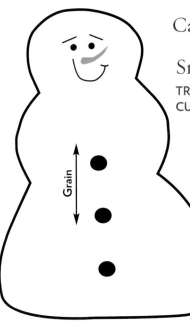

Snowman
TRACE 2—PAPER-BACKED FUSIBLE WEB
CUT 2—FUSED WHITE-ON-WHITE PRINT

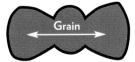

Bow Tie
TRACE 2—PAPER-BACKED
FUSIBLE WEB
CUT 1—FUSED BLACK SOLID
CUT 1—FUSED RED SOLID
FLANNEL

Tree
TRACE 2—PAPER-BACKED
FUSIBLE WEB
CUT 1—FUSED GREEN
SOLID
CUT 1—FUSED GREEN
MOTTLED PRINT

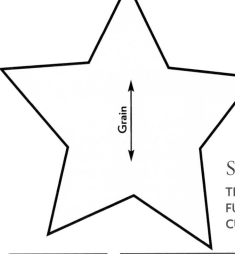

Mittens
TRACE 4, REVERSING 2—PAPER-
BACKED FUSIBLE WEB
CUT 1 EACH MITTEN—FUSED
BLACK SOLID
CUT 1 EACH MITTEN—FUSED
RED SOLID FLANNEL

Star
TRACE 1—PAPER-BACKED
FUSIBLE WEB
CUT 1—FUSED TAN SOLID

Small Heart
TRACE 1—PAPER-BACKED
FUSIBLE WEB
CUT 1—FUSED BLACK SOLID

Large Heart
TRACE 1—PAPER-BACKED FUSIBLE WEB
CUT 1—FUSED RED SOLID

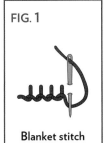

FIG. 1

Blanket stitch

FIG. 2

Stitched snowflake

7. Thread hand-sewing needle with white pearl cotton and stitch a snowflake on each appliqued mitten. See Fig. 2 on page 219 for stitch illustration.

8. Remove paper backing from appliqued squares. Position the squares evenly spaced along bottom edge of sweatshirt. Fuse the squares in place.

9. Machine-sew around each square with matching thread and a wide zigzag or long blanket stitch.

10. Using black or white pearl cotton and leaving thread ends on the front, hand-sew a contrasting button to the bottom of each Christmas tree and to star. Tie ends of pearl cotton in a small bow.

11. Hand-sew remaining buttons where shown.

12. Use orange dimensional craft/fabric paint to add a small orange triangle to each snowman for nose.

13. Use black dimensional craft/fabric paint to add two tiny dots for eyes and to add three small dots for coal buttons on each snowman.

14. Use black marker to add eyebrows and a mouth to each snowman.

Ways to Reuse Christmas Cards

As you pack away the holiday decorations after the New Year, it's tempting to simply toss all of the Christmas cards you received into the recycling bin.

Instead, read through those greeting cards one more time and put them in a box. Over the summer or in fall, pull out the cards and use them in one or all of the following creative ways:

Merry Markers. For beautiful bookmarks or gift tags, reach for the scissors and cut out images or words. Use a hole punch, then tie on a tassel. These homemade bookmarks make special stocking stuffers.

Pretty as a Picture. Framed photos of holiday scenes are a great way to liven up your decor at Christmastime, but they often can be costly. An easy and inexpensive alternative is to frame images from greetings cards. Use a traditional photo frame as a tabletop display. For an eye-catching wall hanging, purchase a larger matted frame.

Seasonal Stationery. The front, inside and even back of Christmas cards can have pretty images that would work well as postcards, note cards and recipe cards. (Be sure to check with your local post office regarding postcard size restrictions.)

Fun Felted Handbag

CRAFT LEVEL: INTERMEDIATE

FINISHED SIZE: Purse measures about 10 inches wide x 9 inches high without handles.

You'll have Christmas gift-giving well in hand when you fashion this attractive tote. Begin by crocheting a simple wool purse. Then felt it and add purchased handles and beads.

Taste of Home Craft Editor

MATERIALS:

100% wool worsted-weight yarn (Patons Classic Merino Wool yarn shown—see Crafter's Note)—two 3.5-ounce skeins of New Denim

Size 1/9 (5.5mm) crochet hook

Set of purse handles

Four silver beads (Blue Moon Large Dangle Charm-Spiral beads shown)

Yarn needle

Scissors

GAUGE: Before felting, 15 scs and 15 rows = 4 inches. Slight variation in gauge will change the finished size a bit.

DIRECTIONS:

Bottom:

Row 1: Ch 46, sc in second ch from hk and in each remaining ch across, turn: 45 scs.

Rows 2-9: Ch 1, sc in each sc across, turn: 45 scs.

At the end of Row 9, work 8 scs evenly spaced across short end of piece. Work 45 scs along opposite side of beginning ch. Work 8 scs evenly spaced across remaining short end: 106 scs.

Sides:

Working in rounds, sc in front lp only of each sc around until purse measures about 12 inches from base, ending at one side of purse: 106 scs.

Sl st around top of purse to beginning sl st. Fasten off.

Felting:

1. To shrink and felt the crocheted piece, machine-wash piece in hot water using laundry detergent, running piece through a complete cycle that includes a cold rinse cycle. Without using detergent, repeat this process until piece measures about 10 in. wide x 9 in. high or desired size.

2. Smooth out wrinkles and lay felted piece on a flat surface to dry. Check piece while it is drying and shape as needed to maintain desired shape.

Finishing:

1. With matching yarn, hand-sew handles centered along top edges of front and back of purse.

2. Hand-sew beads just below handles.

Crafter's Note: For successful felting, use 100% wool yarn. "Superwash" wool does not felt. Bleached white yarn does not felt as well as off-white and colored yarn.

ABBREVIATIONS	
ch(s)	chain(s)
hk	hook
lp	loop
sc(s)	single crochet(s)
sl st	slip stitch

Stenciled Santa Sack

CRAFT LEVEL: INTERMEDIATE

FINISHED SIZE: Bag measures 16-3/4 inches high x 10-3/4 inches wide.

I prefer doing projects that are reusable, which can be enjoyed both now and years down the road…and this Kris Kringle sack will be great to use over the years for your family's presents. Whenever my family sees the painted Santa Claus on the bag, they know it's from me!

Elaine Torrie ★ Kingston, Ontario

MATERIALS:

Pattern on page 223

1/2 yard of 44-inch-wide 100% off-white cotton twill or unbleached muslin

Matching all-purpose thread

Standard sewing supplies

Black fine-line permanent marker

Three 8-1/2- x 11-inch pieces of stencil plastic

Cutting mat

Craft or stencil knife

Transparent tape

8-1/2- x 11-inch piece of corrugated cardboard

Masking tape

Foam plate or palette

Fabric paints or acrylic craft paints and textile medium—black, emerald green, red, metallic gold, white and colorless glitter (optional)

Paper towels

Waxed paper

Stencil brush

Cosmetic sponge

Blue fabric marker

1-1/4 yards of coordinating cord for drawstring

DIRECTIONS:

1. Wash, dry and press fabric without using fabric softeners or detergents with built-in stain resistors.

2. From cotton twill or muslin, cut two 12-in. x 18-in. pieces.

3. Place fabric pieces together with right sides facing and edges matching.

4. Sew along one long edge (side) and across one narrow edge (bottom) with a 5/8-in. seam allowance. Continue sewing along remaining long edge (opposite side) to 2-1/4 in. from end. Skip 1 in. to leave an opening for cord and complete sewing the seam.

5. Clip bottom corners diagonally.

6. Press side seams open.

7. Press under 1/4-in. for hem at the top of the bag.

8. Turn 1 in. to inside for casing and press.

9. Sew close to the edge of first fold to form casing.

10. Turn bag right side out and press.

Making Stencils:

1. Use black marker to trace entire pattern on page 223 onto each piece of stencil plastic, labeling the pieces Nos. 1, 2 and 3.

2. Place stencil No. 1 on cutting mat and cut out only the shapes labeled No. 1 with a craft or stencil knife. (To repair tears, tape both sides with transparent tape and re-cut the shape.)

3. In the same way, cut each of the shapes labeled No. 2 from stencil No. 2 and each of the shapes labeled No. 3 from stencil No. 3.

 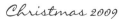

Stenciling:

1. Slip cardboard inside bag to prevent paint from seeping through to the other side.

2. Use masking tape to secure stencil No. 1 to front of the bag, positioning the top of Santa's hat about 5 in. from the open edge.

3. Place a small amount of red paint onto foam plate or palette, adding textile medium as instructed by manufacturer if using acrylic craft paints.

4. Dip a stencil brush into paint and wipe on paper towel until brush is nearly dry.

5. With brush handle held upright, position brush along cut out edge of hat. Move bristles in a circular motion as you press down onto fabric. Without lifting the brush, continue this motion as you move the brush along the edge.

Work inward to fill in design. For more intense color, add another coat. Stencil Santa's coat in the same way.

6. Mix a little white with a little red to make pink and use a clean dry brush to stencil Santa's face.

7. When dry, remove stencil No. 1.

8. With design lines aligned, tape stencil No. 2 to bag.

9. Referring to pattern for colors needed, stencil each cut out shape as before. Use a clean area of the foam plate or palette and a clean dry stencil brush for each paint color.

10. When dry, use cosmetic sponge to apply colorless glitter over white paint on beard, eyebrows, pom-pom and cuffs if desired.

11. When dry, remove stencil No. 2.

12. Tape stencil No. 3 to bag. Stencil each cutout shape as before, adding

colorless glitter over white fur on hat if desired.

13. When dry, remove stencil No. 3.

14. Use blue fabric marker to add eyes as shown on pattern.

15. Remove cardboard and let dry overnight.

Finishing:

1. Turn bag wrong side out.

2. With a dry iron and cotton setting, press stenciled area from the wrong side to heat-set paint. Let cool.

3. Turn bag right side out.

4. Pull cord through casing and tie a knot at each end for a drawstring.

Crafter's Note: To cut down on cleaning stencils and brushes, do several bags at once. You can make three bags from 1 yard of 44-in.-wide fabric.

Santa Sack Pattern

ENLARGE PATTERN 200%
EACH SQUARE = 1 INCH

Eyebrows - 2

Santa Template
TRACE 3—STENCIL PLASTIC

Nose - 3

Snowflake Afghan

CRAFT LEVEL: ADVANCED

FINISHED SIZE: Directions are for throw size, 42 inches x 46 inches. Changes for afghan size, 58 inches x 64 inches, are in parentheses.

The snowflake design on this snuggly blanket makes it just right for wintry decorating. And, you can easily make it either an afghan or throw size because it is knit in strips.

E.J. Slayton ★ Cadet, Missouri

MATERIALS:

Chart on page 225

Worsted-weight yarn in 3-1/2-ounce skeins—8(15) skeins of green and one skein of white (Brown Sheep Co. Inc. Nature Spun yarn, a 100% wool yarn sold in 3-1/2-ounce skeins with 245 yards/100 grams—approximately 8(15) skeins 1,960(3,675) yards of Monument Green #N27 and 1 skein of Natural #730 shown).

Size 6 (4mm) knitting needles or size needed to obtain correct gauge

Cable needle and stitch markers

Tapestry needle

Scissors

GAUGE: 20 sts and 28 rows = 4 inches in stockinette stitch.

STITCHES USED:

St st = stockinette stitch:

Row 1 (RS): Knit across row.

Row 2 (WS): Purl across row.

Repeat Rows 1 and 2.

BC (FC) = BACK CROSS (FRONT CROSS):

Slip next 3 sts to cable needle, hold in back (front), k 3, k 3 from cable needle.

M 1 = MAKE 1:

To increase one stitch, use left needle to pick up the horizontal strand between stitches, working from front to back. With right needle, knit in back of this stitch so it twists.

GARTER ST = GARTER STITCH:

Every row: Knit across row.

DIRECTIONS:

For throw size, make 3 inner strips and 1 left and 1 right strip. For afghan size, make 5 inner strips and 1 left and 1 right strip.

Inner Strip:

Cast on 39 sts.

Bottom border:

Work in garter st to make 6 ridges on RS, ending with a WS row.

Set-up row:

K 1, p 1, [k 1, M 1] three times, p 1, place marker; k 3, M 1, [k 7, M 1] three times, k 3, place marker; p 1, [k 1, M 1] three times, p 1, k 1: 49 sts.

Rows 2, 4, 6 and 8 (WS): P 1, k 1, p 6, k 1; p 31; k 1, p 6, k 1, p 1.

Rows 3, 7 and 9 (RS): K 1, p 1, k 6, p 1; k 31; p 1, k 6, p 1, k 1.

Row 5: K 1, p 1, BC, p 1; k 31; p 1, FC, p 1, k 1.

Rows 10-57: Rep Rows 2-9 six more times, ending with Row 9.

Row 58: P 1, k 1, p 6; k 1; k 31; k 1; p 6, k 1, p 1.

Row 59: Rep Row 3.

Row 60: Rep Row 58.

Row 61: Rep Row 5.

Row 62: Rep Row 58.

Row 63: Rep Row 3.

Row 64: Rep Row 58.

Row 65: Rep Row 3.

Rep Rows 2-65 four (six) more times, making a total of five (seven) St st blocks, ending with Row 57 on fourth (sixth) repeat.

Decrease for top border:

Decreasing 3 sts across 9 sts of each side border and 4 sts evenly across St st block, knit across next row. Work in garter st to make 5 ridges on RS, ending with a WS row. Bind off in purl on the RS.

Make a total of 3(5) inner strips.

Right (Left) Edge Strip:

Cast on 44 sts, work in garter st for 6 ridges on RS, ending with a WS row as for bottom border of inner strip. On set-up row, place marker 5 sts from right (left) edge. Keeping these 5 sts in garter st throughout, work right (left) edge strip on remaining 49 sts as for inner strip.

Finishing:

1. Using tapestry needle and green, stitch strips together, matching the cable crossings and stitching through Garter st "bumps" to make an almost invisible seam.

2. Following chart below left, use a single strand of white to duplicate-stitch snowflakes in the center of alternating blocks. See Fig. 1 below.

3. Weave in loose yarn ends.

4. Block if needed.

DUPLICATE STITCH CHART

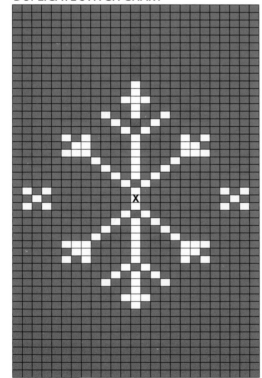

DUPLICATE STITCH KEY

X   Center of Row 29 of St st block

☐   Duplicate stitch

FIG. 1 Duplicate stitch

With tapestry needle and white, bring needle out at base of St stitch, then stitch under both legs of St stitch above, and stitch back into base.

ABBREVIATIONS

BC	back cross
FC	front cross
k	knit
p	purl
rep	repeat
RS	right side
st(s)	stitch(es)
WS	wrong side
[ ]	Instructions between brackets are repeated a given number of times.

Silver Beaded Necklace

CRAFT LEVEL: QUICK & EASY

FINISHED SIZE: Necklace measures about 17 inches long.

Want to bedazzle a fashion-conscious friend this Christmas? Or need a graceful way to accessorize a dress? Try this elegant necklace (pictured at bottom in photo above). The technique is so easy, even a novice beader can create this piece in little time.

Jill Hackman ★ Snow Shoe, Pennsylvania

MATERIALS:

Sterling silver beads—sixteen 2mm beads, sixteen 3mm beads, seven 5mm Bali beads and 160 (1mm x 4mm) liquid silver beads

Two 2mm sterling silver crimp beads

One sterling silver spring ring clasp with split ring

36-inch length of clear beading wire (Jill used Accuflex beading wire)

Flush cutters or very sharp craft scissors

Crimping tool or flat-nose pliers

Needle-nose pliers (optional)

DIRECTIONS:

1. Thread clasp onto 36-in. length of beading wire and fold wire in half, creating two strands of equal length.

2. Thread both ends of wire through one crimp bead and push bead toward clasp until it is 1/8 in. from clasp. Crimp bead closed with crimping tool or flat-nose pliers.

3. Over both ends of wire, thread on one 3mm bead and one 2mm bead.

4. *Separate the two wires and thread 10 liquid silver beads on each wire. Bring both ends of wires together and thread on one 2mm bead, one 3mm bead, one Bali bead, one 3mm bead and one 2mm bead. Repeat from * six more times.

5. Separate the two wires. On each wire, thread 10 liquid silver beads. Bring wires together and thread on one 2mm bead, one 3mm bead and a crimp bead.

6. Thread both wires through the split ring and then back through the crimp bead (use needle-nose pliers if desired). Tuck the ends of wire into the 3mm bead. Crimp the crimp bead closed using crimping tool or flat-nose pliers. Cut off excess wire as close as possible to 3mm bead.

Letter Braclet

CRAFT LEVEL: BEGINNER

FINISHED SIZE: Bracelet measures about 7 inches long.

This sparkling accent lets you wear your heart on your sleeve, thanks to the letter-block beads. You can arrange them any way you like to literally spell out your feelings! We created the bracelet using beads in the birthstone colors of siblings and chose the word "Sisters"…but you could also spell out "Mom" or "Love."

Kelly and Elaine Van Sickle ★ Laurens, Iowa

MATERIALS:

Sterling silver beads—four 3mm round beads, eight 4mm daisy spacer beads, two 3mm rondelle beads, six 4mm rondelle beads and 4mm letter-block beads spelling "SISTERS"

Two 2mm sterling silver crimp tubes

Sixteen 3mm clear spacer beads

6mm bicone Swarovski crystal beads—two of each birthstone color representing each sister (Crafter's Note)

One sterling silver toggle clasp

12-inch length of beading wire

Crimping tool or flat-nose pliers

Flush cutters or very sharp craft scissors

Needle-nose pliers (optional)

Bead design board (optional)

DIRECTIONS:

1. On beading board or flat surface, lay out the letter-block beads to spell "SISTERS."

2. Place a 4mm rondelle bead between each of the letter-block beads and a 3mm rondelle bead at the beginning and end of the letter-block beads.

3. Place a 6mm bicone birthstone bead of each color on each side of the letter beads, placing the birthstone beads in order of birth from oldest to youngest. Place a clear spacer bead, a daisy spacer bead and a clear spacer bead between the birthstone beads.

4. At each end, add a 3mm round bead, a crimp tube and another 3mm round bead.

5. Thread all beads onto beading wire.

6. Thread one half of toggle clasp onto one end of beading wire. At same end, thread beading wire back through round bead and crimp tube, leaving a short piece of beading wire extended. Position round bead snugly next to toggle clasp. Crimp the crimp tube closed with crimping tool or flat-nose pliers. Cut excess short end of the beading wire.

7. Thread other half of toggle clasp onto opposite end of beading wire. Thread beading wire back through round bead and crimp tube. Crimp tube closed as before. Cut excess short end of beading wire.

Crafter's Note: Kelly used green, red, turquoise and two sets of light blue beads to represent five sisters. Clear bicone crystal beads could be substituted for the colored beads anywhere in the design if there are fewer sisters in your family.

Festive Fir Pin

CRAFT LEVEL: QUICK & EASY

FINISHED SIZE: Tree pin measures about 2-1/8 inches wide x 2-5/8 inches high.

Colorful beads and a zigzag of gold wire is just about all it takes to create this lovely evergreen accessory. Would you rather have a thinner tree? Or one with a bit more color? Simply adjust the number and position of the bends in the wire to change the shape of the tree or string additional colored beads onto the wire.

Diane Hesse ★ Mt. Enterprise, Texas

MATERIALS:

15-inch length of 20-gauge gold craft wire

Twenty-one 3mm gold beads

14 assorted-color E beads (two light blue, two clear, three green, two orange, three red and two yellow E beads shown)

15mm red star bead

Tie-tack with clutch back

E-6000 or jewelry glue

Needle-nose pliers

Ruler

Wire cutters

DIRECTIONS:

1. Use needle-nose pliers to make a small loop at one end of the gold craft wire just big enough to fit around the post on the back of the tie tack.

2. Hold the wire with the loop at the top. Referring to the photo at left, use needle-nose pliers to bend the wire slightly to the right, then to the left about 1/4 in. from the loop. Add one gold bead, one E bead and one more gold bead to the wire. Slide the beads over to the last bend.

3. Bend the wire to the right about 1/2 in. from the first bend. Add a gold bead, one E bead and another gold bead to the wire. Slide beads over to the last bend.

4. Bend the wire to the left about 3/4 in. from last bend. Add two gold beads and one E bead as before. Slide beads over to last bend.

5. Bend the wire to the right about 1 in. from last bend. Add three gold beads and two E beads, alternating them as before. Slide the beads over to the last bend.

6. Bend the wire to the left about 1-1/4 in. from last bend. Add four gold beads and three E beads as before. Slide beads over to last bend.

7. Bend the wire to the right about 1-1/2 in. from last bend. Add four gold beads and three E beads as before. Slide beads over to last bend.

8. Bend the wire to the left about 1-3/4 in. from last bend. Add four gold beads and three E beads as before. Slide the beads over to last bend.

9. Bend the wire to the right about 2 in. from last bend, then to the left about 1-1/2 in. from previous bend. Bend the wire back and forth at 1/2 in. lengths for tree trunk.

10. Trim any excess wire.

11. Remove clutch back from post of tie tack. Insert the post end of the tie tack from front to back through the top loop of wire and glue to hold. Glue star bead to flat side of tie tack. Let dry.

12. Insert post of tie tack through clothing and replace clutch back to hold pin in place.

Beaded Grape Stemware Charms

CRAFT LEVEL: INTERMEDIATE

FINISHED SIZE: Excluding wire hoop, each beaded charm measures about 1 inch long x 1/2 inch wide.

The rings fit easily around stemmed glassware to dress them up. If you use different colored beads, the trims give each glass an individual look, so your guests will know which one is theirs. The charms are fun to produce, too. I just shaped beads on wire into clusters of grapes, then attached them to wire hoops.

JoAnn Capella ★ Lake in the Hills, Illinois

MATERIALS (FOR FOUR):

30-gauge jewelry wire—gold, red, green and purple

Size 6/0 frosted iridescent glass pony beads—18 each of yellow, red, green and purple

Four 1/2-inch-long green leaf-shaped beads (see Crafter's Note information)

Small container for each different bead variety

Wire cutters

Ruler

Small needle-nose pliers

Four 1-inch gold wire hoops (see Crafter's Note)

DIRECTIONS:

General Instructions:

Separate different beads into different small containers.

While beading, keep wire taut.

Use wire cutters to cut wire and use needle-nose pliers for twisting wire.

Refer to Figs. 1-10 at right while assembling charms.

Yellow Charm:

1. Cut two 8-in. lengths of gold wire.

2. Using yellow beads, thread bead 1 onto center of one wire piece. Fold wire in half and twist it twice on one side of bead. Thread the same bead onto the second piece of wire the same as before and twist wire twice on opposite side of bead. See Fig. 1.

3. Pull the wire ends up to form a "V" shape with the bead at the bottom. Thread beads 2 and 3 onto the pair of wires on each side of the "V" shape. See Fig. 2.

4. Separate the wires into four separate wires.

5. Place beads 4 and 5 on the two inner wires as shown in Fig. 3. Twist inner wires together twice to hold the two beads in place.

6. Thread beads 6 and 7 onto the lower wires. Referring to Fig. 4, thread bead 6 wire through bottom of bead 5 and thread bead 7 wire through bottom of bead 4. Position beads 6 and 7 on the front and back of cluster.

7. Thread beads 8 and 9 onto the

twisted inner wires as shown in Fig. 5. Thread one wire down through bead 4 and the other wire down through bead 5. Pull all four wires upward.

8. Thread beads 10 and 11 onto the lower wires. Referring to Fig. 6, thread bead 10 wire through bottom of bead 9 and thread bead 11 wire through bottom of bead 8. Position beads 10 and 11 on the front and back of cluster.

9. Thread beads 12 and 13 onto the lower wires. Referring to Fig. 7, thread bead 12 wire through bottom of bead 9 and thread bead 13 wire through bottom of bead 8. Position beads 12 and 13 on opposite sides of cluster.

10. Thread beads 14 and 15 onto inner wires as shown in Fig. 8 and twist inner wires together twice to hold in place.

11. Thread beads 16 and 17 onto the lower wires. Referring to Fig. 9, thread bead 16 wire through bottom of bead 15 and thread bead 17 wire through bottom of bead 14. Position beads 16 and 17 on opposite sides of cluster.

12. Thread bead 18 onto the twisted inner wires as shown in Fig. 10.

13. Twist the outer and inner wire on each side together four or five times to make two pairs of wire. Twist both twisted wire pairs together three times.

14. Separate the wires into pairs and add a leaf bead to one pair of wires as shown in Fig. 11. Twist all wires together again from the leaf to the end of the wire.

15. Insert the wire end through the hole of a wire hoop and twist to fasten. Cut excess wire.

Remaining Charms:

Follow instructions above for remaining charms, using purple wire with purple beads, red wire with red beads, and green wire with green beads.

Crafter's Note: The leaf-shaped beads (item BD-CC-32966-02) are available from Sunshine Discount Crafts, 1-800/729-2878. The wire hoops (item CH122) are available rom Jewelry Supply, 866/380-7464 or at www.jewelrysupply.com.

FIG. 1 Adding wire to bead 1

FIG. 2 Adding beads 2 and 3

FIG. 3 Adding beads 4 and 5

FIG. 4 Adding bead 6 to front and 7 to back

FIG. 5 Adding beads 8 and 9

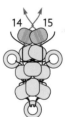

FIG. 6 Adding bead 10 to front and 11 to back

FIG. 7 Adding bead 12 to front and 13 to back

FIG. 8 Adding beads 14 and 15

FIG. 9 Adding bead 16 to front and 17 to back

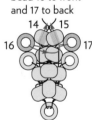

FIG. 10 Adding bead 18

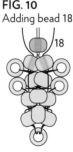

FIG. 11 Adding leaf

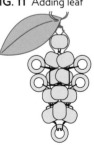

RECIPE & CRAFT INDEXES

There are three indexes for your convenience. The first is a complete alphabetical listing of all the recipes in this book. When you know the name of the recipe you need, simply turn to this index. The second index, General Recipe Index, lists every recipe by food category, major ingredient and/or cooking method. For example, if you're looking for a slow cooker recipe or one that uses beef, use this index. The last index is all you need to find a craft...they're listed by title and type of craft.

Alphabetical Recipe Index

General Recipe Index

Craft Index

Share the Magic of Christmas

Do you have a special recipe that has become part of your family's Christmas tradition? Do you have a special flair for decorating on a budget or make the most superb, original gifts? Those are the types of recipes, ideas and crafts we'd like to include in future Taste of Home Christmas books.

To submit a recipe, craft or decorating idea, print or type the information on a standard sheet of paper. Please be thorough and include directions, measurements and sizes of materials or equipment. Also include your name, address and daytime phone number, photo if available and add a few words about yourself and your submission.

Send to "Taste of Home Christmas Annual", 5400 S. 60th Street, Greendale WI 53129 (with a self-addressed stamped envelope if you'd like your materials returned). Or E-mail your submissions and photos to bookeditors@reimanpub.com (write "Taste of Home Christmas Annual" on the subject line).